CW00944688

Cheers + best wishes
you old pal
[signature]

The Mandala and
the Machine

The Mandala and the Machine

An autobiographical story of the 1960s

Laurie Burt

© Laurence Burt, 2008

STEIP Publishing

December 2008

ISBN 978-0-9560793-0-5

All rights reserved. No part of this book may be reproduced or transmitted in any form by any means electronic or mechanical including, but not limited to, photocopying, recording or electronic storage or retrieval without written permission from the publisher.

Prepared and printed by:
York Publishing Services Ltd,
64 Hallfield Road, Layerthorpe,
York YO31 7ZQ
www.yps-publishing.co.uk

To people alive or dead mentioned in this book – although believing that I have written nothing which might in any way be considered offensive – I trust they or their kin will forgive me should they feel otherwise.

This essence of this story about my earlier years was originally meant for the better understanding of my eldest son, Peter. However, I hope that Paul, Julie, Solomon and Theo, together with my ever loving wife, Angela – on reading it, will also come to know me be better.

I owe especial thanks to Denise Raine for her encouragement and a firm belief in both myself and the story told herein.

And a final thank you to Theo for his ever reassuring interest in all my work and helping edit and design this book.

L.B. 2008

And my last words shall be these – that it is only from the inmost silences of the heart that we know the world for what it is, and ourselves for what the world has made us.

Siegfried Sassoon
"The Complete Memoirs of George Sherston"

Chapter 1
Early background, school, the army and art

The room was brightly lit and occupied by a dozen or more young students busily working on small plaster sculptures. The shelves of the room were crowded with portrait heads, small figures and animals; more clay models stood on modelling stands here and there. At the far end of the room, raised high on a turntable was a four foot clay figure of a Madonna. A tutor, by the look of him, was pressing on more clay, shaping it, stepping back to examine his modelling and repeating the process. Students were busy at a large sink, scooping soft clay out of plaster moulds or occupied on similar tasks. It all looked too good to be true...

Home from work one evening I'd read in the paper that evening classes in sculpture were starting in the College of Art down in Leeds. For the last few months I'd spent hours attempting to model a man's head in three-quarters relief in clay – copying it from a tiny engraving of a Renaissance man found in the local library; mouth agape, he was angrily screaming at some unseen thing. Every detail of his features and wind-blown hair was immaculately drawn; because of the picture's lifelike perfection it fascinated me. In another book in the same library were photographs and drawings of how sculptures were built and modelled in clay from start to finish. Looking at the pictures of the completed models I wondered how anyone using mere clay could transform the ordinary into what appeared beautiful.

As a child I'd dug clay from a nearby wood and on a board on the kitchen table shaped a face. Finished, I pasted papier-mâché over the dried out clay to make a mask. It could not have been brilliant, even painted, but my parents thought so. I was ten at the time; it was four years before the Second World War.

I left school at fourteen but would much sooner have stayed on. Generally either top of my class or near it, I was far too nervous when scholarship day came round – I became too ill to take the exam, or if I did I failed it. This was in the old days well before the timely *eleven plus* was introduced.

My parents therefore apprenticed me to a firm of architectural metalworkers in Hunslet, Leeds, and that was that! Born into a family of time-served craftsmen I followed that pattern. Even my mother as a girl served an apprenticeship in court dressmaking at a shop in Harrogate; she was born in that town. My father, a joiner and foreman shop-fitter by trade, travelled all over Britain working; he spent little time at home. In later years I discovered that my maternal grandfather, surnamed Wray, stemmed from a family of stone-masons – perhaps this was where my family's inherited skills came from.

My first year as a fourteen year old at the metalworks was spent as a general dogsbody – running errands, sweeping up, 'mashing' the men's teas and later the women's when they came to be employed on war work. I hated tea-making – mug by individual mug out of paper twists of tea and sugar, and shopping for twenty or more people, which meant buying sandwiches, buns, and hunting for cigarettes, a luxury in extremely short supply during the war. I also hated the telling off I got if I brought back the wrong cakes, the wrong change, or made some other unfortunate mistake. More than once I ran off to hide in the lavatories up the yard where I could be alone in tearful misery.

Two years later, out of a sense of youthful excitement engendered by the war, I let another sixteen year old friend talk me into joining up. What helped me to decide on this step was that three brothers older than myself were in the services; I mistakenly imagined I too would like to be in the thick of things – the war; being in uniform seemed a much more interesting future than stuck in a rotten old workshop.

My friend and I, without parental knowledge, doctored our birth certificates. With a knowing wink we could not quite understand why we were turned away by the Navy recruitment chap and went to try the Army. The sergeant at this recruiting office said nothing at all about how young we must have looked, and after a brief medical signed us both on. Having made us swear an oath of loyalty to King and country he gave us the King's shilling. The only other thing I remember about the occasion was hearing the sergeant telephoning someone and shouting over the phone, 'I've got a fine specimen here for you, Fred!' The fine specimen turned out to be me.

So I became a soldier. To my dismay my friend's parents somehow managed to cancel *their* son's enlistment. A month later, alone, I went by train up to Berwick on Tweed and into the base-camp and training battalion of the Royal Scots. It was first time away from a cosseted, secure home-life and I found the tough army regime and hard rigours of infantry training in January snow and ice were no joke. What did little to help the situation was that I turned out to be the only Englishman in a platoon of thirty Scots who were by no means all quiet and sober chaps. To add to my misfortune the very young platoon officer turned out to be a loyal Scotsman. Sadly, a true national, he was not overjoyed at having a Sassenach in his platoon.

The following five years in the army were not at all the romantic adventure I had imagined they might be; and as for being a soldier – I was never remotely near action on a battlefield.

To backtrack – the Leeds elementary school that I attended, Quarry Mount, must have been pretty good of its kind. I can recall every one of my teachers, *and* their names, remembering them with retrospective affection – even those who caned me, clouted me over the ears, and particularly Old Ben who whacked one stingingly hard on the bottom with the flat of a pencil box. After the war I was sad to hear that Old Steve – teacher of the oldest class of boys in school, was killed at Dunkirk. I had liked Old Steve although he was strict; he also loved *our* much hated singing lessons. The patriotic 'Drake's Drum', a folk song telling of Francis Drake's tragic burial at sea was his favourite. Since then, and up to this day, hearing it, an image of Old Steve with hands raised beating time comes into my mind's eye, and I wonder exactly how he met his violent death in battle – bravely I am sure.

There'd been Old Wilson too, gassed in the First World War and as a result was understandably a bad tempered old devil. He'd once given me two on each hand for being naughty in class when a student teacher happened to be taking us. I was in the wrong and could not blame him; but the cane most certainly hurt, breaking the skin and raising great welts on either hand; yet, I'd deserved it and in the long run it did me no harm.

During those five years in the army, after one year in the Royal Scots I swapped regiments and became a REME – the Royal Electrical and Mechanical Engineers. Out of despair and the boredom of repetitive infantry life I'd applied for the transfer at a time when the army badly needed tradesmen – mentioning my brief apprenticeship as a metalworker. Successful, I was sent down to London on numerous courses. This was in 1942 when there was a lull in the German bombing raids so that I all but escaped this horror. After the tough regimented life of an infantry battalion, my time spent in London in civvy digs and learning things with the REME felt like a brief taste of paradise. My true, great regret in having left a front line battalion was that I was never put to the test in battle.

Instead of that opportunity to prove whatever I was, my postings were abroad in relatively safe, enemy free arenas. After sailing by troopship to Port Said and entraining for what was then Palestine, my company was transported by truck over the Sinai Desert for four days to arrive in Baghdad, Iraq. From there, serving time in Shaiba near Basra, Saudi Arabia, and finally North Africa, I spent the years abroad in army workshops. My sole view of any battle during the 1940s' war was that of the appalling aftermath of the North African desert campaign. Travelling by train from Cairo – the track ran alongside the Mediterranean coastline right up to Benghazi, I saw innumerable battle scars; these were bombed and burned up tanks, guns, trucks, and ships half sunk in Tobruk harbour. Worst of all the horrors were the pitiable sights of Arab children with white bandaged stumps where young hands or feet had once been before being blown off by a land-mine or a discarded grenade picked up as a play thing. I also came across other joyless yet poignant sights of human destruction – the true symbols of war's ghastly harvest. In the near distance, away from the railway lines were mass cemeteries closely packed with regimented white crosses, each marking the lonely death of a serviceman, and sometimes a brave woman's grave. I had cause to remember Rupert Brooke's 1914 world war poem – for here, literally, were thousand upon thousand of dead soldiers lying in faraway *foreign fields;* the only difference here was that they lay in desert land.

My years spent in the army were not always mindless and monotonous, although I suspect my youth transformed much of the time into what seemed like a prolonged, often unpalatable dream wherein few parts were less acceptable than others.

Of the more worthwhile times – I remember camping in the desert, lying back and looking up into a night sky overburdened with bright stars which spread from horizon to flat horizon, suspended high in a vast indigo dome. Years later, in Madame Tussaud's planetarium with two young children, I recalled sleeping out on the coast of the Persian Gulf and experiencing the overwhelming awe such a sky imposes on mere humans. I was grateful that I had been there, seen the real thing, and also known the vital emptiness of the desert.

But that was years ago, before oil and the Gulf War spoiled the natural beauty of much of the vast desert of land between Kuwait and the ancient town of Basra. Now I presume, those previously unspoiled, vast, unlived in areas are irrevocably littered by the ugly remnants of twentieth century war, together with the skeletal remains of violently slaughtered humans. In 1943 I volunteered to be part of a small tented workshop and signals detachment stationed in the middle of the Saudi Arabian desert. We were stationed there to service the transport of a locust mission whose task it was to kill off the voracious insects before they grew to maturity and swarmed. The camp consisted of about fifteen men of the REME and the Royal Signals, a corporal, a sergeant and one officer (an entomologist). Among us there were mechanics, drivers, a medical orderly, the signals people, and myself a metalworker and jack of all trades – there to undertake non-mechanical repair jobs on the trucks.

Each month, turn and turn about, two personnel from the lower ranks were allowed to convoy wagons five-hundred miles up to Basra – in order to collect supplies and mail. The trip, taking three to four days, provided a break from the monotony and rawness of the isolated situation in which we lived (survived might be more apt), stuck out in the middle of a barren sand swept nowhere.

Driving North to Basra it was necessary to pass through the small state of Kuwait. When my turn came to make the trip I accompanied a driver called Drummer Drake. Some years older than myself, in the recent North African campaigns he'd been shot up while driving an armoured car; the experience, although he was not yet thirty, greyed his hair prematurely. But he knew how to make the best of things under desert conditions. Camped out within sight of Kuwait, at that time merely a mud-walled township, he quickly contrived a fire out of petrol-soaked sand and camel

7

weed. On this he cooked small pancakes made up of flour, sugar and water; they tasted delicious compared to our usual monotonous diet eaten directly out of tins.

After a night spent on blanket and sand we were to deliver a message to the only European living within Kuwait at that time – the British political agent. In order to visit him we needed permission from the Sheikh of the small, independent state. Entering through the town gate accompanied by an armed guard, the two of us were shown into a long narrow throne room; it appeared to be bursting at the seams with white-robed bearded Arabs squatting cross-legged on benches along the wall of each side. The guard ushered us up the length of the room where the royal ruler sat centrally enthroned. Attempting slight self-conscious bows and speaking in very limited Arabic my companion and I gave the ruler a tentative salaam; he responded with a beaming smile, a handshake, and the immediate offer of a cigarette – Russian, as it turned out – and by the look of the blue, barely breathable atmosphere in the throne room, every one there was seriously chain smoking. The cigarette in my hand appeared to be an extraordinarily long one; feeling nervous under the many curious eyes I placed it between my lips. What I unhappily failed to realise was that most of the cigarette's length consisted of a cardboard tube containing a mere smidge of tobacco at one end. True to form I put the wrong end to my mouth so that given a light by a good natured, grinning Arab, the thin cardboard tube burst into flame, bringing peals of delighted laughter from the whole room, including the Sheikh of Kuwait; the event helped ease any tension the two of us might have felt in the undoubtedly friendly yet alien situation.

There were other unique adventures while on the locust

mission. On one occasion, placed in charge of a convoy of five three-ton trucks I was told they were to be driven by Arab drivers up from the Red Sea port of Jedda. 'These chaps don't seem to know their arse from their elbow,' the sergeant told me just before the convoy set off, 'So watch them!' Neither apparently had they ever travelled far from Jedda. This point was proved when once in Basra I was horrified when one of these same drivers drove the truck, in which I was passenger, very fast down the busy main road, expertly weaving in and out of other angry, hooting vehicles whether to the right or the left, coming or going – he was oblivious of the fact that it was law to drive on the left side of the road. Needless to say I survived the ordeal.

These Jedda drivers were quite friendly and likeable individuals when one came to know them. At that time I could just about make myself understood using hand signs, facial contortions and a smattering of basic Arabic. All the same, I was anxious – stuck on my own in charge of a convoy driven by five Arab, non-English speaking drivers dressed in ankle length gowns, wearing loose turbans or embroidered skull-caps. Together we were to travel over four hundred miles across open desert guided by a single Saudi policeman. His guidance was a *must,* because at that time, apart from a single engineered road leading from Jedda to Mecca, there were no others. Our way would be along open desert track often obscured by sand storm; it was therefore dangerous and easy to become lost and without water. If this happened the trick, we were told, was to drive one mile East, then two miles West, hoping by so doing to hit the track at one point. The dire consequence of getting lost without any means of communication could be terminal. It almost was on one occasion when two Saudi drivers drove off track and ended up drinking the water from their truck's radiator.

I was taking the convoy across from the middle of Arabia to the Persian Gulf and to an American oil company where the truck loads of empty ten-gallon petrol cans the convoy carried would be refilled. Crossing flat, sun-baked desert, involved hours of driving in conditions of intense heat; temperatures might well rise to upwards of a 130 degrees. At midday, all that I and the Saudi drivers could do to escape the blazing sun was to lie in the meagre shade provided beneath the trucks. The water we carried was drawn from deep ancient, infrequently situated wells, where the life-saving precious liquid often swarmed with tiny pink tadpole-like creatures. It was necessary to strain them off through mutton cloth or one's hanky'. Water was kept in four-gallon metal cans and floppy canvas bottles; the water in the cans became quite hot; the canvas bottles (chargels?) were hung on a truck's bumper, the contents supposedly cooled by evaporation. Most times however they were a dead loss and what one thirstily gulped down was foul tasting, tepid water. Desert travel in those conditions brought one to value civilisation and the taken for granted miracle of a cold water tap – an impossible mirage in the mind's eye.

During this trip to the Persian Gulf various other happenings are perhaps worth a mention. One was an invitation to take coffee – a hospitable invite impolite to turn down. However I usually found the ceremonial a trying business, the wickedly strong taste of the coffee essence reminded me of ghastly compulsory doses of senna pod when a child; otherwise it was not an entirely unpleasant procedure. The several tiny ceramic bowls, encircled in the hand of the server, chinked musically together as with the other he expertly poured out a minute measure of black, almost caustic liquid, offering it between thumb and forefinger to the guest; the ritual was performed three times before custom was served – to accept less than three doses, we were told, was insulting. Fortunately three small glasses of very sweet tea followed, which counteracted the bitter dregs of the previous brew. On this particular occasion I had been invited for coffee immediately after sunset, at the lovely Eastern time of twilight when longed-for cooling winds supplanted the stark heat of a sun scorched day.

The convoy had stopped for the night at a town called Hof-hof. My young host – possibly about my own age of nineteen or twenty years – was the son of the local sheikh. We sat cross-legged high on the wide ramparts of the town wall at either side of a camel weed fire on which was balanced the archetypal Arabian coffee pot. The carefully nurtured fire, bursting into occasional spurts of bright flame, and the keen fragrance of roasting coffee helped create a special haven in the warm enclosing darkness of an Arabian night. It became one of those rare magical moments when one becomes intensely aware of actually *being*.

Later that same night, the Saudi drivers and their Arab friend in whose dwelling we were to sleep, drove us a short distance to bathe in a nearby hot-spring. It was housed in a domed building resembling something straight out of an Eastern fairy tale of magic and genie. Inside, a naturally formed pool steamed at the bottom of a small volcanic crater; narrow steps carved in the rock led down to it. A slab-tiled floor and flat stone benches circled the crater in which gently steaming water bubbled temptingly up from a small fissure in the rock. One or two bathers stood with obvious pleasure in the waist high hot but bearable water of the small azure lagoon thus formed. Having already bathed, half naked, bearded and brown skinned men lolled on the benches drying themselves and chattering noisily.

Stripped to my underpants, self-conscious, having no real choice but to enter the water, longing to do so after an appallingly hot day, I was aware that my pink white skin made me odd man out among the Arab host. There was no doubt that I was attracting general attention. Feeling incredibly Western I would like to have shouted out 'Bollocks!', a good old English swear word but thought better of it. Instead, I carefully edged down the crater's steps and slid into the deliciously steaming water, smiling and attempting to ignore the stares of the hospitable but naturally curious audience.

The hot spring was an enjoyable experience, but there was a more demanding one to follow. That night I had set up my camp bed in the friendly Arab's long, single room abode. The following morning, dressed and ready to get out to the wagons, a young boy, or it might easily have been a girl, sidled close up to me. It was certainly not easy to determine the true gender of the owner of the dangling hennaed curls, the powdered face and kohl-blacked eyelashes. *He,* as the creature seemed more likely to be, stood shyly merely a hand's breadth away giving off an explicit sense of the erotic. The boy-cum-girl was not unlovely and I experienced a moment of unease, thinking – what on earth was expected of me. The painted young person continued to stand disturbingly close looking searchingly into my eyes, leaving me at a complete loss as to how I might escape the situation, and wondering what the hell I was supposed to do...

Fortunately, the incident passed off when the exotic creature gently reached to lift out a recently acquired fountain pen from my shirt pocket, obviously admiring it as though it was some rich, jewelled thing. Without words

I pressed the pen as a gift upon him (I was later told that it *was* a boy) a gesture which happily brought the alarming episode to an end, much I suspect to the relief of the Arab drivers who closely watched the incident.

One other memory of the trip had been the unwanted attraction I seem to have inspired in one of the Saudi drivers. Very black in colour he might well have been the descendant of an African slave from times past. At least six-feet tall he looked giant-like dressed in a loose turban and an ankle length galabia – the common Arab gown; it was evident that his manner towards me threatened more than overtures of friendliness.

The test of this came when – camped outside the perimeter of the American oil base, the Saudi drivers were allowed in to buy cigarettes and other luxuries from its canteen. Alcohol, strictly forbidden under Koranic law in Saudi Arabia, was sold in the American canteen under the guise of a brand of very liquid hair oil. By the time the men returned to the wagons later that night they were far from sober. On this occasion my bed was made up in the back of the truck in which I rode daily. It turned out to be the first port of call for the now drink encouraged admirer, who, grinning, reached up and began to clamber over the tail-board of the truck.

I had never before felt quite so isolated in this strange land. Under cover of the blankets on my camp bed I had earlier hidden a twelve-inch machete – just in case – to be brandished as a warning weapon should need arise; I reached for it. The darkness practically hid the giant's face as he climbed, yet accentuated the whites of his eyes, the mouthful of gleaming white teeth, lips drawn back in a frightful rictus grin; the danger was real. Later I liked to think that it was an observing god who saved me, because the huge man over-balanced, falling from the high tail-board of the truck, to crash heavily onto the rock hard ground. The fall must have brought him to his senses, cooling his drunken ardour if that is what it was, for he staggered off into the night. Come morning all was well; what occurred appeared to have been forgotten and we went on our way.

One other vivid memory from my time overseas as a soldier remains with me; this was a brief, fondly remembered romance. Called Mary, she counted as a first serious love affair, although with hindsight, infatuation might better describe it. A young Greek woman living in Cairo, she was a few years older than my self and the mother of a very small child; there was never any father in evidence. Compared to my own naive and inexperienced years Mary was world-wise. She spoke four languages, was blond, slim, respectable, intelligent and very fanciable.

Our meeting took place when my locust-mission army pals and I were shipped off across the Red Sea to enjoy a much needed two weeks leave in Cairo. Heading out of the railway station complete with kitbags and cases, the six of us piled into a horse-drawn gharry to be driven through the literally teeming streets of the city to a *pension* loudly recommended us by our Egyptian driver. In broken English, using excited hand gestures, he emphatically promised that it was, 'Very, very best place British stay Cairo!' Once there, as soon as we clapped eyes on Mary the proprietress no one chose to question the driver's wisdom. Cool, slim, and extremely beautiful in an immaculate white dress, Mary appeared to us who had spent the last year in appalling desert conditions without sight of a single feminine face, all that any man could desire.

Up several flights of marble stairs, the *pension* was situated in a large tenement block bang in the middle of bursting at the seams, over-populated Cairo. On one particular night of our stay there was the lack of a bed for a new arrival. By some means or other, to the green-eyed envy of my pals I was invited by Mary to stay at her place for the night – thus providing an empty bed.

Shyness could not have totally hidden my acute awareness of Mary during the time of our short stay in her *pension*. Perhaps, I thought afterwards, she in turn admired my own youthful appearance in well-bleached summer-khaki shirt and shorts. Leaving with her that evening I ducked down in the taxi out of sight of possible lurking Military Police – her home, a modern flat complete with a stout black-clad female Arab servant, was in the out-of-bounds district of Cairo. That night, from my arrival there I cannot recall the events preceding the moment I finally found myself in bed – *alone*. The promised night of romantic bliss, vividly created in my imagination, proved to be a lonely, sleepless vigil. I lay awake unknowing what might happen... anxiously wondering how I would react if anything did? My only experience of the kind during my comparatively few years on earth had been a sullied, unavoidable one in a Basra brothel not too long ago, one forced upon me by the married man who'd needed the support of my presence in order to visit the place. The initiation proved to be a sordid introduction into the mysterious act I had heard so much about.

The night at Mary's turned out to be a frustrating experience; but disappointing or not I comforted myself later, it had been an unusual out of the ordinary adventure. Back at the *pension* my army pals refused to believe in the innocence of a night spent at gorgeous Mary's place; giving me a rough-ride, declaring a total disbelief when I persistently shouted that, 'Nothing at all happened!'

After our leave ran out we sailed as drenched, third-class deck passengers on the prow of a small steamer across a storm-swept Red Sea to the port of Jedda – our final base camp in Saudi Arabia. Later, posted to North Africa, I received a couple of letters brashly lipstick kissed beneath Mary's signature; we'd had one or two other brief meetings; one was during transit when I took French leave by climbing over a Cairo barrack wall in order to spend an evening with her. We dined romantically in the open air on a lovely Egyptian night within sight of the pyramids. However, after completing three years abroad, given a month's leave back home in England, then spending my 21st birthday sailing back to Egypt across the Mediterranean, somehow my dream of Mary faded, came to an end. It remains in time an occasional conjecture as to what *might have been* had I returned to Cairo to marry her? Later on, sent home from North Africa on a hospital ship with stomach problems, I was eventually discharged in 1947 with no higher rank than corporal and rewarded with an ill-fitting brown de-mob suit and a minute pension. Settled back in dear old Blighty I returned to the metalworks where I was once apprenticed. Later, I worked alongside an older brother, Roland, repairing and re-building motor cars. Over the following seven years I learned a great deal about shaping and forming metal. By that time I had also become aware of a useful gift I possessed in devising inventive practical solutions for out of the ordinary problems – connected that is, with making things.

Once, when still in the army in Barce, North Africa, this fact emerged to prove of value. I was asked by the captain of our small REME workshop to devise an orthopaedic bed for setting broken bones. Given a scribbled idea on the back of an envelope of how it was meant to operate I was left to my own devices. Intended for the local Egyptian hospital, the bits and pieces necessary for engineering it were to be salvaged from an aircraft graveyard nearby, where the skeletal remains of crashed Nazi, Italian, and RAF planes were laid to rest. Involved in constructing this bone-setting machine, it crossed my mind how better used these parts were when taken from machines originally meant for the hateful purpose of killing people, and to be now used instead to contrive a machine for healing.

Back in civvy-street I was comparatively well paid for my skills in the workshop. But the joy of being a civilian and free from the army was short lived. Whereas life should have been good, for some reason it was not. The exact cause of dissatisfaction I could not possibly have explained at the time. The nearest I got to it was that there seemed to be an ever present lack of purpose, or any remote sense of fulfilment in whatever I was doing. Although I had married, fathered two children, and worked in a well paid occupation – worthy as these things were they were insufficient; there remained a constant nagging feeling that there must be more to life. Looking back I was totally incapable of thinking out whatever the trouble was. The only vague clue as to the dilemma appeared to be in a long standing wish that I had been born an artist. It seemed an unattainable and useless wish when thinking about it because I was convinced that artists were born as such – weren't they? Like the boy I knew during my schooldays who could sit down and draw practically anything, without effort it seemed; he had definitely been an artist – *born* and *gifted* with that envied ability.

This was what was at the back of my mind at the time, yet, on second thoughts I questioned – what about the clay models I'd worked on recently in my living room. They were not all that bad, and at least they'd persuaded me to respond to the advertisement I'd read about evening classes at the College of Art in Leeds. And now here I was, standing in this incredible room where people were actually engaged in making sculpture.

Chapter 2

Evening classes and opportunity

The year was 1949 and from that time on life became a mad dash three evenings a week. Clocking off at the garage at six, dashing to the wash room to eliminate the muck and sweat of nine hours hard work shaping and welding metal, and then a hasty journey across town to the College of Art by six thirty. Two nights a week I would be using clay, one of which was spent life modelling; a third evening was drawing from life. My first visit to a life class took me completely by surprise. Sitting at the back of the life-room, pencils, board and paper ready, even knowing it was a life class I was still astonished when a middle aged, dark haired woman walked sedately from behind a screen, disrobed, and allowed herself be directed into a pose by the tutor. Although married I had never in my life seen a completely naked woman, and here was one to be looked upon, observed intensely in fact for a couple of hours. The strangeness of the experience fled the first moment I realised just how difficult a task it turned out to be – getting anything remotely worthwhile down on the immaculate sheet of cartridge paper. There was little time for lewd thoughts; by the end of the class the model had taken on a naked ordinariness which surprised me as much as her first unclad appearance.

Over the next four or five years all my spare time was shared between family life, my job at the garage, evening classes, and making whatever sculpture I could at home. I became a workaholic and my existence a busy journey balancing out these widely differing activities. At work I became increasingly fed up with the job, which, whilst not uninteresting, felt more and more like an activity preventing me from doing what I really wished to do. The fact that it represented a way of making a necessary living became incidental. It was hard to envisage the present as an unalterable pattern governing the rest of my life. At thirty years of age the thought of the sameness of the next thirty-five proceeding remorselessly on until I was sixty-five and ready to retire, did not bear thinking about. There seemed to be no possible way of escaping the deadening succession of the years ahead. It was a problematic time. The elementary education I received up to my fourteenth birthday, nor my time in the army, equipped me in any way to *think* or perhaps work out a plan shaping a more agreeable future. I found material and practical matters relatively easy to deal with; I was intuitive when it came to ideas needing original solutions. The main problem was that I had never attempted to reason out ideas or concepts of the slightest intellectual nature simply because I had never associated with people who did. If complex or vaguely abstract thoughts entered my head then they were generally worked on with an emotional bias and more often than not a romanticised one. There was never any longing to be clever or brilliant, only an an unexplained desire to create something meaningful, perhaps beautiful. In the jumbled way I thought at the time it seemed to be a need that came directly from a strange inner entity called the *soul*. The influence of this personal soul arrived in one's consciousness from a spiritual source without obvious material existence, but was connected in some way to both body and mind. At least, that is what I believed, having been convinced of its existence by various books read and a few parsons I'd heard sermonizing.

Meantime, after five uninterrupted years of evening classes in sculpture I must have become fairly well known to the lecturers and looked upon as a serious part-timer – whatever that might mean. The first signal offering opportunity for change arrived when it was mentioned during one evening class that the College wished to include my one and only carving in an exhibition of full-time students' work; the exhibition was to be held in the City Art Gallery. Never having been a great believer in myself I recall being more worried than happy at the prospect. The work in question was a twelve-inches high alabaster carving; the original idea came from a tiny Madonna I had modelled in half-relief and laboriously cast in lead; the Madonna's hand was held out in supplication. The week following the exhibition I was congratulated and told by the sculpture staff that the schools collection had bought the Madonna for the sum of thirty-pounds, an amount particularly valuable to me in the early 1950s. In due course, the cheque arrived, (my first ever) presenting me with the difficulty in finding anyone in my circle with a bank account able to cash it. Nevertheless I was surprised and pleased that someone actually wanted to own, even buy the work.

One Thursday evening shortly after, I was patching up a

plaster cast at the studio sink when the lecturer teaching that night walked up and casually said, 'Look, there's a studio assistant's job going, are you interested?' Fully realising the dismay he'd caused, the tutor turned away, smiling and saying, 'Well, think it over. But let me know within the next couple of weeks if you'd like it.'

I caught the tramcar home in a mental flap, knowing there was a virtually unacceptable choice to be made. The lecturer who approached me about the job, Alf Park, a helpful sympathetic man, wishing if it was in his power to help me without being over persuasive, had dangled the proverbial carrot before my eyes. Should I take the job it would obviously bring me into direct contact with Art, particularly sculpture... and wasn't that what I wanted above all else? However, the wage on offer was poor compared to what I was then earning. At this later date, in retrospect, the problems to be faced look so much less than the implications taking the job presented at that time. There were others to consider besides my self – how would it affect them? Not well in the long run.

And did I really wish to be more or less a lackey, a labourer in the studios at the beck and call of student and staff. Thinking about some of the tasks I would be facing, which, as an evening student I had seen George, the existing studio assistant, doing – such as cleaning up the appalling mess left behind when a class worked with plaster, casting it or filling moulds. Plaster of Paris when a large group of fifteen or sixteen years old students were using it left the studio looking like a snow storm had swept through; both hard set and slushy plaster covered floor, studio furniture, tools, and just about everything in sight, and plaster is a thousand times more messy and worse to shift than gentle snow. Did I really want to be landed with that kind of job? Thinking of this anticipated chore as one among many similarly envisaged, I was forced to question, that apart from a big drop in income, would it really be worth the swap? I left it at that, hoping the problem would go away; but of course it did not. At the following Monday evening class, I was asked if I had decided about the job yet, was I going to take it on? Unthinking, I immediately replied, 'Yes!' and the next moment felt alarmed at the answer I'd given, yet feeling incapable of reversing that decision. It was done, no matter what difficulties (and there were many) turned up in the future it would be a matter of making the best of it.

*

Some months later, accustomed to the routine and work in College I was not particularly happy. Instead of the exciting, enjoyable job I'd imagined it turning out to be, directly connected with all the things I wished to do and believed in – it was not enough! Apart from the old familiar sense of frustration, the work often involved physical tasks such as humping innumerable sacks of clay and plaster, each weighing a hundredweight, up two staircases sometimes three, and I was never a Hercules. There was a hand-hoist but that was as physically demanding. A further regular chore needing attention at eight each morning was that of attending to the clay bins – which meant breaking down hard clay with lump-hammer and spade, adding water and thumping the mass, adjusting it to the correct consistency for easy modelling.

The damp cupboards were also an important item morning and evenings. In the days before the glut of polythene, these wall-length, ceiling-high cupboards, lined with zinc, sheltered portrait heads and other clay models when these were not standing out on modelling bankers to be worked upon. The cupboards prevented wet clay drying out and were to be kept constantly damp by a twice daily spraying using a brass garden syringe. Numerous other important tasks were to do with the hundred and one items necessary to keep a sculpture studio working well. One job I did appreciate was looking after the many tools in use such as carving chisels; these were regularly tempered and reground down in the basement workshop and foundry – a place which would eventually become my base of operations, helping with the innovative teaching soon to take place in the College.

Not so good were times when a particular tutor, obviously disapproving of me for some reason, changed his routine when I arrived on the scene by noticeably allowing students to leave the studio before any attempt was made to clean up the shambolic mess they invariably left. But things eventually changed for the better; my gradually acknowledged usefulness as a metalworker gave me a greater sense of fulfilment by my taking part in the new kind of work going on. Further help came by way of the Head of Sculpture, Harry Phillips, an incredibly kind bearded man of true Bohemian appearance and character. Adopting me in the first instance he spent considerable time teaching me the rudiments of moulding and casting small sculptures in metal.

The small foundry down in the College basement was suitable for melting about seventy pounds of bronze ingot, sufficient molten metal to cast an average portrait head. Whilst exciting, metal-casting became a frightening process when the furnace was noisily blasting away, melting down its charge of bronze; the temperature and colour of its glowing firebricks changing from a sinister dull red to one giving off an intense white heat. The tiny sweltering foundry vibrated with excitement resembling something like a cavern in Dante's Inferno, *and* all but felt like that when operating. On casting days, students crowded in just before the crucible of molten bronze was to be tonged up out of the furnace preparatory to pouring. When the ear splitting furnace-blast was switched off, the ensuing silence could almost be heard. The near to brimming crucible of glowing liquid bronze was lifted slowly out of the furnace; the suspense of this obviously dangerous moment when accident might turn quickly into tragedy, caused those watching to catch their breath.

It took two of us, Harry Phillips and myself, using huge iron-tongs, to lift out the heavy container of boiling, bubbling, metal, which gave off black smoke and glowed a sinister iridescent green and gold, the air around it quivering with the intense heat. Working in unison we would lower the crucible steadily into its holder, an iron circular band with long rod handles at either side of its diameter which sat ready and waiting, resting across low walls of bricks at either side of the casting area.

After fluxing and skimming the liquid metal free of impurities and dross, the holder containing the brimming crucible was carefully lifted – the person on each handle warily manoeuvring it until its milkjug spout was aimed over the funnelled inlet of the prepared and waiting mould. The crucible was then tipped, *quickly,* and out poured a continuous golden stream of molten bronze, into and filling the negative space inside the mould in order to produce the eventual art work – splashing out as it did so tiny red-hot globules of metal which curved like meteors in space, It could be a dangerous moment; if only rarely, a mould could explode should it contain even a speck of moisture – the sudden expansion of steam blasting its way out; fortunately I never saw this happen.

Eventually I rigged up a one-man system in which I could melt, handle and pour a bronze or aluminium casting without other assistance. All these activities helped add a new dimension and sense of excitement within the College – which was already primed and poised to *step-out* and away from the confining years of traditional teaching and its resulting tendency to bring about academic standstill.

Once reasonably adept at metal-casting, as a perk I was allowed to cast small bronzes of my own – a fish, a Greek horse, a fawn, and other creatures, all finely finished, patinated, waxed and polished. Harry Phillips persuaded me to travel down to London to show the bronzes to Heals on Tottenham Court Road; the huge department store included an art gallery and might well offer to sell the small sculptures on a commission basis.

But no, the lady in charge was charming once I overcame my natural reluctance and plucked up courage to enter the posh up-market store 'No...!', they already had more than they could show or sell of things like this she said, sympathetically; she thought the bronzes were lovely things, but, 'Sorry... No!'

Embarrassed, I fled, inwardly cursing the great weight of the bronzes in my backpack; I resisted a momentary impulse to dump the things in the nearest litter bin and caught the first train home.

Back in College, over the following months, I became instrumental in introducing new methods in the actual making of sculpture. One was in the building of armatures;

these were the iron, aluminium and chicken-wire skeletal structures over which clay is modelled; the armatures often bore masses of very heavy wet clay. Previously, these were cunningly but laboriously fastened together with innumerable twists of 20G galvanised wire, a method probably used since Renaissance times. Having persuaded the college to invest in oxy-acetylene welding equipment, I found that willing students quickly grasped the rudiments of constructing armatures by this quicker and more secure method. Looking back my arrival in the College came at a timely moment in that it helped bring in newer industrial skills, so replacing existing age-old traditional ones. It was a sad change seen in one sense, but necessary in that it helped break the back of a long, overplayed mystique of craftsmanship, which, whilst admirable in its own right, would anyway soon have fallen prey to the speed of twentieth century technological developments.

Although the long years spent working in industry and workshops served me well in many practical respects, otherwise they had done little if anything to allow me any real understanding of the complexities and concepts underlying Art. Employed in industry meant an unavoidable consideration of the practicalities of making or repairing objects, a process which gave me my weekly wages, and of course my employers, their profits.

*

Apart from the less attractive aspects of being a studio assistant the work had its lighter moments. Although no longer an evening student I was still able to spend time up in the life modelling studio helping the evening tutors in various ways. Thursday was overtime night and also evening life modelling class so that most times I enjoyed the last two hours of the working day.

Evening students, arriving at six-thirty worked until eight-thirty, with a short break between for coffee and to give the model a longer rest period. Beginners in life-modelling were always politely but emphatically warned *never*, on any account, to touch the model when using the callipers to take a measurement. These callipers, consisted of two long, slender, curved aluminium arms, pointed at one end and hinged at the other by means of a single bolt and tightening wing nut. To take a measurement before reducing it down in scale to the half or quarter size of the clay figure in progress, one approached the jock-strapped male model, or naked female, gently closing the points of the callipers to within no more than a fraction of the life-model's vulnerable flesh. One Thursday evening a new student arrived to join the existing evening class of half a dozen others. He was a forty-ish, business suited man, plump, balding, and looking as though he had at that moment stepped out from behind an office desk. On this particular evening the model was an amply proportioned blond woman posing for her first time. The new mature student, obviously excited, preparing to manipulate the callipers eagerly approached the model. There was an immediate cry of, 'Oh-h...!' and 'Do-oo... be careful!' as the model jerked away to escape further contact with the cold points of the callipers which, quite literally, between them, had pinched both her belly and her shapely bottom. A titter came from somewhere in the studio, while the culprit, apologizing profusely, insisted that it had been an accident – the callipers slipped! Following a quiet word of warning suggesting the man be more careful next time, the evening tutor calmed the model and the class continued working. Ten minutes later there was an abrupt scream, the sound of a slap, and the model, hand to tingling breast fled in tears to hide in her cubicle. The seemingly unabashed offender, one cheek bright red, was asked to leave – for good! The distressed model only resuming her pose after assurances that what happened hardly ever did, and was unlikely do so again. At coffee time the group of students enjoyed a ribald argument – *had* it been an accidental slip, or couldn't the chap help himself – the points of the callipers substituting irrepressible male fingers?

However, apart from such episodes livening up the occasional college day, it began to look as though my comparatively new situation, although directly in contact with my love – Art, once again seemed to offer little further promise of anything ongoing happening in the near or distant future.

Chapter 3
On understanding Art

Surprisingly innovative methods of teaching began to appear in Leeds College of Art; they were offered in place of the usual academic studies. Becoming actively involved on the practical side with these new directions helped subdue for a time my habitual discontent.

It had became obvious that something was badly needed to rescue the fast sinking ship of Art Education in the latter half of the 1950s. The thought of accepting anything new if its origin was in *Modern-art* was devastating to numbers of the lecturers who for years had settled back into happy uninspiring patterns of teaching. It seemed that little originality was demanded from students, or for that matter questions asked of them about Art at any level of thinking, such as – *what* is Art; *what* purpose, if any, does it serve in society; or *what* is the meaning of Art? The result, or non-result of such a lack of inquiry was that much of the work produced in College lacked the sparkle one might expect from fresh young minds bursting to outpour and express feelings in a creative, original way.

Suddenly, new alternative lines of study were being offered. These differed greatly from the old teaching of imitative and unquesting methods which might or more likely *might not,* produce new *Old Masters.* Dynamic, more open-minded lecturers were appointed, and practising artists also brought in to teach on a part-time basis. These innovations related more to Modern Art and contemporary artists came about due to the evangelistic fervour of the lecturer, painter and committed educator, Harry Thubron; he had been appointed Head of Painting in Leeds. Almost overnight the previously uneventful College days became times of intense, unending excitement. Art became a great adventure – a voyage of discovery into previously unconsidered uses for materials and daring new ways of painting, and making, shaping, and constructing things. New images expressing ideas more relevant to the present – the mid-50s (it was 1956) were appearing. Out of the sheer joy such innovative changes generated the students buzzed with energy and excitement. Without in any way excluding the traditional and academic finer points of painting and sculpture, these new lines of inquiry into the methods and concepts underlying Art now were startlingly different. They contrasted sharply with the previous hours a student spent in College – often seeking to emulate the work of past generations of art and artists. Magnificent as the Art of the past might be, *they,* the students, lived in the here and now of the mid-twentieth century and wished to demonstrate an awareness of what this meant in their terms.

The eventful changes within the College mirrored other extraordinary happenings in the outside world, reflecting also the anticipatory mood of the times and the many post-war events and innovations taking place, of which – Sputniks, Dr. Spock and Rock were just a few; the Beatles and the Rolling Stones were yet to come. Men and women similar to myself, not long back from the war, were waking up to dream of a brighter future and experiencing a sense of release from the restrictive disciplines of years spent in the armed services; we were arriving at a newly discovered sense of individuality. What was taking place was a foretaste of *things-to-come* in the following decade – the incredible Sixties.

My own understanding at that time of how the kind of work the students were doing was connected with what I knew as Art, appeared, to my unlearned mind, complete rubbish. They were to do with Space the students informed me when asked, but I failed to see any vague resemblance to Art in the bent bits of wire or the drawing of meaningless lines and dots scattered there on paper. Students were being taught to do this instead of what I felt they should be doing, like painting or making sculpture, creating worthwhile images portraying everyday things ordinary people could recognise such as portraits, landscapes and sculptured figures. What on earth had Space got to do with Art? I conceived Space as being the place where the sun, the moon, stars and the planets hung, up where scientists were nowadays busy shooting rockets.

Gradually however, doubts crept in, and in the end I was forced to question the strange ideas now being taught. By this time I had been, not unwillingly, dragged in to show students how to weld, braze and fasten wire and odd shapes of metal together; the curved bits of wire bent this way and that, turned suddenly at right-angles and perhaps back again, or upwards, downwards, or in any odd direction – it all appeared quite mad! Students told me that the exercises were to make them more consciously aware of the *space* they occupied, daily. Space was not a separate item up in the sky where I with my limited, unthought-out understanding considered it solely to exist. No, in the studies the students were pursuing they were dealing with the everyday space we occupy in order to live and wherein we move.

One more patient student when I self-consciously asked him to explain what was *really* going on, said, 'Just try to imagine a block of space.' He held both hands apart, separated by twelve inches or so, then moved them to a position above and below then sideways – I suddenly realised he'd described an imaginary block, a cube of Space, as though it really existed; which of course it did! Another said, 'If you can see and accept that a cube of wood or some other solid exists, why not a cube of space – empty space if you like, but it's there? The shape and volume of it needs to be sensed in the mind's eye – then using the imagination to project it yet unseen in front of you it becomes conceptually real.'

Thinking back, my thought processes seem to have been incredibly simplistic; but many of us were ignorant of many things only fifty years ago. To my unlearned, 1950s, untaught mind, madly attempting to understand these strange new concepts, it all sounded unconvincingly daft until the proverbial penny dropped and I was able to imagine – along with other abstract ideas, that intangible block of apparent nothingness theoretically defined as Space. It remained a difficult image to grasp until such concepts, along with others equally difficult, actualised within my mind, and the various insights grew to become minor yet seemingly huge revelations. This bending of wire in all directions (an exercise in spatial awareness as it was called) *if* one was able to sense and internally visualise three-dimensional space, was not so weird after all. Formulating the various proportional and dimensional aspects of objects in space was like working out how to manipulate and place objects in a room, or arrange forms within the limited two dimensional space of a canvas or painting. Grasping the idea of Space as a thing one would become better able to organise forms – shapes in space, arrange the various masses of a sculpture, a building, or a whole architectural complex for instance. It seemed to boil down to a matter of visualising the space in and around an object as well as a total awareness of the phenomenal object itself. I found if I could do this then Space became a reckonable item and a realisation of the fourth-dimension – time being an inescapable part of it, together they seemed to measure our own veritable existence.

Recognising that I was in process of learning, of *finding out*, these sudden insights were exciting. It was not information taken and digested by having read a book; rather it was the delight of actually arriving – with a little on the spot help from younger intellects than mine – at an understanding of various abstract concepts undreamed of previously. The pleasure such hard earned knowledge brought was the harbinger of an immediate second, unwelcome insight. This was the sudden perception of the enormous gap in my very real understanding of Art. I was shocked by the fact that I knew next to nothing of the complexities underlying and surrounding the meaning of the word. The five and more years attending evening classes, while not entirely wasted, merely taught me what I needed to know about modelling a figure in clay and other means and methods of producing a sculpture – that was the whole of it; about the ins and outs of Art and its underlying principles and concepts I knew little, if anything.

Fortunately, for the time being, I was kept too busy and in demand to worry about this real sense of inadequacy. And shortly, a more important degree of help arrived in the appointment of full-time lecturer to the painting staff. It was intended that he should take over the three-dimensional side of the painting school's work. This newly appointed lecturer, Tom Hudson, was to become my boss and mentor in the future.

A naturally friendly man he was easy to get along with if sometimes demanding; and proved to be, a along with Thubron, a committed art educationalist with a fixed determination to change and improve the existing system of Art Education. The great thing was that he would always take time out to explain things to me of which I was ignorant at the time. So that, slowly, very slowly, owing to his enormous patience and my own desire to learn, I eventually began to grasp more of what the tutors were talking about when discussing Art or a student's work.

However, a further problem arose, which was that owing to my increasing involvement with the practical aspects of the teaching, it was becoming more and more impossible to cope with the workload of everyday studio tasks I was expected to carry out.

*

There had been occasional easier working periods during this passing year working as a studio assistant; the tasks slackened during college holidays when students and staff were away. There was still much to be done but a more relaxed attitude prevailed.

Often, I was able to escape early from College and find time to work on sculpture at home, take on jobs about the house, and still have time to read or play games with the children.

One favourite day was Sunday when Robin Hood was serialised on television just before tea-time, and Sunday tea-time was always a special occasion when the children looked forward to a feast of cold meat, cakes, jelly and custard perhaps, and other special goodies. Before that feast however my customary task was to sit squeezed on the settee with a child on either side, our collective attention riveted to the nine-inch black and white screen. Towards the end of the programme a threatening change in audience attention and behaviour took place. Pent up excitement and anticipation not altogether to do with the adventures of the bold Sherwood Forest outlaws gripped each child. The arousal reached its peak before the cliff-hanger end of the serial arrived moments before the last notes of the theme music accompanied the ennobled Robin as he disappeared gloriously over the far horizon.

Until then the childrens' eyes appeared to be glued to the flashing black and white pictures but were also slyly diverted eye-corner-wise straining to peer expectantly at Dad. A tense hush ensued, quickly and alarmingly followed by a simultaneous unmusical outcry of, 'DA-DA-DI-DA-DAA...!' trumpeted out through closed fists by one adult pretend-sheriff, and two small pretend-outlaws.

This was the recognized, nervously awaited signal each Sunday when all hell broke loose. Unseen, before the signal sounded, tiny hands cunningly grasped cushion-corners ready to fling these missiles hard at the appointed target – Dad! The ensuing battles barely lasted minutes, during which time loud triumphant cries could be heard issuing from the mouths of the ever victorious mini-outlaws. The wicked sheriff generally surrendered, groaning with assumed pain flat on his back behind the sofa, puffing out breath after breath, spluttering away airborne cushion feathers until an ever tolerant wife and mother would shout, 'Enough, that's enough of it! The cushions'll all be ruined..., anyway, your tea's ready. Come on!' They were days remembered with everlasting fondness.

*

Approaching the end of Summer term just before the long vacation began, having finally made the difficult decision, I realised that the time had come to hand in notice of my leaving. I was fed-up with being a general dogsbody; secondly, money was becoming more and more of a problem. I intended returning to some kind of industrial work although knowing deep inside that I would regret losing much of what the past year had meant to me. I wondered what it would be like to return to the old hum-drum, day after day of working to live rather than being involved in creative work and ideas, even if it was only on the periphery of the scene.

During my time at the College, in between the ordinary tasks one or two others of an unusual nature cropped up. One was when the Principal called me in to to tell me about a problem with a lead statue of Peter Pan in Leeds Roundhay Park. Someone, children most likely, had swung on Peter's outstretched arms, breaking them completely off. It would cost a fortune to get the enormously heavy sculpture down to London for the necessary restoration work by experts. Someone in College then thought of me; could I fasten the arms back on and restore it to its original appearance? There would be a fee for the work of course. Thinking it over, doubting I could make a perfect job of it, I agreed on condition that they find a plumber to give me a hand with any tricky soldering work required.

In the end the job had been fun. The city works department lent the plumber and also set up a screen around the broken statue. And because it was late Winter and cold, they'd installed a glowing coke brazier and a supply of coke to help keep the two of us from freezing to death.

Sadly, I have forgotten the name of the plumber who turned out to be a good, down to earth Yorkshire craftsman and an invaluable help. The lifesize arms, which, continually bent up and down, creased, flattened, and finally broke off completely. The plumber and I opened up and reshaped the ends, made brass sleeves as inserts to strengthen the rejoining, and soldered the arms back together, finally filing and sanding down the solder until the joinings no longer showed except for a difference in colour. The final task had been getting the metallic shine of the repair dulled down to match the original black patina of the sculpture; lead and solder do not react similarly chemically. The colour match had not been perfect but the park people were very pleased with the result. There'd been a photograph of the statue in the Yorkshire Post and a report about its repair; I had also been paid twenty guineas for the task – a badly needed and useful amount of money at the time.

Another tricky job had been that of repairing the broken base of a bronze portrait head in the collection of Leeds Art Gallery. Making the repair I recall thinking how amazing it was that I, me, was actually handling and mending a sculpture by the famous artist, Epstein.

Nevertheless, these sideline events failed to outweigh the disadvantages of my employment as studio assistant. I eventually sought out Harry Phillips, Head of Sculpture, telling him I wished to leave at the end of the present term.

From then on, for the first time, lacking any real interest in what was going on in the studios, I almost wished I had never set eyes on the place. Yet, at a deeper level I knew this not true; working and associating with lecturers and artists had undoubtedly given me something valuable. I knew for instance that I would never again consider Art from a previously unquestioning point of view and out of complete ignorance.

However, one morning shortly after this firm decision I was told that the Principal wished to see me – would I go up to his office. I imagined it was to collect my employment cards or for some similarly connected reason.

But no, after a few comments about how I had helped with the new work in college, to my complete surprise and near disbelief he asked what would I say to an appointment on the teaching staff as a part-time lecturer? The thing would be at the lowest grade to begin with of course, but it *was* a lectureship, and I would only be teaching four days a week which would allow time for me to carry on with my own work. The lecturing fee would also provide a salary of more than I might earn in industry, not a lot more, but certainly more than enough to satisfy my needs. How incredible! It was one of those more than rewarding moments life rarely offers up.

I walked out of the great man's office in a daze. Was it true, was I *really* to become a lecturer. I experienced a profound joy and a sense of gratitude for this gift just now received, for it *was* a gift, this sudden change of fortune, perhaps hard won but nevertheless it could not be mere luck, could it? I felt that someone, somewhere was on my side.

Chapter 4

A new life, Art, and Art Education

When one of the most significant Summers of my life ended, and the day arrived for a turnabout from studio assistant to lecturer, the material aspects of existence immediately improved, otherwise, life in College to begin with did not. The opposite held in fact simply – because crossing over from the caretaking staff to the academic side was not all that easy. It was my own particular temperament that got in the way; in the 1950s social barriers, although on the decline, still existed.

But as the weeks and months sped by the situation eased off somewhat. My teaching time in College was mostly spent working with my adopted boss Tom Hudson downstairs in the bronze foundry, which was now more a workshop for three-dimensional art. Tom and I in combination made a good team in a sense of the coming together of his art-educational background and my varied experience and know-how of industrial skills. Such skills were more related to sculpture but also connected with the unique

Constructivist aspects of the early twentieth century together with concepts promoted by the Bauhaus in both Art and Design. These relatively startling ideas, Thubron envisaged, would magically transform the old ways of teaching visual art in Leeds College and bring them sharply into line with a rapidly evolving post-war world. Similar ideas about teaching were being tried out by the painter Victor Pasmore, Professor of Fine Art up in Durham University. These collective ideas and methods of teaching would, in years to come, develop into the nationally accepted Basic Design Course which introduces students to the essential, formal language necessary for the creation of all visual-images in two or three dimensions.

Both Hudson and myself were products of English working class families. Tom had survived the Second World War unscathed and afterwards attended art college. He was an expert on colour, the history of art, and appeared to possess a photographic memory; to my naive mind of the time he seemed to know just about everything there was to know about Art as well as almost everything else!

For myself, as someone aspiring to make sculpture, despite vain attempts to claw my way up to achieve a more creative way of life, I remained virtually chained to my less elementary educational background. I suppose that was until being pitched head first into a group of creative people comprising both artists and lecturers; people involved in replacing largely redundant methods of teaching art in order to introduce others more directly relevant to later twentieth century.

My appointment as a lecturer in a college of art was an undreamed of miracle as far as I was concerned. I was intelligent enough to foresee the greater benefits yet to come, the most important of which was the chance to get to know more about Art in its wider sense. Although a lecturer I would at heart remain a student, directly learning just as a student might attending art school – and acquiring in the process that vital knowledge of the visual grammar all original artists must possess.

*

I think it was in 1957 that Hudson told me one day of a major exhibition on in London to do with the new technology of plastics – materials fast becoming increasingly important in the post-war world. Considering the innovative teaching we were engaged in, seeing the exhibition was a must. The trip down to London would be during College time with all expenses paid; it should be a useful, pleasant two days experience. Also, while we were down there Tom planned to visit London Zoo in order to take slides and film various exotic animals; both were needed for a lecture on colour he was to give shortly.

On the train down to Kings Cross I sat daydreaming as the outside world flashed by, my thoughts dwelling on how life had changed, and on the inconceivable luck of the job which had come my way. Also lately, I had sold two or three small sculptures so that everything seemed to be too good to be true, and now here I was on the way to London and being paid for it, it was pure magic!

But, that aside, sitting back into my seat I recall trying to work or puzzle out various things in my mind, things to do with sculpture generally. Having learned by experience that *buts* are useful words concerning doubt, and *doubting* I had come to know forced one to really think things out. The most immediate problem nagging at me needed some kind of resolution. It was to do with my ever present thoughts about the *things* I was working on at home. Not exactly sure what they were in explainable terms of images and objects in the sculptural sense, all I could say about them was that starting out from a formal idea they ended up resembling neither animal or human form.

What I was attempting to do was to build something of visual interest which might also be considered a meaningful image. This was the simplest most direct explanation of an art object that I could think of, leaving behind any previously fixed ideas I'd had about Art. It seemed a simple, reasonable enough concept to do with an art work.

In College we were taking first year students through two and three-dimensional exercises utilising space, shape, and the iconic forms – point, line and plane. These add up to the basic elements comprising all visual images. Out of College, using the front room of my half a Victorian house as a studio, I determined to construct something based upon almost similar instructions given out to the students over the past few weeks. Choosing the cone as a basic shape I sought a way of evolving an idea from this geometric figure into an object. Whatever image or work came out at the end of it I hoped that it would resemble an acceptable sculpture, abstract in one sense maybe, but nevertheless a work of art.

Drawing out the surface pattern of a truncated cone on white card I transferred this to 20G brass sheet and allowed the idea to develop from there on. What eventually came out was a small block-like object, which, filed, cleaned up and polished took on an appearance of near mechanical perfection. I then patinated the metal by applying hot chemical solutions until its colour was a rich dark brown with glimpses of olive green showing through here and there.

Standing back to take stock of the object, small as it was it was certainly unique and unlike anything I had made or even seen before. Geometrically satisfying it obviously possessed more guts in an aesthetic sense than those fancy decorative wire nothings I had made and sold recently. Yes, I concluded this thing was much more worthwhile. Not a particularly pretty object thank the lord, it was quite the opposite in fact! Within the apparent block of metal, observed through any of its four conical pierced flat sides, was a tiny shaped inner chamber; the descending cone suspended pointing downwards within this almost secret inner space became mysteriously significant, helping make the visual experience of the whole image a special one. The near to geometric image, its colour and tiny crab like feet lifting it slightly from the its slate base, was abstract on one level, but it otherwise reflected a human/animal presence. Minutely sculptural, it certainly gave off a sense of a self-important yet undefined material existence.

My further meandering was interrupted by a nudge from my companion on the train. Tom on the seat opposite was pointing to a page in his Guardian at a headline stating that the Russians were going to be the first to shoot a satellite up into Space, 'There'll be men up there very soon,' he said, turning back to continue reading.

Arriving at Kings Cross I recalled my last trip to this immense, frightening city – London; it was less than a year ago when I travelled down trying to sell those animal bronzes at Heals?

On by tube to Russell Square, Tom booked us into a rather plush hotel. Thirty-nine shilling for bed and breakfast seemed to me to be fantastically expensive in 1957; it was my first stay in such lavish surroundings. On by Underground we arrived at the plastics exhibition where I found the beautifully engineered technology of the plastic producing machines incredibly impressive; yet their extruded products gaudy and unlovely when produced by the thousand in garish primary hues. I became quickly bored; Tom was not, examining in the most absorbed, concentrated manner just about everything there was to see and touch – particularly if relevant information leaflets were there to be picked up.

That evening I was treated to a meal in a Lyons Corner House just off Piccadilly Circus and listened to Tom enthusiastically discussing the plastics industry and how it would reshape civilisation – in time it did; he was right in so many ways but not all of them good. To bed; and after a typical English egg and bacon breakfast next morning in the baronial dining hall of the Russell Square Hotel we were on our way to Regent's Park and the great London Zoo.

Here, everything went according to plan. It was a lovely day full of brilliant sunshine and both of us took innumerable slides of any creature displaying tone, colour, or texture, all of which might help Tom's forthcoming lecture on the science and theory of colour. After a particularly good session photographing and filming ridiculous stomping round male peacocks unavailingly displaying their grandeur for the female of the species it was back to Kings Cross to Leeds and home.

*

Back in College, the result of our London visit was that the subject and technique of working with plastics became Tom's immediate obsession. For myself, forever single mindedly inclined towards Art in any form rather more than in techniques and materials, I was less interested.

But of course, there was no escape from a direct involvement with plastics in that they came to be used a great deal in the students three-dimensional constructions. There was one particular plastic product which I came to loathe – this was resin reinforced glass-fibre. In the early stages of its development in the 1950s the process was a hit or miss affair. Often, what had been moulded in the smelly, sticky resin which soaked the strands of glass fibre and which was eventually *supposed* to harden – often *didn't!* Instead, it remained *adhesive* and stayed overpoweringly *smelly* – spreading its spiky, feathery strands of gluey glass-fibres to every available surface in the studio including shoes, clothes, and hands; the stuff seemed virtually impossible to remove. Also, apart from the unpleasant fumes and mess involved in the process, there lurked the hidden danger of creating a minor explosion. Back in the early days of the process it was necessary to mix the catalyst and accelerator – each separately contained, into the resin; *never* never, under any circumstances were the 'twain to meet' or be mixed together. Dire and repeated warnings were given to students against this hazardous mistake.

But naturally, one day, a less aware student committed the cardinal sin of mixing the two incompatibles together in an empty Heinz bean tin – quite suddenly, the small basement studio erupted with a horrifying shout of, 'Oh dear, help! It's bubbling and getting hot!' Tom, fortunately was working downstairs at the time and shouted, *'EVERYBODY OUT! Quickly, quickly out!'* Grabbing the virtually boiling tin from the shocked student's hand, which by now, was crackling loudly and spewing out foul smelling black smoke, he flung it into the sink and fled to join myself and students outside the studio door.

'Back, get back!' Tom warned once more while I peeped around the door jamb, ready to retreat further if it became absolutely necessary to do so.

In the end, it was not actually a false alarm, or an event which resulted in a catastrophic minor atomic explosion; yet, what did actually happen was unnerving, causing all the more fearful students to panic and flee the building.

The unhappy bean tin containing the antagonistic chemicals, now in the comparatively safe haven of the deep sink, continued to pour forth foul black smoke in repetitive puffs equal in intensity and sequence to the ever louder guttural crackles given forth – until the tin finally split asunder with an enormous 'BANG...!' The exploding tin simultaneously gave off a sinister black but beautifully shaped mushroom cloud of smoke – which rose into the air, appeared to bounce off the studio ceiling a couple of times and then disperse in a rolling pall of black, repulsive and noxious fumes. I suspect this same event occurred in more than one other college of art throughout the country in those early polyester resin days.

*

Term upon term followed and work continued. The weeks of free time during the lengthy vacation periods – arriving at regular intervals together with my shorter working week enabled me to get on with my own sculpture. There were also other incredibly useful advantages in the very different life I was now leading.

For one thing it provided me the invaluable opportunity to become much better informed; there were lectures and exhibitions to attend; conversations to listen to concerning subjects I'd never heard of previously. The information

I absorbed came in on many and various levels. Working in the studios – *with* and not *for* other lecturers and artists became a precious learning time. Teaching itself was indeed learning – learning about the formal aspects of Art which arose during the innumerable critical discussions about any and every student's work in two or three dimensions. Occasionally I would even be asked for my opinion – which immediately demanded an analytical response forcing me to assess rightly or wrongly whatever visual image was in question.

Outside of gaining knowledge about Art with a capital 'A' I remained relatively ignorant in respect of many other intellectually demanding subjects – particularly that of language and the meaning of words. My grasp of English was barely more than elementary. I remember with extreme embarrassment what from this distance in time appears as a farcical incident that happened once on a short train journey. Funny in retrospect it was the result of a sheer lack of schooling and my limited knowledge of the English language and the meaning words. At the time it caused me to more than regret my short years of elementary schooling which, although good, ended when I was a mere fourteen years of age.

Tom Hudson would sometimes ask me along to attend a lecture with him, help with a weekend teaching course, or visit an occasional exhibition. Such invites were, I realised later, not only for the sake of my company, but were also a generous attempt to help fill the gaps in my sheer lack of learning; Tom was always a concerned helper and natural teacher for the less aware. This particular occasion, occurred following a lecture concerning social conditions in Britain Post World War One. The talk was given by a professor of sociology from a nearby university and it took place some distance away, necessitating a short train journey; Tom and I travelled part of the way back with the lecturer. Tom's other pet subject at that time, which seeped into all his ideas relevant to art and teaching involved growth and shape variants of *organic* and *inorganic* forms – plants, rocks, or anything either term might classify as such. His conversation on the train with the professor on the subject was decidedly *heavy*. Listening intently I attempted to grasp bare fragments of the discussion I thought I'd understood. During a short pause in the talk, having remained utterly silent throughout, determined not to appear completely subdued and thick, I spoke out about some organic item Tom had mentioned a moment or two ago. 'Is that really an orgasm?' I asked. Later, Tom, to my ever remembered horror, gently, straight faced, explained to me that the word I meant was organism, and how close the spelling and saying of the two terms was.

But whatever the imagined problems and innocent gaffes of the period were, for me it was a very important, informative time. With it came the realisation that there was a need to become increasingly aware – by observing, listening, learning, reading, thinking and reasoning and doing all of these in order to better understand the complexities of not only Art, but myself and Life itself – could it be that all of these three were one and the same thing?

Chapter 5
Artists and making sculpture

One morning – it was 1958, I was seated among a group of people lounging on chairs loosely gathered at a scruffy cup-ringed café table. Round the corner, away from the red-brick college of art building with its mock Greek mosaic over the entrance, this tiny café was an ideal hideaway for the clique involved in the new teachings now well established in Leeds College of Art. The group comprised Tom Hudson, the art-history lecturer Norbert Lynton, Harry Thubron, myself, and four practising artists.

My beginners state of mind at the time put me in awe of these latter four who, in my naive eyes, resembled minor gods – because each was a comparatively well known, established artist. Invited by the far sighted Thubron they were here to teach for one or two days a week. The nearby University of Leeds awarded Gregory Fellowships to practitioners of all the Arts; Herbert Read, I believe, was a deciding factor in the Visual Art awards. Two of the present Fellows were among the four artists in the café. Terry Frost a St Ives painter was one, the other, Hubert Dalwood was the Gregory in Sculpture. A third painter sitting at the table – Alan Davie, had preceded Frost's fellowship at the University. The fourth artist, Victor Pasmore, down from Durham, was teaching in Leeds for the day. Pasmore, together with Thubron and Hudson, would all eventually be effective in bringing about the great national changes in the system of teaching Art and Design. Under the more liberal and encouraging economic climate provided by the Labour Government of that time, British Art Education in the 1960s would develop the most enlightened methods of teaching the Visual Arts compared to anywhere else in the world.

In the late 1950s, the presence in Leeds College of Art of artists exhibiting both in London and internationally, created a vital, enthusiastic atmosphere; it also brought a sense of real contact with the contemporary, real world of Art – outside and beyond the College.

Sitting in the café on that particular morning I could not fail to compare my present situation with that of the not too distant past. Teaching, many years later, I invariably told students to associate if possible with the kind of people they wished to become – people who were involved and doing the things they themselves wished to do, because such contact somehow rubs off; fortunately, it did so for me.

Recalling this occasion in the café should I ever feel down, it taught me that the virtually impossible can actually happen. I remember also that the conversation was full of a general air of excitement to do with the fact that the first Russian Sputnik was that very day up in outer space – orbiting Earth. Years later, asked to write a few paragraphs for an exhibition catalogue explaining why a particular sculpture of mine was shaped as it was, and also describe the idea behind it, Sputniks and Space came directly into the statement – bringing to mind once more that very special morning in Leeds.

The Gregory in sculpture, Nibs Dalwood, on more than one occasion sought my advice on technical matters when I worked as studio assistant. Later I welded up a fifteen feet high armature for him and also helped clean up rough aluminium casts directly delivered from the foundry. Yet, although doing so earned me money I soon opted out of further help – deciding I needed the valuable time to carry on with my own work; money while not plentiful was no longer in desperately short supply.

There were similar offers of studio work which I also refused. Successful and reputable artists were always on the look out for good studio workers capable of assisting in the task of finishing sculptures. One offer I received was that of a job in Hepworth's studio in Cornwall – if I fancied it? The temptation to work with the famous was attractive, but, 'No!', I said, 'I'll stick with what I've got. Thanks all the same.'; although it was rewarding to be asked.

With my mind still in a conceptual vacuum in those early days as to what my work was about, I continued to make objects and images resembling contemporary sculpture. These were not entirely without interest and were – I believed, finished works quite worthy of exhibition; my technical know-how gave the objects a sense of permanence and presence.

I realised that I was greatly influenced in both idea and attitude by the sculptor Dalwood. I consider him to have been an imaginative artist and still do. Although once winning the John Moore's Open Exhibition I think he never ultimately received due credit for the original, tactile style of the work he evolved. Modelling sculptures in clay these were cast in aluminium or bronze and worked on by himself after casting – which added to the hands-on quality of the finished works.

I retain one fond recollection of Nibs apart from the original sculpture he produced. This was the knack he possessed, if present anywhere in College, of invariably turning up in the life-room should a new attractive female model be posing for her first time. Unused to the strain new models were not unknown to faint in the first half-hour – slipping sideways off the throne maybe. Somehow or other Nibs Dalwood would be there, open armed and ready to catch the distressed lady.

With regard to my own work, I remain indebted to Dalwood, whose indirect influence taught me that strength and toughness in a formal image could be far more effective than contrived attempts to create conventionally attractive images. In the immediate post-war decade artists appeared to be searching for more unique, extreme forms of expression far removed from the old. In the confusion of concepts that arose at the time figurative images of the real often approached ugliness, particularly in sculpture. A sense of novelty in the choice of materials also became fashionable. But these less traditional images often seemed to openly contradict the outworn aesthetic aimed at figurative perfection and the ideal of the beautiful. Such new works of art proved to be the real creative signposts as to what in fact constituted the truth of the time – stark alternatives perhaps rather than continuing efforts to churn out palliative conventional images. It could have been that fresh from the traumatic years of the last great war artists were out to cleanse and re-establish a more humanitarian world – by a cathartic search for forms and images expressive of the tumultuous carnage of the first fifty years of the twentieth century; attempting to do so by depicting images which vainly hoped to parallel and express the tragedy of trench war, of Hiroshima, and the horrors of the Holocaust.

Dalwood working as an artist in the 1950s in Leeds was certainly a product of post Second World War art, his early figurative work fell totally within the above concept. His sometimes macabre figures (which I failed to understand at the time) looked like an attempt to create the raw antithesis of humans popular in romanticised classical sculpture. The only practising sculptor I was likely to meet he was therefore someone that a person such as myself, an aspiring sculptor, would have in mind as an example.

He exemplified the working artist, one wholly involved in the creation of art, sculpture. He represented an actual artist rather than a teacher or lecturer as were those I worked with. Naturally indebted and grateful for the opportunity given me by the College people, I knew that art education as such was never the real thing. Admittedly Dalwood's living was provided by a fellowship grant, occasional gallery sales, commissions, and the odd lecture, but no matter – he was first and foremost directly committed to making sculpture. Up to Dalwood's appearance on the scene Leeds College of Art was the one and only place where I was exposed to Art – where it was talked about and practised.

The affect of these realisation served to strengthen me with a greater determination than ever to make Art – to create original works; *what* they might stand for in meaningful terms was the question I held perpetually in mind. At this point Dalwood's influence ended; his ideas were of no help in coming anywhere close to defining even vaguely what feeling or concept underlay the art objects I was rarely happily producing.

Compulsively continuing to make sculptures regardless of being in the conceptual dark, I would have been hard put to it to explain them to anyone who was more than curious to casually inquire. The only firm conclusions I came to about anything created during this period was that I should give up the attempt of trying to understand what they were about and get on with it. Neither, I convinced himself, should I bother about the fact that all the works being produced, although original in image, were very different one from the other and lacked any obvious similarity of style. The importance of the objects, I decided later, was that by creating them – dreaming the images up from scratch and working through the problems of bringing them to a balanced conclusion, then I was acquiring the formal experience and language I once had the insight to see was the tool-kit of the original artist. It was a language which would be needed if I was ever to accomplish anything worthwhile in the way of Art.

*

My circumstance having improved I eventually bought a build-it-yourself concrete block garage to use as a second studio. The house had quite a long garden which opened onto a quiet, leafy residential lane. On a slight incline, it was always a pleasure to leave busy roads behind and walk up it on a balmy summer's day – arriving at the double gates my father had made and put in place for me. My father, retired but still active, had also laid out the concrete foundation ready for the garage components when they arrived.

Once these were delivered I took on the hefty task of erecting the blocks and getting the roof in place. Completed, the garage-cum-studio was not all that big as a working space, quite the reverse, but it was better than nothing in addition to my front room. A great drawback was that in Winter the place was deathly cold and virtually impossible to heat satisfactorily. The two Aladdin paraffin heaters I purchased barely kept the resident spiders warm.

Nevertheless, with everything at last organised for work, I strode up the garden path one late November day – feeling that it appeared to be another of those magical moments life offers up too infrequently. My day off from college – the children were at school and my wife at her mother's, I was therefore alone and free to do whatever I liked.

The first thing after equipping the new garage come workshop with a bench, tools, and the materials needed to construct armatures, was to order a hundred weight or so of modelling clay and two galvanised dustbins in which to store it. All therefore was ready and poised, awaiting a determined surge of creative activity – inspiration being a more doubtful visitor.

A few days previously, giving into impulse I had gone into an antique shop near the tram stop to ask the price of a three-feet long, strangely shaped wooden object. An inch or so thick in the middle, six in depth, thinned down and rounded at each end, its centre was slotted to provide a hand hold. It was an African shield the antique shop owner informed me, pointing to where shallow-cut tribal symbols decorated one edge of the thing. I'd noticed it propped in a corner when looking through the shop window each time in passing on my way to College. Lured and creatively interested by its exotic shape I bought it at what I thought was a give-away price.

Recently I had been impressed by one of Dalwood's cast-aluminium sculptures. It was a material and casting process I had introduced into the college foundry work recently and which Nibs had taken up with alacrity. Using great ingenuity he had evolved a way of producing metal sculptures at an affordable cost. Aware of this I was about to begin modelling a work of my own in clay based on the African shield. If what came out looked reasonably promising as a sculpture I would get it cast in aluminium at the foundry; I could just about afford to do that!

Up in my new garage studio at the end of the garden it was cold, very very cold; I moved about continually to keep warm and help the chilly air circulate. The electric fire I'd plugged in and the two permanently lit paraffin stoves were definitely not giving out enough heat to warm the place. Relying on the physical effort to warm me up I constructed an armature five feet high out of iron rods, galvanised wire, and chicken wire. Firmly secured to a wooden base-board and set up on a ground level turntable the thing was ready for the addition of clay. Resembling an enlarged skeleton of the African shield the armature rose vertically from a narrow ovoid stem – widening to body width then narrowing again vertically to become a slender shape a hand might grasp. I spent the rest of the morning spreading an inch or so of clay over the chicken wire; modelling the work solidly in clay would mean placing a tremendous weight on the slender armature and dangerously overloading it.

After a quick solitary lunch along with a book propped up as added luxury, I returned to the studio and began the formal composition of the sculpture. Modelling directly from one's imagination is a hit and miss affair of adding and removing clay – of altering, shaping, and continually trying out this shape or that to see if one or the other works formally and contributes or destructs the already existing composition. This intuitive process is immediately creative in the sense that clay is a naturally plastic medium which may even replicate the artists fingerprint in the final cast of the reproduced sculpture – even in bronze. In a manner of speaking the sculptor brings the clay image eventually to life – inanimate life but seemingly representative of the animate, which we may then call Art. *Presence* was a term of expression artists used at the time when describing a sculpture which gave out an emotive, unique sense of its own phenomenal existence.

Ending up dissatisfied with the final look of the day's modelling was not an unusual state of mind. Even at this early stage of attempting to create work someone somewhere might actually call Art, I realised that the effort to do so would never be an easy option. I knew that people who often imagined how pleasant it must be to have such an occupation were wrong; they were certainly misguided about the kind of art I wished to dig out of my psyche – or wherever the yet indefinable images presently lay. If Art meant simply imitating a pre-existing idea – recreating an already familiar image... well, that was fine, but for me it would never be that easy, not if I was to do anything really worthwhile – what ever did turn up would have to come uniquely out of me – which necessarily might take some years. But I intended achieving that end wherever or whatever that end might be? Any normal disappointment with the day's work happened! at the moment it was something to be expected and stoically accepted.

I worked on the clay of the sculpture for most of the following month, changing the composition for the better, yet sometimes for the worse, until the thing was nearing the stage when I needed to say that it was finished and as complete and as good an image as my present level of creative know-how would allow.

What the final image was meant to represent or give out I could not have said, but there and then I decided to call it The Sentinel. The clay was ready to take a plaster mould – providing a pattern for casting in aluminium at the foundry. I expected to undertake the moulding during the coming weekend.

Before then however the weather took a turn for the worse and calamity struck. I had once been told that clay, once frozen, completely disintegrated on thawing. I then understood why farmers welcomed frost at this time of the year – it broke up the frozen lumps of claybound soil.

Glancing out of the French-windows onto the frozen garden this particular morning the scene looked quite beautiful in tonal greys. It remained beautiful up to the moment my imagination informed me of what might possibly be taking place up in the cold silence of the garage-studio. The paraffin stoves were lit twenty four hours a day but *what if* the paraffin had run out.

Dashing up the garden it felt infinitely colder inside the studio than out – the stink of burnt wick was acrid and almost *felt* black. Unfortunately I needed to leave the door open to get rid of the fumes – the temperature in the studio dropped yet more...

Thank God! The damp cloths draped around the clay sculpture normally there to prevent drying out were icy cold and stiff, but not yet white with ice. Unwinding them one by one, horrified, I changed my mind instantly – realising that the clay surface *was* hard, but not hard in the way that clay dries out normally. Instead, I felt an icy cold crystalline hardness against my fingers. My spirits not only sank but seriously crashed at the thoughts of all the time and work wasted – the model was all but lost...

Urging myself on, not to give in, murmuring a series of strongly expressed, tension releasing swear words I very quickly refilled the paraffin stoves, cleaned the wicks, relit them, and moved them close in to my precious clay model. I had already switched on an extra electric fire and stood back watching, with a sinking heart.

Waiting for the first sign of whatever was going to happen if anything did – I concentrated upon the finished modelling of the clay surface. Sensing a slight rise in temperature I thought the heaters were doing the trick and it seemed as though no obvious change was taking place. I peered closely at the clay, then closer still... it seemed as though the clay was resuming its natural wet look. Good! but no, something was very wrong – the surface texture of the clay, normally appearing tightly cohesive was becoming decidedly granular – tiny fissures were appearing. I quickly arrived at the awful conclusion that freezing had already taken place, expanding the mass and body of the clay. Now, due to the slight rise in temperature and thawing out, the clay mass had lost its natural binding property – I was about to witness the model, the Sentinel in its death throes and slowly disintegrating – unless...

How I saved the thing eventually I remain altogether unsure. Thinking back, I remember watching a great chunk of clay on the lower part of the model begin to come away, fall in slow motion, parting gradually from the wire mesh of the armature, the surface modelling of the sculpture distorting slightly as it fell. Quite remarkably with a lightning reaction I caught the piece in both hands, holding it gently in an attempt to save the clay's modelled shape as it fell with a slither towards the cement floor. Quick as a flash and with little thought I carefully but firmly pressed it back onto the armature exactly from where it came away – it was as though fitting in a wet piece of a three-dimensional jig-saw puzzle. Much of the modelling was damaged where my fingers sank into the soft clay surface due to unavoidably pressing it back on, but the general shape remained. Quickly, I moved away the heaters, grabbed a flat piece of wood and pressed, batted and bashed the whole surface of the model, compressing and binding the clay once more in order to re-establish its grip on the mesh of the chicken wire.

A month later when the Sentinel stood confronting me in the studio, cast in silvery aluminium, fettled up and finished, I thought – what an odd thing to have made, I must be mad, and wondered if others might have similar thoughts or equally incredulous ones.

Chapter 6

Brussels and a small exhibition

That summer, Tom Hudson and I went by plane to Belgium as part of a student group organised by London University. From the airport we travelled on by coach to Brussels and then Luxembourg. Halfway through to completing a commissioned decorative sculpture for a local business man I had come across a notice about the trip in the Observer – there were spare seats to be had.

The work I was constructing was made up of thin rods brazed together to form parabolic curves; lacking interest in the job it became unwanted work – taking up valuable time. On seeing the notice in the paper I suggested that if Tom helped me finish the commission we might share the fee – it would pay for us both to join the trip to Belgium where we could visit the recently opened Brussels Exhibition. It was an important late post-war event where many countries would be showing examples of the state of their national arts and trends in design and technology.

The two weeks trip proved exceptionally worthwhile. I found myself living for the first time in close contact with intelligent young people which, among other things was a valuable learning experience. I remember opting out one day from a collective bus ride around the Luxembourg vineyards – I'd felt like spending some time alone. Despite having no other language than English apart from a now forgotten smattering of Arabic I made my way to the local swimming baths. There, a youth befriended me and we conversed happily in broken English and sign language. Although it seemed an insignificant event it was rewarding and one I recall happily.

Back home, the start of the new term and the pace of work both at College and in my own studio helped a return to normality. By this time I had accumulated twelve or more sculptures – the largest being the Sentinel. The others were relatively small and I was not exactly sure what to do with them. Self conscious about actually doing so I knew that I needed to let people in College see them – who else but artists might offer any worthwhile critical opinion? Working in comparative isolation at home and attempting to judge my own work with any real level of objectivity was far from satisfactory. All I could honestly say of the works was – that while a few were original and interesting, the others, while not without interest were not very remarkable.

Having worked hard to produce the sculptures they undoubtedly showed a sense of commitment. Accepting the fact that while some of the pieces were certainly objects of art, what they collectively lacked was a consistent style attributable to one person – me; that was what I felt was wrong. It was an unfortunate conclusion but a necessary perception if I was ever to find my way and work with more consistent intention and purpose. Perhaps I was at the beginning of a long ego-trip – yet, without that element of *selfness* (not necessarily selfishness) which inevitably urges an artist to abandon all else in order to express his or her innermost feelings, there would be neither artists nor art.

The problem of showing the work became foremost – what must I do? I lived with the question for days on end, believing that I had reached another timely impasse when one knows intuitively that something has to happen, and that generally the person who must make it happen is oneself. I had also realised by this time that dwelling upon a problem fixedly in the mind rarely fails to pay-off. Working up in the Sculpture School one day, showing a student how to construct an armature, the obvious solution arrived in a flash... why not? That's what I would do. My fair-sized front room on the first floor at home would become an art gallery, a small one admittedly, but rooms in private galleries were never all that big. There'd be just enough space to display the sculpture. I would set it out as it might be exhibited in a gallery and invite people along – special people whose opinion I valued.

That same weekend I called over to see my eldest brother Maurice, a signwriter and house painter. As a child back in the early 1930s I can still see Maurice unrolling white lining-paper and pinning it horizontally the length of the living room wall in order to paint a sign for the local cinema. After quickly sketching in the outline letters he would place a Wills Woodbine between his lips, light it, take up maulstick and paintbrush and without the slightest hesitation commence painting in the huge letters – to watch them appear in colour was like magic. The most fantastic thing I recall was that the cigarette never left his lips. Burning slowly down the end glowed bright red with each succeeding inhalation and outward puff – while the grey ash, once tobacco, remained intact, assuming a gentle downward curve. As a small child looking on, the amazing thing was that the ash, a complete grey ghost of the original Woodbine remained, whole and rarely dropping off unless Maurice happened to cough – even then, miraculously, it did not always do so.

On the occasion of the present visit I was there to ask him for a price for painting the whole of my front room pure white – an unheard of choice of decoration in 1958 and quite mad in Maurice's opinion; although I believe he had long considered me that. However, if I insisted of course he would paint the room all white. We agreed a price and after the room was stripped of its contents, the plain floor boards sanded and varnished, the work went ahead. Later that week I was shouted to, 'Come up stairs and have a look...!'

The four-storey Victorian house my family and I occupied had once been divided down the middle, making it into two tall back to back dwellings. Therefore the room intended for a gallery was one flight up from the living room. Excited, dashing upstairs, beckoned in by my brother, I entered the dazzling, pristine room. The effect, not to put too restrained a word on it, was brilliant! Happily, Victorian architects gave rooms ample height allowing the space a proportional dignity – this space was now an immaculate white.

But I needed plinths or stands on which to display the small sculptures – each separately in its own small portion of space so that its individual effectiveness would not be lost. Unable to afford box type plinths, and anyway they would have looked bulky heavy and perhaps dwarfed the images; my solution was to order a hundred-feet of two-by-one timber and a length of thin planking; I intended to design my own lightweight plinths.

It took the weekend to saw, glue, nail and screw together

a number of slender but adequately suitable vertical stands; the half-inch planking, cut up, acted as top surfaces. Painted with a coat of white emulsion they were of a reasonable design, unobtrusive and easy on the eye.

Each time, entering the empty all-white room before filling it with sculpture, its virginal whiteness was uplifting. The noiseless, unsullied space felt peaceful, religious and spiritually persuasive. Overwhelmed on one such occasion I recall wondering if there really was something humans possess called the Soul, and if so – then was the feeling I experienced on walking into this immaculate room an echo of that other world entity?

In succession I had been a Wolf Cub and a Boy Scout, and finally, in order to be with friends I later joined the Boys Brigade. These youth movements together with parental insistence on attendance at Sunday school and a ten-minutes Bible story most mornings at elementary school, although providing moral instruction and implanting a few lifelong responsible codes of behaviour, were, eventually, unconvincing as to the existence of a mythical man-God; I had never seriously bothered to question such a belief. But this is not entirely true – for in direful times for safety's sake I sometimes felt it necessary to mutter the Lord's prayer under my breath, which must at least imply a faint hope that there *might be* a Divine existence hanging around.

Setting the sculptures out in my beautiful white front room – arranging them and rearranging them time and time again became a trying process. It was probably an attempt to make the things look better than I felt they actually were. But eventually, once the exhibition was set out the overall impression was not too bad! It looked an intriguing show of small sculpture if a rather crowded one. The style remained varied but there was nothing I could immediately do about that; given time I would!

Considering that this self-proposed exhibition was ready for viewing I decided it lacked only one item. Walking down to the local off-licence I glanced over the shelves with a reasonable eye to cost. Spotting acceptably labelled Cyprus sherry at under a pound a bottle I bought three, stopping on the way back to buy half-a-dozen suitable glasses. It being the first time I had ever, ever, done anything vaguely like what I was about to do, I worried excessively whether sherry was an acceptable drink to offer – even after the chap in the shop assured me that it was. Walking home, the labels on the sherry bottles brought to mind Stass, a Cypriot painter friend and fellow evening-student still around in College, now studying part-time; I would invite him round.

After arranging glasses and bottles casually but with care on the marble mantel-shelf I felt my tiny one-room gallery was complete and only awaiting visitors.

*

Terry Frost accepted the glass of sherry. Glancing round to take in the general look of the room and its contents – his initial expression of surprise echoed the immediate pleasure he'd shown on entering. 'This is marvellous! Good lord... I wasn't expecting anything like this. It's good... great!' he said, with the usual gusto and evident joy he contributed to every event in his eventful life. Painting in St. Ives before accepting the Gregory at the university in Leeds he was some years older and much more worldly than myself. He loved painting and sculpture without having fixed opinions or conventional ideas about what Art *was* or was not; he also possessed a critical yet constructive eye when it came to looking at painting or sculpture. An inmate of a German prisoner of war camp during the last world war, painting had become his life – along with all that such a way of life encompassed he invariably conveyed the impression that the creative act was a great, joyful one.

Now, he slowly went from sculpture to sculpture, contemplating each without comment, sipping sherry and silently holding out an empty glass for more – a good sign the stuff was palatable. Finally, he took great pains to point out which of the works he liked and which he thought the lesser of and giving specific formal reasons why and why not. His comments were generally reassuring, to the point, and he talked as one artist to another which was as valuable to me at that time as anything else he might have said.

A useful item of learning I gathered was – that as two or three other invited artists or lecturers from College came to look at the work over the next couple of weeks, although expressing preference for one particular sculpture as against another, each arrived at the same conclusions as to what was formally right or wrong with any one image. It was evidently the practising artist's acquired language of form coming up-front once more; it had nothing to do with the imaginary talent or the skill I once imagined an artist was gifted with at birth. If that was already there – good for whoever was granted it! But equally necessary was the hard work and effort to observe, learn and understand about the use of space, mass, marks, shape, colour, tone, balance, texture, contrast, etc., etc., – all the available aspects of language comprising the visual arts which must be studied and acquired. But of equal importance, if not more so, this knowledge needed to go side by side with a compulsive drive to express one's feelings in whichever media and discipline of the fine arts seemed appropriate to make manifest the idea – in my case in the late 1950s it was hard fought for works of sculpture.

Continuing to search for meaningful answers to the many deep seated thoughts bothering me, I came to the conclusion that after an artist attempted to bring into phenomenal existence his or her original conception, then its image must be relatively unique. Yet at the same time it must conform to certain established principles loosely defined perhaps by the key words – *aesthetic* and *art*. Both terms implied order, formal order – without that the artist's artificially contrived world in whatever media fails – dismally! I concluded that if the *thing* – either object, image, or other sensory experience in art-form fails to excite the emotions convincingly, it fails. Art reflects life when humans beings reshape and reorder the Tao's* 10,000 forms in order to create moving spiritual symbols.

Opposing these positive products of human creativity, disrupt and oppose Nature's laws and Man's dependence upon the Natural world out of sheer evil ignorance, error, or still worse by intention, then the end product can only result in disorder, disharmony, and in the end Chaos! And didn't the Holocaust and the devastation caused by the *Bomb* erupt from causes like these – great catastrophic events devised because of unwise human negative intelligence, jumbled thinking, engendered fear and hate?

Coming back down to earth I contemplated my insignificant sculptures. Looking seriously at them all I could think was that each – complete in its own small world – was a creative attempt to bring order and some kind of formal harmony out of the vague images contrived in my mind's eye. The attempt to make works of art I realised, not for the first time, is a progressive way to sort inner things out and, I hoped, a way to true self-discovery.

Back in College Terry Frost spoke well of my work, which brought others along curious and interested to see it. Tom Hudson preferred, as I might have expected, the more basic abstract sculptures. But most of all I was appreciative and pleased when Harry Thubron, asked to see my – *One Man Show* as he smilingly referred to it. I had enormous respect for him as a person, as an artist and also as a great teacher. A visionary, he inspired both student and artist – preaching and teaching a new way to look at and understand Fine Art and perhaps by that process ones world. I think he wished above all that Art might play a direct and important role in the lives of people – changing the environment and Life as a whole – by making it more meaningful so that the lovely and the beautiful became more common possessions.

Regarding his natural gift for teaching, often indirectly – a tiny incident occurred one day which comes clearly to mind these many years later. It seemed insignificant at the time consisting of a simple sentence – yet it was significant enough to eventually inform and turn my mind around. Surprisingly sought out and asked by Thubron to go with him to advise on an exhibition space in a building some way away from the College, I only half-heartedly responded to the invitation. Very busy – involved with students in teaching the actual making of sculpture, I implied in a round about way that I would much prefer being in the studio actually *working* rather than spending valuable time talking about things; I passed on this last bit of information as we were outside and on our way to look at the proposed exhibition site. Stopping in his tracks, resting a hand on my arm he turned to face me and said quietly, 'Look Laurie, this is *working! This is work!* Talking is working!'

This incredibly important (to me) insight he was offering – of what lay behind his words, simple as as they seem in retrospect, only really broke into my mind later on. The understanding they imparted added a further piece to the jigsaw of the more informed sense I was gradually acquiring. What had happened seemed a non-event, but Harry's words subtly hammered home a mistaken attitude imposed by my brief education and working-class background, both of which implied that *work* was a physical hands-on activity necessary to earn the wage to buy the bread of survival – both of self and of family.

*

In early Autumn sunshine I led Harry up the garden path to my front door. Travelling by tramcar from College I'd felt constrained and worried during the ten-minutes trip – being completely apprehensive about showing my work to this specially important person. Up the steps and into the hall, breath held, I showed him into the white room where the sculptures were arranged. Mumbling some quite stupid self-conscious remarks I was kindly but firmly told to, 'Shut up, Laurie!'

After providing Harry with a generous glass of sherry I hovered in the background, watching the great man go from one sculpture to another, looking with intense concentration, oblivious to all else. Later, both thankful and pleased when the ordeal was over, I could not recall a word of what Thubron had actually said – excepting that he was definitely encouraging, implying that I must keep on making art.

The two of us stood talking outside on the front door steps for what seemed an age – I think that I was talked intensely *at* rather than *to!* Harry absent-mindedly wandered off somewhere to behind and beyond the thin gold-framed spectacles which graced the prophetic world within his Leonine head – a beautiful world wherein idealistic dreams were formulated in order that they may become reality.

Unnoticed by Harry it started to rain, 'It's raining!' I informed him, taking his arm down the garden path to the gate where I pointed out the way back to the main road and tramcars. His only response was a vague smile from behind the rain-spotted spectacles not quite hidden beneath the peak of a flat cap, and an indistinct goodbye and faint wave as he walked off – completely in the wrong direction.

That he eventually found his way home was evident next morning when he came to me asking if he might bring someone else to see the work that evening, after College. The person he brought was Victor Pasmore – renowned modernist painter and Professor of Fine Art who was introducing an evangelistic course of art education up north similar to that evolving Leeds. Although these events happened many, many years ago I can still recall my surprised and astounded feelings on seeing Pasmore and Harry Thubron conversing closely while determinedly walking up my garden path. Nervously showing them in, after supplying them with drinks from the fast waning supply of Cyprus sherry, I left them to it.

Returning after a sensible interval I realised that Pasmore had looked at the work intelligently and critically – without enthusing in any apparent way he was complementary; a wise response I afterwards thought. He then pointed out that some works were more successful than others. However, just before leaving the house, talking aside to Thubron he mentioned that it was the London Group Exhibition next month – it might be worthwhile my sending two of the sculptures down and suggested I submit the Sentinel and one of the constructed brass cone works.

The idea of showing sculpture publicly presented me with a sudden, worrying crisis, it had never seriously entered my head that I would do so; I had until then concerned myself solely with making sculpture and was much too preoccupied with the task to think beyond that point. To bring the objects out into the open to be judged critically perhaps, even ridiculed, was a different matter altogether. But I was forced into asking myself the obvious questioning – why had I ever made the sculptures in the first place if not to have people look at them.

In years to come, teaching, I invariably pointed out to students reluctant to exhibit, that exhibiting work was of equal importance to the practising artist as the act of making it. Showing finished work was like writing an open letter to the people of the world – describing ones most intimate thoughts; it was like writing a love-letter and pinning it up on the wall for everyone to see, to read; it was bravely exposing one's deepest feelings to the common gaze. Playing safe and failing to exhibit in order not to risk that kind exposure might well indicate a lack of conviction and belief in the purpose of one's work, and in Art.

After Pasmore's visit, advised by people in the college I sent for details on how to submit work to the London Group. I learned also that it was quite an important show in which to exhibit at the time – if a work was selected for exhibition it gave the lesser known artist an opportunity to be seen alongside the famous who were invited to show.

Packing the two sculptures Pasmore had suggested I organised transport to the nearest collection point for the exhibition – and that was it as far as I was concerned. Being exceptionally busy I forgot about the whole thing over the following two weeks until approached by Alf Park, the lecturer in sculpture who had been my first kind mentor.

I was working in Sculpture on that particular morning when he brought the Guardian over – holding it out to read he pointed to two or three relevant lines in a long paragraph on the Arts page and said, 'Look here! Congratulations! You've received a good little mention about your sculptures in the London Group Exhibition.'

Chapter 7

A trip to London and the I.C.A.

After my complementary mention in the Guardian I felt no gratifying change within myself except a little natural pleasure. I did however begin to quibble when described in another paper as being a sculptor – I somehow did not wish to be classified so positively so soon. And anyway I thought – a sculptor was really someone who carved in stone, chipping away with hammer and chisel until the figure or whatever it was appeared as though having been hidden for ever inside the block of stone. I only once carved anything seriously and that was when, as an evening student I carved the little alabaster Madonna bought by the Leeds Schools Collection. Regardless however, after four years employed as a lecturer in sculpture in Leeds College of Art I seemed well established as an integral part of the life of the college, its students and staff. Yet I still remember feeling a certain amount of envy for the rest of the people there – they, compared to the whole of my evening class attendance's had had the advantage of attending art school day in day out, year after year. To them, making Art had become a daily task – it was like having a job in fact. It was difficult and virtually impossible for me to consider Art as though it was an every day ordinary, occupation. I felt totally incapable of a habitual output such as churning out each and every day something called art. Having an ordinary job and using one's various skills was another matter entirely; I had done this long enough in industry. But even after these last four years teaching in the college I often remained inspirationally tongue-tied – which might be one way of describing my creative state of mind late in 1959. For me, the impulse to make sculpture arrived only occasionally – in compulsive bursts of creative energy. Continuing to be unsure and in the dark about whatever I was trying to accomplish I experienced depressing doubts as to whether I was capable of producing art at all. And that worry was only a part of it; the real problem nagging me was that there were no specific concepts or images present in my mind waiting to appear – like those a sculptor sought out in an uncarved block. In fact, if asked what the word concept meant I would have been hard put to it to attempt an explanation; my briefly schooled mind could not yet have coped with such a demand.

In this case to carry on art-making meant choosing which of two paths. The first, and I knew it well, was falling into the trap of doing nothing at all; that way led directly towards failure and frustration. The other path was to work hammer and tongs at a vague idea – literally hammer and tongs because it meant picking up tools and with no explicit image in mind attacking some kind of material or other; better this than endlessly awaiting the non-arrival of inspiration. Working without a specific idea in mind was a hit-and-miss affair of hoping – hoping that by virtue of manipulating the chosen media, clay or metal for instance, that something of interest might emerge, take on shape to become the vague beginnings of an image worth pursuing. It was a wishful-thinking way of making art which very, very occasionally produced results or most times did not! The trouble was, that if this chancy hit or miss method failed then it often brought on a more completely negative state of mind than if one had never begun in the first place. Once more I realised that creating original works of art was never going to be easy! Yet, until I understood more fully what I was actually about there was no alternative way of working.

*

By the time the late 1950s came round my life generally appeared – not for the first time, to have gone into slow-drive. Teaching had become something of a routine; the earlier day to day excitement caused by the many remarkable changes introduced in College was gone! The teaching which not too long ago seemed to be an exciting visual adventure, although not losing ground educationally, had lapsed into an almost predetermined pattern.

So that when one morning Terry Frost, in College teaching that day, came down unexpectedly to the workshops, things took a temporary turn for the better

'Look here, Laurie' he said, 'I'm driving down to London on Friday and coming back late Saturday. Would you like to come? I'll be seeing a few people and meeting them might be good for you. And bring along a few of those sculptures, the brass cone things. We might get time to call in at a couple of galleries, and you never know?' He left it at that and walked away, offering little opportunity for refusal.

He was taking new paintings down to the gallery where he was contracted to show on a regular basis – Waddington's

I believe, and intended paying a few social calls while down there.

It is difficult to remember all that Terry and I talked about driving down in his van, saving that some of it concerned our teaching back in college. He was keen to point out the differences between practising artists and those people whose mission appeared to be to teach Art – they were the educators. He went on to say that unlike the artist whose recognition and success depends upon painting and sculpture, their careers rested upon teaching, the success of their students and the changes and improvements they were able to introduce into the art education system. Thubron and Tom Hudson were great visionary teachers he implied, and although artists in their own right, particularly Harry, both were more intent on improving the quality of art education than practising Art. And what a good job that was for the students and for the likes of people like you and me – art education provided paid teaching work for artists; it was the twentieth century patron of the Arts and invaluable for both art and struggling artists.

That evening, arriving in London I encountered a way of life far removed from the ordinary – if seen in the light of someone like myself who happened to be the product of a northern working class background! Arriving with Terry Frost, the reputable St. Ives painter, was very different to earlier visits paid to this sprawling, often frightening city – particularly that trip one or two years when desperately broke I was trying to flog animal bronzes to Heals. With that in mind I was reminded how visiting London cut one down to size, mini-size – its people and place-scale diminishing the most cherished illusions built up by any normally provincial ego.

I felt exactly like this when Terry pulled up outside a three-storey house somewhere in Chelsea. Let in by a small, thin, bespectacled man, he led us upstairs after exchanging old-friend greetings with Terry and giving me a quick inquisitive glance. He turned out to be Roger Hilton, a painter later to win the prestigious John Moore's Exhibition. Once upstairs Hilton crouched down to resume what must have been his occupation before Terry knocked at his door – kneeling beside a small blackened Georgian fireplace he held a tiny saucepan over sparse yellow flames. The pan contained red wine he informed us, grimacing to show toothless gums bloody and fresh from a visit to the dentist; the wine was apparently his version of more acceptable pain killer.

Later, the three of us ate at a small King's Road restaurant where the two close friends talked over memorable old times – swapping stories and recalling and retelling past pleasures and painful trials. Hilton, I realised, was a man who like Terry Frost had fought in the last war; captured, both were confined in a prisoner of war camp in the 1940s; listening to their conversation I imagined they must have shared appalling experiences behind barbed wire. I found the meal itself and the completely unfamiliar atmosphere of a King's Road restaurant strange – and soon distinctly uncomfortable. Presented with a menu listing dishes previously unheard of I had unknowingly and unwisely chosen devilled prawns – which of course left my mouth and tongue feeling as though they had been stroked by a red hot poker. A further surprise was when Hilton, wishing to pay the bill, summoned the attractive young waitress he'd chatted up during the meal, grabbed her, and gave her a smacking toothless and no doubt bloody kiss, to which she raised no objection. I suspected she knew him of old, that he was fun and gave lavish tips.

Leaving the restaurant we walked down the road to a corner pub in the heart of Chelsea – the Queens Elm I think it was called. It was the meeting-up and drinking place for a group of successful Sixties artists. Once inside the door of a small bar, Hilton squeezed Terry and myself through a jostling group who waved casually, acknowledging the two painters; I assumed the role of a very silent witness – knowing that I was among those who were artists of the contemporary elite. There was no halt in the babble of conversation going on, much of the talk was literally over my head. Most was to do with who had exhibitions coming up, what prices which artists were selling for, or else who had gone off with whose women. The gathering comprised all males until a well built women arrived – the sculptor Elizabeth Frink who had once been a student of Harry Phillips before he arrived up in Leeds College. Another sculptor present was Kenneth Armitage – I believe that the others were all painters. The events and never ending flow of known artists was becoming a bit too much to take in – and more so when Francis Bacon was pointed out, drinking over at an adjoining bar. I was glad of the apparently never ending supply of beer shoved down in front of me, it finally helped null a gradually overwhelming sense of the unreal.

My lasting impression of that night was that the people I was fortunate to be drinking with resembled a club, not one easily joined but not impossibly exclusive either; yet it was certainly special. The qualifications to join I judged, required each member to be a hard working, hard-living creative individual, committed and relatively free from conventional constraint. They would also have to possess an original and unique point of view – be an artist in fact and live as near as possible off the rewards and proceeds gained by practising art. The artists present in this Chelsea pub occupied a world far removed from that of the art world I knew in the college up North. The people gathered here – working, socializing, chatting about the latest happenings on the professional art-scene, existed at its centre, its heart – they were ultimately connected with Art – living it in fact!

What was presented to me was a sip of the flavour and texture of the true face of contemporary British Art. I was seeing artists as real people and not as a separate species read about in art-mags and set-up as distant minor gods on imagined pedestals. Although I did not fully understand it at the time this must have been Terry's intention arising out of his innate kindness.

There is no clear memory of what happened after the pub. I probably slept on the floor at Hilton's or on some other friendly floor. Next morning, Saturday, I was driven around visiting one or two artists studios. Of these, one was that of the sculptor Armitage, briefly met at the pub the previous night, who acknowledged me and then chatted with Terry whilst I was free to take a quick look at the sculptures standing around in various stages of completion. Armitage had been Gregory Fellow in Leeds prior to Nibs Dalwood.

One further important reason Terry was visiting London was in order to visit the American Abstract Expressionist Exhibition only recently opened; I think but am not sure that it was in the Tate. More than impressed by the exhibition – its scale and incredible colour, Terry raved about it. Myself, knowing little of the state of modern painting and not altogether interested in what was happening on the other side of the Atlantic, I certainly recall being overawed and visually moved by the hugeness of the surrounding vast canvases – painted with powerful uncomplicated images comprising masses of lush and beautiful colour. Thinking about this recently, attempting to equate the power of spiritually lifting music with the other Arts, the nearest I could come to it was a recollection of these greatly affecting American paintings. They seemed the closest to what are sometimes called 'oceanic feelings' and the way music can subtly break through to raise ones appreciative psyche to new spiritual heights. Literature and poetry although often intensely moving never quite seem to reach the effective level of feeling a Bach cello suite achieves – to me anyway!

Before leaving for Leeds and home, we drove into the heart of London to Gimpel's – the top London private gallery specialising in modern sculpture. Once inside Terry introduced me to its director, Peter Gimpel, and while those two swapped news about the Art world it was suggested I went out to the van to collect and carry in the few small sculptures I'd brought down. Terry had persuaded Gimpel to look at them which he did with an expert's eye, becoming most interested in the constructed brass objects. Nodding approval he said, 'Yes, come back with more of these in a year's time and we'll see what we can do about an exhibition.' Outside the gallery on our way home once more, 'There you are...,' Terry remarked, 'Do that and you'll have it made!'

Bewildered by the events of the last two days I felt as though I had been thrown into this new world at the deep end. In one sense I had – so that it was virtually impossible to take in actually all that was on offer. Unready for such a plunge into the mind toppling happenings of the weekend's extraordinary scene filled with art and artists, I was not sure how to react and respond intelligently to such unexpected, extraordinary events. Perhaps I failed to respond! I was much too new to it all to be fully aware of the various nuances of the opportunities placed before me, almost on a plate. The chance of a lifetime was there – a guaranteed way to make a name and quickly achieve a reputation as a sculptor. That is if I wished to take up the glittering prize of Gimpel's offer and so become among other things relatively well known – even almost famous.

But, within a week or two after the London trip I forgot all about Gimpel's kind offer, or any such thoughts about having an exhibition in that important gallery. That I would do so never seriously entered my mind – I was far too busy and it was as though the prospect had never arisen. Whatever the future held in store for me, well it was not going to be as cut and dried as that. *Had* I considered falling for the diversionary temptation of an exhibition comprising more of the brass and cone sculptural constructions which were of interest to Peter Gimpel but of little further interest to me, how different life might have been? But I did not because the created objects belonged to the past, the things were incidental images which happened along the way... the way to where? That was what was important – the undetermined and undiscovered path, the future, the way ahead; the idea of churning out numerous, slight variations on a theme merely for the sake of doing so was not something I wished to undertake, contemplate! To continue searching for the yet invisible, the obscure, was a much more worthwhile goal. To seek out the way forward – seeking to unearth whatever latent images and evolving ideas might emerge – this was the true way forward rather than blocking the mind by loading it with the less creative manufacture of variations on redundant, past images.

*

Around mid-term in the Winter of 1959, Harry Thubron and Tom Hudson cornered me down in the workshop with a request which was more or less a command. Leeds College of Art together with innovatory work carried out by Pasmore's students up in Durham University, were to share an exhibition at the Institute of Contemporary Arts in London, on Dover Street. Opening in 1959 the exhibition was to be called 'The Developing Process'- and demonstrate to the world the recent innovatory modernistic teaching of the visual arts as practised in Durham and Leeds by Pasmore and Thubron respectively. The vastly different approach to art education, reinforced by the often extraordinary students work on show, was meant to contrast the existing programme of study for taking the Intermediate Examination in Art and Design. Successful study at this level meant admittance to a three-year course leading to a National Diploma in the particular discipline chosen. This diploma was finally replaced by the present B.A. courses in Fine Art and Design. The Developing Process exhibition of 1959 would be the deciding factor for change and largely instrumental in bringing about the innovative Basic or Foundation courses introduced in the 1960s. The more modern, exciting, and original students work on show was intended to demonstrate and promote new ways and means of teaching the Visual Arts. It would provide the many principals, lecturers and teachers in other Colleges of Art with an opportunity to see the exercises and more completed works carried out by students at Leeds and in Durham. Unhappily, jealousy had reared its ugly head. It seemed to stem from a natural yet competitive desire to grab credit for the work to be shown in the I.C.A.

Regarding the reason for my forcibly suggested trip to London I assumed that an argumentative battle for honours had surfaced and was in full flair between Pasmore, Thubron and Hudson. Apparently there'd been something of a difference of opinion over the telephone, and neither Tom nor Harry wished to travel down to London to help Pasmore hang the exhibition. There was perhaps a loss of face somewhere along the line so that I was seconded to represent Leeds College and give Pasmore a hand in hanging the many paintings, drawings, sheets of exercises, and display the 3 Dimensional works carried out in Leeds College. With hindsight and in view of my inconsiderable stature in the art world I should have felt flattered given such responsibility, but I did not – it seemed like just another of those unexpected undesired chores which kept turning up from which there was no possibility of escape. It also meant travelling to the vast, intimidating, teeming metropolis of London once more which to me still remained a largely unknown quantity. Taking the tube from Kings Cross I managed to find my way to the Pasmores' house in Blackheath. Having by this time met both Victor and Wendy Pasmore more than once when they were teaching down in Leeds, I survived the formal dinner and finally escaped to bed. But my brief stay with them turned out to be unforgettable because of one of those stupid, funny incidents which pave and annoy one's life-history. Almost ready for bed I found that in packing I had forgotten both toothbrush and toothpaste. It could not be helped so I picked up a likely looking tube from the bathroom shelf, squeezed a strip of its white contents onto my finger and rubbed hard at my teeth. Disaster struck – the repulsive acrid taste not of toothpaste but of creamy hair shampoo lingered on in my mouth throughout the night, flavoured breakfast next morning, and remained strongly present even later in the day while hanging the exhibition work.

However, once up the exhibition looked great! I was glad to have been concerned not only with getting it there and hanging it, but more so at having played a good part in teaching and helping the exhibited works exist. Observing Pasmore sort and select sheets from innumerable folios of drawings and colour studies was an experience in itself. His ability, without hesitation, to judge, reject, or select a sheet immediately for its interest and aesthetic value was remarkable. Approaching midday when all the work had been pinned up or hung and I was busily tarting-up the dejected gallery walls with a brush and white emulsion, Harry Thubron and Tom arrived. Perhaps the various disagreements had been mutually ironed out by telephone, although I never found out further details of the affair.

I continued to work on my own sculpture and managed to have two or three more pieces cast in aluminium. As for exhibiting I did so only locally. On one occasion I was pleased when Thubron told me that when selecting work for a local show together with Herbert Read, that Read had chosen an experimental architectural piece of mine. Abstract in form it *was* actually called Project for Architecture and eventually bought by the schools collection in Leicester.

Towards the end of the Summer term in 1960 I was disconcerted when Tom Hudson told me that he was leaving Leeds College to take up a more responsible job in Leicester. Having worked closely with him for all of five years the idea of his leaving was something of a shock. During that time, even though progressing from studio assistant to lecturer, I had felt intellectually shielded under his mature and wiser wing. We had shared lots of teaching, trips, ideas and dreams together – mine more related to art, his more seriously devoted to the valuable broadening and improvement of the many aspects of Art Education in Britain. Assessing my own position at the time – not having stinted on my teaching efforts at Leeds College the rewards had been great. Regarding my somewhat better informed mind, much of it was due in effect to the working relationship and friendship with Tom. I found the idea of continuing to teach in College without his dynamic presence difficult to imagine. That apart, the past five years of learning, teaching, and attempting to make works of art had set in motion an ongoing state of expectation for new things to keep on happening; it was not likely to be easy accepting the fact that Tom's leaving seemed like the end of a very significant period in my life, and that once again things seemed to have come to a sudden, unexpected full stop!

Chapter 8

Leicester 1960

'D. H. Lawrence lived for a short time on this street,' said the agent, handing over the keys to the first floor flat in Leicester. I suspected that saying it gave the man a feeling of contact with fame; and why not – anything above the humdrum reality of the ordinary helped add interest to one's life. Having been fortunate enough to escape the struggle and monotony of a working lifetime spent in industry five years ago – my good luck seemed to be holding out just when I imagined it had not!

Yet, was it altogether luck? Perhaps not! My years as an evening student in Leeds College of Art led up to a providential time when the place was ripe for change. Those who were about to bring about that change arrived at a time when a fundamental lift of the system of Art Education in Britain seemed vitally necessary. They also came at a timely moment for myself – partly because of my obsessive interest in sculpture but also because the skills I possessed were to prove of value in what was to happen in Leeds College.

Now, these five years on I was teaching in Leicester – once more with Hudson and directly responsible for the three-dimensional side of the Basic Course as it was then called; it was taking place in Leicester Polytechnic. This establishment included a painting and a sculpture school that at the time was able to offer successful intermediate students a Higher National Diploma in Fine Art and later a B.A, award. The new Basic Course that Tom had been appointed to organise and direct was concerned with a study of the basic language and formal grammar of the visual arts; in part it would replace the earlier first year course of study. A one year course it was prior to a student choosing to specialise in Fine Art or alternatively enter a creative aspect of Design.

My ever patient wife Jean, although hesitant about moving a hundred miles away from family and friends, finally agreed to move to Leicester – hence a rented flat on Dulverton Road, a road where D. H. Lawrence reputedly once stayed. The children, Peter and Paul, would be fine, there were good schools in Leicester according to Tom.

The new job – and the offer of it had come as a happy surprise, was a much better one than the appointment back in Leeds. It was a full lectureship on a higher scale – which meant quite a bigger salary. But equally valuable to me was that it involved only three days a week contact teaching; the rest of the time except when demand called for it was more or less free; there would be ample opportunity for making sculpture. Tom Hudson invariably and wisely preferred his staff to carry on with their personal work. This in fact meant that the Basic Course in Leicester comprising on average one hundred-plus young students was taught by ten, sometimes more, practising artists or designers. And generally, apart from Tom, myself, and two other full-time older members of staff, the part-time lecturers were young, aspiring, creative people of an age likely to stimulate a student's wish to emulate an inspiring teacher.

Apart from the improved status, salary and the gift of valuable time, the challenge to move to a different college was in all respects helpful. Chance and Leeds College of Art had certainly transformed my life, yet, while working there I remained a kind of local boy made good. This was my *very own* hang-up – a self-conscious self-imposed chip on my shoulder I suppose; how difficult it is ever to change oneself! Only hindsight, insight, and one's ongoing and steadily accumulating years can do that – to whatever little or large degree.

*

After overcoming the initial worries of my responsibility for any three-dimensional studies taking place on this newly established course, I settled down reasonably well in Leicester Polytechnic. There were many unknown people to meet, and although my customary reserve was a handicap it was not too exacting a problem. The reason for this more relaxed attitude was that here I arrived as a lecturer and was also known as a sculptor with an existing reputation – however slight; my original working-class *hang-up* melted back into the past.

Due to the temporary chaos resulting from the change of place, people, and employment, my own work had come to a temporary halt; I needed the space and isolation of studio or workshop. Once more, circumstances acted favourably for me. Tom, needing part-time staff, invited four recently ex-postgraduate students of painting up from London for interview. It fell to my wife and I to put them up for the night. All in their early twenties – three males and one female, they somehow managed to squeeze in and bed down on our tiny front room floor.

One of these, Mike Sandle, did in fact stay on as a self-invited but not unwelcome lodger for six months. His one unforgivable sin while staying had been to wear out my favourite record – Puccini's Tosca, presented to me as a part of a handsome going away gesture made by the staff at Leeds College of Art.

The last mentioned event came as complete surprise. Persuaded to go for coffee in the College staff room one morning a few days before I was to take my final leave, without warning the room filled up with people. Realising all eyes were on me the penny finally dropped. To my considerable embarrassment, even horror, Eric Taylor, the recently appointed Principal, and Harry Phillips, Head of Sculpture, spoke briefly about my usefulness to the College over the previous five years. After a moment's silence Harry Thubron then said, in a manner typical of his invariable understanding and kindness, 'And what about Laurie's work as an artist?' I was then presented with a handsome amount of record tokens. A good memory in retrospect. Later, thinking back to what happened, pleased with the unexpected, kind gesture the staff made, yet what Thubron had said was an equal if not more valuable gift to me. In future years, whenever hearing a particular Puccini aria from Tosca it is always a significant reminder of my humble but yet more than fortunate beginnings. The music also brings to mind the intangible platform from where I literally stepped out into the unknown to begin the ultimate search for my self.

*

Three of the postgraduates – Sandle, Terry Setch, and Mike Chiltern were appointed as regular part-timers to teach on Tom's Basic Course. They turned out to be valuable assets both to the College (the Poly) and to me when not in it. Their early years and an unspoiled desire for fame as successful artists were their most appealing qualities. Recognition would be a more suitable word than fame, implying a genuine desire to create original and worthwhile works of art – which they did. They became valuable colleagues and close friends and by virtue of association contributed to my learning process both as a person and in respect of my work – as an artist. They were the first art-people with whom I felt completely at ease and more or less on equal terms; we were perpetual students in a manner of speaking – intense, idealistic and involved in the visual arts, hoping to make our way in the contemporary world of art by creating something of notable value. Teaching provided a living and the time and space to attempt to do just that.

Early in our relationship it must have been obvious to the three of them that I was speaking from a less informed background when talking and discussing ideas about life and culture generally. Consequently they were influential teachers when the knowledge *they had* and *I had not*, often surfaced. In return, I was able to offer them an actual experience of teaching and a great deal of know-how or expertise when it came to making things. At the same time as this I imagine I showed them a total commitment to Art – sculpture, which possibly helped them commit themselves. Incidentally, all three, for a short time created three-dimensional work in combination with painting. During our times spent teaching together and at other times spent out of college, they proved invaluable friends in helping shape and improve my mind

– and often they would reinforce my creative efforts should I flag or waver occasionally.

Mike Sandle, who became a semi-permanent lodger and friend contributed usefully and forcefully to my family life. Incredibly opposite in background, reserved and extremely sensitive, he provided a presence in the flat of someone with similar interests and aspirations. He fitted in in a not unpopular manner with my wife and two young sons, contributing to the household in various happy ways – that is if a persistent scratching away at my Tosca record might be discounted.

The other two – Chiltern and Terry Setch once they were sure of employment teaching, hunted for digs and found a suitable first-floor flat within reasonable walking distance of my own; it was also not all that far from our place of work. The ground floor of the house they were to move into was occupied by its owners – a pleasant elderly couple who appeared delighted to have people living upstairs who were art lecturers working at the Poly. They were never known to complain about any of the goings-on up on the first floor which, to put it mildly, whilst never noisily outrageous were never exactly conventional. The place was heaven sent for the two part-timers, and similarly became something of a haven where I might sometimes call in for a coffee and a chat; the house was also to provide me with somewhere to work.

The reason for this was that below the ground floor wherein lived the landlord and his wife, there was a large basement consisting of three fair sized cellar-rooms. The first of these had a sink and a necessary water supply. It was entered by a normally unused outside door situated within a high-walled, green-gated yard leading off a quiet narrow back alley-cum-street; it was very private. Once through the first room with the sink was a long passage with doors leading into the two other quite large cellars. On the left of the passage a flight of stone steps led up to the first floor and a door leading into the upper floors. The middle cellar had a low cement slab bench in the centre; it was once used for laying out and making tiled fireplaces apparently. The bench would be useful I thought when looking with a mind to renting the place as a studio. The whole of the basement was painted out white. One slight worry was that the place seemed cold and felt graveyard dank in a sinister though not off-putting way. However, the plus factors were that it was relatively bright and clean, and notably, the first large cellar off to the right of the passage had a tiny but serviceable looking fireplace. The cellars would make an ideal studio providing I was sensible about using the place and there was no worrying interference from the elderly owner couple on the floor above; as it turned out there never was! The rent was by no means excessive, and quickly renting it I moved in bench, tools, materials, welding equipment and my few existing sculptures.

The cellars were more or less perfect because of the space and privacy they afforded. As soon as I was settled in I collected firewood, a bag of coal, a kettle and mugs, sugar, tea, coffee and tinned milk, and got a fire going which soon warmed and cheered the place up, I felt that I was about to start work in my first real studio. The young painters came down from their flat two floors up to see me installed, and it maybe have been that they too felt a more real involvement in the practice of art – aside from their task when teaching it. The studio gave me a more absolute connection with Art, and I felt a vague kinship with people like Dalwood the sculptor and Armitage whose studio in London I'd momentarily visited with Terry Frost; they were the only two sculptors I had ever directly met.

*

Work on the new and evolving Basic Course in Leicester Polytechnic was both exciting and rewarding; the teaching was still breaking new ground – experimenting with and trying out previously untried materials and techniques. At the same time the many unexplored formal aspects of visual art and its wide open range of images were excitedly tried out. The difference here compared to Leeds College was that the staff were generally young artists more aware of the art of this century than that of the long past. More detached, less involved than Tom, I remained active in working with the range of ideas being tried out – simply because it was a way to help my own continual learning process. The newly devised exercises opened up ways and means by which beginner students of the visual arts might visually try-out and experiment with both media and methods – therefore learning and understanding the essence and make-up of the images they wished to create; discovering for themselves the knowledge which I was once horrified to find I totally lacked. Seen as a language it seems a bit like the vast amount of experiential information a London cabby acquires and carries in his head called the 'Knowledge', which implies an intimate knowing of a vast area of London space – his territory. As a more abstract model – as well as any intuitive ability an aspiring artist might posses, they also need to experience and formally order the visual images defining their particular territory – the space on paper, a canvas or three-dimensional art work spatially spread. The serious artist must be a minor god, god of each minute part of that space on whatever scale – bringing its contained imagery into a state of the perfect order a conceived image needs to manifest as a work of Art and express it's purpose directly or indirectly.

I quickly realised that students on the Basic Course in Leicester, not long after coming out of art lessons at school were, for the first months, often completely baffled as to *the actual why* of the seemingly abstract exercises given them like – point, line, and plane with an emphasis on space. Yet generally, after a month or two of intellectual confusion, turmoil and often doubt, at some point the penny dropped, allowing the student a sudden illuminating insight and a real grasp of some aspect of a previously incomprehensible formal problem. It was always a joy to observe this life-changing moment in a student and see the sudden click of understanding about some concept staff had been attempting to teach and get across for weeks on end. The moment was always a huge step on the way to becoming a super-creative person. I was able to relate this example of a student's sudden awareness to my own recollection of such an event years ago – when a momentary flash of insight allowed me the idea of a cube of space by a student simply miming with his hands.

There were other less serious days in College – easing our heavily committed teaching days. Coming out of the Men's toilet into the main entrance hall on more than one occasion I was forced to marvel at the conscientious spirit of our caretakers. Their brown overall coats reminded me of my days as studio assistant – stirring up sympathetic feeling. However, my attention centred on one man perched on the top of a step ladder giving such undivided and concentrated attention to the cleanliness of the glass partition above this one studio door; it was decidedly odd. It apparently took two men for the job – one to hold the bottom of the short step-ladder while the other, in turn and turn-about, mounted the steps to re-polish the glass above the door with undivided attention. Occasionally performing the task in what appeared to be slow motion they would pause now and again, staring intensely at the glass – checking-up one supposed on their conscientious and untiring efforts to clean it. It was obvious what was happening. The particular room under top-of-the-step-ladder observation was where life-drawing classes took place and this was what the busy, busy caretakers were occupied with – a tantalising peep-show in the nature of an unclad female; one could not blame them, but well...

In Leicester in the 1960s male models were in very short supply. An advert in the local paper eventually brought two contenders. Both apparently exhibitionist, they might well have been members of the gay minority during that insecure, unsafe period of time for them before common sense won the day. One of the two, a pleasant, handsome forty-ish man, when asked to take up whatever pose he liked placed a low stool and simply arched backwards over it. The result was that his shiny peacock-blue jock-strap presented an apex of brilliantly coloured sexuality to the sixteen-years old students comprising the drawing class. Most of the students, perhaps twenty in number were impressionable though curious teenage girls who, at that time were considerably less sexually aware than would be their peer-group today, The event became something of a departmental joke in that the life-drawing tutor, Victor Newsome, a painter I had known in Leeds College of Art, amused by the bizarre situation persuaded the students to close in with their easels and drawing boards. After the giggles subsided the end of the evenings exercise was a number of graphically detailed, beautifully executed pencil and charcoal images of the model's upper thighs and and his evidently well filled jock-strap.

One other amusing anecdote concerning models was the events surrounding an extremely shapely female lady. Of a sweet nature but not vitally intelligent, she persisted in naively donning a short robe barely covering her crotch whenever leaving the life-room to saunter across the common hallway of the entrance hall to pay a call of nature. Invariably one or two male members of the caretaking staff usually happened to be loitering within the immediate vicinity. The model was eventually kidnapped by students during the Leicester University Rag weekend, which resulted in glamorous almost page-3 pictures of her appearing in the daily papers. She afterwards received innumerable letters from various parts of the country sent by desirous males. The most remarkable of these was from a man who ran a suspect beauty parlour. Posted from a distant city it offered her the quick removal of any superfluous hair on her body – *free of charge* should she be in the vicinity of the writer's establishment at any time. Life during the 'swinging Sixties' was rarely boring.

My day to day existence continued to be incredibly eventful – not entirely happily eventful but certainly packed with all manner of new experiences and opportunities for learning. I continued to soak up the influence of the number of younger artists I worked with who were wholly committed in their vocation, and like myself caught up in the seething cultural excitement of the early years of that decade. As well as the painters living two floors above my cellar studio there were numerous others teaching with us who regularly commuted from London; they kept us directly in touch with what was happening down in that vital centre for the Arts.

Teaching was always an opportunity to discuss and explore a wide range of ideas. Such discussion often carried over into the pub where imagination, stimulated by a few beers, helped trigger lots of original conversation. Our talk varied from ribald humour to ideals and serious reflections on contemporary living ranging in subject matter from politics to education, the opposite sex of the gender of whoever was speaking, and of course it invariably turned back to a subject never far from our thoughts – Art.

Such ideas – arising in the lively questioning minds of these younger uninhibited people I was closely associated with, often demonstrated a serious concern to discover what life was really about; what they themselves were about, and what they were attempting to do creatively. In the complex process of living they intended to extract the uttermost enjoyment and fun despite life's incongruities and the inevitable ups and downs. At the same time when not teaching they were attempting to express relevant social or spiritual comments in the unique works of art each was attempting to create. Or if working with less serious concern then they were intent on coming up with something visually beautiful and uplifting in its sheer imagery. Not too long ago, talking to a woman who knew very little about art or artists, and who recently came into contact with one or two for the first time ever, she remarked, 'They're a different race, aren't they? They're something else entirely!'. I did not fully grasp her meaning until these many years later when now, out of touch with other artists I seriously miss their unconventional upside-down Zenist minds, their less conditioned behaviour and ever stimulating friendship.

The Sixties were undoubtedly a dynamic period of growth when viewed from this distance in time and in the opening years of a brand new uneasy millennium in a vastly changed world. For myself, it was not always a time of untroubled easy progress – there were some difficult times and grave personal troubles ahead.

As for making sculpture – I was beginning to appreciate the relative quietness and isolation of my newly occupied cellar studio. I would be there on days off from teaching and also after finishing College in the evenings. And if any other spare time turned up I would arrive there to enjoy its atmosphere – Christmas day and Bank holidays were no exception. Once the fire was lit warming the place and dependent on the mood of the moment, the sounds of Puccini, melancholy Elgar, or more lightly the Modern Jazz Quartet would be emotionally vitalising its solitary state.

When first settling into the particular cellar in which I intended to work I reorganised the workbench, purchased welding equipment, filled clay bins and set up modelling stands so that all that was needed was even the tiniest speck of inspiration to activate a dormant creative urge. I still could not summon up the necessary drive to work without any definite sense of direction or vague image in my minds eye – no matter how strong the urge was! And sometimes, when spirits were low, despondent, I wondered if this new life I had taken on was what I really wished for – or was it all a very big, bad, sad mistake?

On a higher note, when looking round Leicester junk shops in those early weeks, scanning long dusty book-filled shelves, I came across a small, old, pocket size hard-back. Bound in fading indigo its title was on the front in red print on a once white time-stained label; the book's pages were hand cut and irregular and I enjoyed the feel of the roughly trimmed edges – in fact I immediately fell in love with the tiny volume regardless of its contents. Opened up it was filled with the poetry of a man I had never then heard of; his name was Walt Whitman and the book was called Leaves of Grass. Costing one shilling and sixpence it became one of those few things in life one possesses upon which no material value can be placed and it seems wrong to do so. Such priceless treasures belong under the profound designation of *earthly delights*. Sadly, I no longer own the little book; in a stupid sentimental moment I gave it away to someone I also valued; I wonder if they still have it... perhaps not!

Now, down in the studio, half seated on the slab bench close in to a newly lit fire, drifting through the tiny book's hand-cut pages, scanning a line here and there one particular poem I read was inspirational in expanding my mind – proclaiming Whitman's great vision of the world, the Universe! The words of the poetry stirred up a feeling of the significant spiritual element I perpetually sought but never seemed able to grasp or express in my work. Needing to make a gesture to both poet and poem I quickly nailed hardboard to the inner side of the cellar door, painted it white, took a black pencil and wrote the poem on it in big scrawling handwriting. The title of the poem was Assurances, various lines read -

'I need no assurances, I am a man who is preoccupied of his own soul;'
'I do not doubt but the majesty and beauty of the world are latent in any iota of the world;'

'I do not doubt I am limitless, and that the universes are limitless, in vain I try to think how limitless.'

The ultra significant words of the second to last line of the poem, *'I do not think Life provides for all Time and Space...'* shouts aloud the prophetic poet's underlying universal message – down from the poet's own troubled times and to the many confused, insecure people beginning this uneasy, third-millennium.

My appreciation for particular poetry or music changes over the years, verse tending to be an occasional need, music the more necessary. But on that particular morning Whitman's verse fuelled a deep sense of purpose. The words, scribbled on the studio door, read over if I happened to be in a solemn or self-doubting mood, invariably re-established my individuality and my validity among the innumerable other struggling masses attempting to make sense out of the human nonsense of our collective, yet often, very separate worlds.

Looking back, there is little healing in thinking what a great pity any higher thoughts of mine were not always able to prevent feelings much much less noble from raising their destructive heads. My struggles, apart from those when desiring to make sculpture, were to do with instinctive yet less worthy aspects the body demands – and which are directly opposed to the *good* moral values reflected in ones psyche. This darker side of the personality encourages and allows acts of extreme selfishness – inevitably destructive to the happiness of others. Excuses were never soul-saving if I did something harmful, even inadvertently. After such events I well knew the abject portions of guilt and mental punishment wrong actions unfailingly extracted. People at the East of the world manifest great wisdom in accepting the Hindu law of Karma – a religious belief understood to measure an individual's right and wrong behaviour and accordingly grant happiness in life or conversely suffering.

All that aside, undeterred by an inability to produce anything I considered worthwhile as sculpture I continued to work in clay, modelling haphazard shapes without having any lucid idea or intention in mind; I felt I was merely going through the motions – parodying a sculptor.

What eventually turned my efforts in a more determined direction was the result of the influence of the painters upstairs. By this time there were actually three of them living in the first floor flat. Mike Sandle had joined in with Terry Setch and Mike Chiltern, and soon, a fourth addition to their household was Chiltern's partner, Joy. It was a friendly, delightful household to visit for a coffee and a natter about the College, art generally, or the people we knew and all the latest 'goings-on'.

The painters, more knowledgeable about the art-scene in London – having lived down there as post-grad students not long ago, knew of a private gallery run on altruistic lines by an art-loving female proprietor. She being a painter was known to be generous in helping promote aspiring, unknown artists – she might be interested in seeing their work and might even give them an exhibition. The first I heard about the idea was when the trio from upstairs clumped down the cellar steps, crowding into my studio one Saturday morning. I was sitting by the fire sipping a freshly brewed mug of tea, wishing above all that something different, *anything*, would happen – perhaps their arrival implied that this was it! The three of them appeared to be wound up in some way and my curiosity was rewarded when one of them said, 'Look, we've got a gallery woman coming up from London next week, coming to look at our stuff, would you like her to see yours as well while she's here?' They had all been busy over the past months working on two and three-dimensional paintings using canvas, wood and other materials, and now had sufficient works to have someone see them; naturally, they were anxious to get the stuff on exhibition in London.

Of course I said yes to their offer of bringing the gallery lady to see my cellars and work. I spent the next few days tidying up and arranging what sculpture I possessed around the studio; most of it was that I'd brought down from Leeds and I despaired once more at its diversity of style. Having learned from my front room exhibition – now two years ago – I made every effort to please. Although the cellars were a less presentable setting than my immaculate white front room in Leeds the work did not look at all uninteresting, varied as it was.

Borrowing various electric fires and digging out my old paraffin stoves I managed to take the overall chill off the cellar basement, and in a further attempt to make the place more cheerful banked up a blazing fire in the actual working studio. There was also a choice of white or red wine on offer with an alternative glass of sherry if she so chose; for memory's sake and good luck I tried to find the Mosaic Cyprus vintage of that earlier occasion but failed.

On the day of the gallery woman's visit the painters were to meet her at the station, taxiing her round here to the house and studios. The visit was a great success, particularly so for me. She was a lovely, lively spirited Polish lady called Halima Nalecz whose gallery was in Porchester Place near Marble Arch – it was called the Drian Gallery. Although not on the most reputable list of the top art-critics of the time it was a certainly a well known, user-friendly, gallery and ideal for a beginner artist on the scene – and it was free. Pleased with what she saw, Halima selected various pieces of the painters' work; she would show them in the Drian when next she put on a mixed exhibition artists work. In my case for some reason I never learned she had quite taken to me, or was it the work, and had gone round from one sculpture to another marking the half dozen she wished to have in the gallery. It was an important day for all of us and of great import for the future.

Chapter 9

About images, art, and the Drian

It was fortunate that coinciding with the luck of finding a gallery to show our work I had recently passed a driving test. Costing fifteen pounds in cash for five lessons I managed to pass the test first time round – the driving instructor was an intelligent one. Also in the business of selling cars he found me a reasonably priced Commer van which proved to be one of the best things ever!

But the particular night, picking it up after dark provided a few bad moments. Not having driven any car since my five lessons and when taking the test the previous week, I fully expected the driving instructor selling me the van to drive it and me back to my flat across at the other side of Leicester. But nothing of the sort – having paid over the cheque the van was mine and I must drive it home he told me, laughing and saying, 'I'd passed the test, hadn't I!'. Not having driven solo in a car never mind a van – a vehicle without windows apart from those on the doors, it lacked all-round visibility. However, I quickly learned to drive it after the nerve-racking ordeal of getting the vehicle from one side of the city to the other, traversing the busy city-centre and near-missing endless glaring headlights and careless unpredictable pedestrians. In a highly nervous state I arrived (thanking God) in Dulverton Road in time for the childrens bedtime.

The light blue van became my closest friend. At times I would jump up from wherever I was sitting – anywhere or everywhere, and feeling a sudden impulse to drive the thing just shift it up the road and back. Even when it was parked I would sit there thinking that I actually owned this kind of chariot, this incredible moving machine which possessed the magical power to transport me practically anywhere; it was not quite a magic carpet but near enough. Late that Summer I drove across Wales with my wife and children, camping or bed and breakfasting each night; it was a memorable, happy holiday.

Soon, the van become a work-horse, helping transport the three painters' work and my own down to London to the Drian Gallery. Coincidentally, Britain's first motorway, the M1 had just opened – with great political ceremony. The first journey from Leicester to London so soon after my few driving lessons and the speed of getting a licence proved to be a nightmare. It was certainly so for my uneasy passengers because tense and nervous myself I wavered a bit and persisted in hugging the edge of the new MI for the hundred and more miles trip as though the rest of the road did not exist. The back of the van was packed with large paintings and wooden constructions along with my own sculptures, and jammed between these was one of the three painters – the other two squeezed on the front seat beside me. The whole drive was traumatic – not only was it my first time on a busy highway outside of Leicester, it was also my first drive of any great distance. I trembled as literally dozens of cars flew past at what seemed astonishing speeds far exceeding the happy thirty miles per hour I was used to in town. Consequently my passengers were pale and shaken by the time we finally crept down the Edgware Road – but very grateful to have got there! Turning off to the right a little way before Marble Arch we arrived at the Drian and unloaded the art works.

The gallery consisted of three not over-big rooms downstairs and a similar three up – but it was reasonable hanging space. Halima had a tiny office hidden behind a discreet lace curtain in the first room entered from Porchester Place. The gallery came to be somewhere I would often visit over the following years. I recall it with fondness and remember it and charming Halima Nalecz as a generous helpful women herself a painter; she helped many a struggling artist to put on their first show. Her life was devoted to Art and everything about it, she loved associating with artists. The Drian Gallery openings were always well packed – and it was not only for the liberal supply of drinks that people attended them; and the gallery was not without its friendly critics who would write favourable articles or mentions in the Art and Artists or Studio International.

*

The cellar studio suite seemed comparatively empty with half the work gone. It was almost as though some essential parts of me were missing. I always felt that a sculpture completed and standing there upon its plinth, reflecting its final polish, was both a mental and a physical battle resolved – not always successfully but nearly. Given this kind of thinking

I was forced to accept the fact that I was undoubtedly a confirmed romantic. I persuaded my imagination to believe that each sculpture would in a strange way contain Psi information in the form of an etheric essence – extracted from the sensory experience and recollections of everything I as a person experienced up to and during the period of the sculpture's creation. The Psi quota of paranormal energy was the intangible spin-off accumulated during the process of every day awareness – of perceiving, thinking and of doing during all my living time; it was redeemed energy – Psi. It could communicate, subtly – the value of its effect would be equivalent in power to value of the accumulated, subconsciously computed information and experience I might have extracted from the books I'd read, by films seen, music heard, by intense days spent teaching, time spent in close people relationships and the highs and lows of all of life generally – I hopefully imagined the subtle effects of which would mysteriously imprint within the material phenomenon of the particular art work I was seriously involved in making. The more intense the creative input, intention and effort which went into the sculpture then the more power and presence its image gave out. What I did realise was that such inner fantasies reinforced the creative drive – and what is Art if not intuitive, spirited and intense fantasy no matter what kind its tranquil or tortured imagery represents.

I would always and will continue to believe that some objects and images more than others do possess an extra special way of affecting the people confronting them. So do unique humans with extreme personalities, special qualities or great charismatic wisdom such as a prophet might be gifted with.

Yet, despite all this doubtful conviction of magical or mythical powers the first works I churned out in my brand new studio showed that I was still conceptually lost. What materialised were half-baked reflections of art objects – they were nondescript *things* whose value was the proof of a stubborn persistence of mind and a determination to continue making and searching until something worthwhile did shine through.

*

Later that year, established in a routine of teaching and dashing to the studio during time off, I began a new series of works. Unbelievably the images derived from a most mundane, insignificant source – it being the dreamy contemplation of a hammer.

Quite early one morning, half sitting on the slab bench, lost and wondering what line of work to pursue, I held a hammer loosely by the end of its shaft while tentatively sipping a mug of very hot tea. Called a planishing hammer the tool was one with which I once earned a living as a metalworker. Preoccupied, half listening to the radio I was toying with the thing – casually swinging it up and down from the wrist – up and down, enjoying the repetitive feel of its balanced weight. A most recent discovery was that at this early time of day if I was fortunate, ideas sometimes appeared from out of thin air. Maybe, I considered – it was because sleep rested and refreshed the brain and the mind had not yet begun its habitual daily round of useless chatter; thus, inner mind-space was available for more imaginative and creative thoughts to enter. On this particular morning for some reason I became acutely aware of the object consisting of steel and wood casually swinging from my fingers. A time-

111

designed and proven tool the metal head – square at one face and round at the other, was firmly fitted and wedged on at the end of a shaped beechwood shaft a hand might comfortably grasp in order to fulfil the tool's function which was to hammer and planish thin sheet metal.

It seems ridiculous to say, (and anyway, who wants to know?) it was as if I really saw the thing for the very first time. The *seeing* came as a sudden realisation on a mini-scale as it must have done so for Kubrick's ape-cum-man in the film 2001 (but on a maxi-scale) when it hammered away at the bones while Strauss's cosmic Zarathustra crashed out upon the spellbound cinema audiences ears – literally blowing the audiences mind in the enlightened moment of the discovery of the first tool – the cinematic event uplifting *the mind* in the way that great Art invariably does!

My very much mundane hammer experience with the planishing hammer was, in comparison, not in the least mind blowing or even remotely spell binding. Using Kubrick's memorable Time/Space cinematic moment of enlightenment provides a good model for explaining an ordinary yet illuminating moment of *seeing* on one unspectacular morning in a cellar in Leicester. It was the matter of fact of casually looking at a quite ordinary thing that one normally takes for granted – when, for some odd reason the mind (bored perhaps) decides to zoom in and focus the eye consciousness upon this *thing*, amplifying its importance and bringing it to extra special notice. In this case the object was an everyday tool of all things. Its steel head, forged from square to round by some distant in Time blacksmith was no longer a mere hammer – it imaginatively transmuted in my mind which was starved of images to become an object of shape offering innumerable sculptural possibilities!

If this sounds like a long winded explanation of the source from which an artist's idea stemmed, then it is, but it *was* like that! It was also at a long ago time when making sculpture remained a hands-on *tactile* pursuit of manipulating materials such as stone, or wood or clay, until the chosen material assumed an acceptable and meaningful sculptural image.

Regarding my hammer, or hammers, I always anyway felt an innate sense of satisfaction in using hand-tools. Having worked with metal for most of my working life I enjoyed the feel of a well balanced hammer – especially one shaped to serve a special purpose and perform a singular task. The particular one in question having stimulated my imagination was now triggering off a range of mind's eye visualisations from which sculpture might hopefully, actually emerge. The contrary shapes of the hammer's steel head allowed for a variety of formal interests if scaled up; furthermore the direct contrast of square to round carried all kinds of symbolic connotations – the most obvious was male to female.

At this point I welded up three small thirty inch armatures on which to model clay. Perhaps I should explain here that I never imagined myself as a sculptor in a final sense – someone producing monumental or monolithic outdoor works in granite or other everlasting material which would be passed down to posterity. Although I did produce a few larger works occasionally – someone later, rightly I think described my activities as those of an *image-maker,* which, in view of the broad range of images and concepts I would work through seemed right and a more valid and comfortable description.

The period I am immediately writing of is 1962. I said

earlier on that sculpture at that time was more of a tactile, hands-on activity and generally of a scale suitable for exhibiting in galleries rather than planned for architectural sites. For some time after the last war money was tight – which explains this early trend of smaller works. The cost of casting modelled sculptures into bronze or other permanent material was comparatively high – which obviously restricted sculptors who were not particularly wealthy. It would be the later Sixties before it became possible to produce large scale works relatively cheaply in resin-reinforced glass-fibre – a technique which became common practice for the post-war generations of young sculptors the art colleges would turn out. Until then the scale of work and chosen medium was most times limited to the size of one's pocket.

*

Meantime, a few days later I found the postman had pushed a larger than usual envelope through the letter-box – surprised because it was the days before the infestation of pulp mail crashed down most morning's behind Britain's front doors. The A4 envelope contained a catalogue for an exhibition opening in January 1961 at the Drian Gallery. The title of the exhibition was 'CONSTRUCTION: ENGLAND: 1950-60'. Constructivism was a movement born out of the 1917 Marxist revolution in Russia. The concept underlining the movement gave rise to unique and extraordinary works of art. Created by Russian artists working during the early post-revolutionary years the intention behind the art-forms was to re-apply the Arts usefully within the environment in a twentieth century modern style. The idea was to help the revolutionary order in Russia create a brand new peoples state, a Communist state wherein everyone would work, be fed, and therefore live happily ever after! However, dreams rarely come true and all that remains of this 1920s Utopian dream are the works the avant-garde sculptors and painters of the 1917 Revolution left behind. Particularly important, even today are the three-dimensional constructions created by the artists Gabo and Pevsner. These were also revolutionary in both concept, media and image and eventually led to Constructivism. The catalogue for the Construction exhibition Halima planned in the Drian in 1961 was to present the work of contemporary English artists whose work related in some way to the concepts established by those early twentieth century Russians.

I suppose it was important career wise and also reassuring when reading the list of exhibitors I found my own name; and overlooking the fact that not for the first time the spelling of my Christian name was wrong it was still an odd feeling to see it in print alongside artists of considerable reputation. Most surprising and coincidental, topping the list of people showing was Victor Pasmore who once visited my front room in Leeds. Reading through the titles of works to be shown in the exhibition I saw that two of my early works were included; they were those based upon the cone and constructed about 1958. Certainly, they *were* constructions in the way they had been shaped and pieced together, but they were never conceived as being in any way related to the concept of the historical art movement Constructivism. Although differing greatly in image they seemed to fit in with the other very formal images Pasmore, Kenneth and Mary Martin and others were showing. The fact of exhibiting with these well known artists was suddenly a remarkable thing; on the other hand it felt like something distant as though it was happening to someone else. I supposed it *was* a sign of approval, yet, it felt like no more than that! After all it was not that important considering my search for the metaphorical pot at the end of the rainbow; that remained the all important reward if ever there was to be one – not a pot of gold, just some inkling of a self determined truth?

*

The hammer sculptures progressed well. Of these, and there were three variations, one did in fact become a work simply entitled Hammer. In time I associate it with two odd incidents giving me good cause to remember them. One occurred when I drove down to deliver or try to deliver the Hammer to Halima at the Drian. I had been unusually pleased with its final form – about twenty-four inches high it was an unusual and adventurous work. Around the exposed iron rods of the armature which supported big, opposite variations of square and round shapes, I'd bundled and glued strips of wood, afterwards carving and smoothing these down to vaguely resemble a fair sized hammer shaft. Finally, when the thing stood vertical, held there by a complementary metal stand supporting the wooden shaft, I considered it finished, yet something about it remained unsatisfactory. The shapes and composition were acceptable but there was a problem – the graphite finished cement fondu did not sit at all well with the polished wood of the carved shaft. To overcome this I took the unusual step of glazing the graphite with pale primary colours – even though colour on sculpture was still something of an innovation. The idea of painting the work was certainly due to the influence of my painter friends upstairs who were always enthusiastic and happy about about trying out new ideas. Unfortunately however, Halima at the Drian was far from happy; arriving at the gallery with the Hammer sculpture I was met with a blast of disapproval. She was furious, 'What *have* you painted it for?' she demanded. 'Take it away, take it away! Take it out, I don't want it in the gallery!'

I could not quite understand her rage and put it down to a Mid-European temperament together with a conventional attitude when considering Fine Art – even though her choice was usually towards the *modern*.

I lodged the work with a close painter friend who taught part-time in Leicester and shared a flat and studio with another painter and his wife in Bellsize Park. The flat was high on the third-floor of a large Victorian terrace house; it was where I used a sleeping-bag on odd weekends in London. The fact that it was three floors up was to prove a desperate trial of strength for poor Hammer which had become an integral part of the flat's cultural decor. That is until one late summer night when people back from the pub were partying and a close friend of mine – in a rage for some unpredictable reason, threw the thing out of the third-floor window. Not present on that occasion I finally heard about it on viewing the sorry looking wreck of Hammer. Although badly cracked it had undergone its remarkable flight to crash-land on stony ground in good spirit. In time I was able to restore the thing successfully. Yet more remarkable still it was bought by the Arts Council in Wales regardless of its wild and varied history.

I continued to work in clay using fingers, boxwood modelling tools and a piece of 2" X 1" timber which acted like a cricket bat for quickly slapping the stuff into shape. Next to iron as a choice of material which, if worked with long familiarity is both malleable and plastic, clay was by far my favourite material. Naturally plastic in substance, spontaneously echoing an image of any slight surface indent affected by the gentlest of pressure; and like a pencil accidentally dropped onto white paper which leaves the graphite mark of its impact, so does a clay surface respond to the most subtle touch.

I decided to let myself loose on the clay of the third model of the hammer series. The final image emerged as a slightly larger than life-size head, although on this occasion it became more skull-like than fleshed. Carrying on I modelled in minor forms suggestive of medieval armour, and at the front deeply incised a cross and other symbolic markings. The image appeared summoned up from some archetypal depth, yet, while not exactly sinister neither was it pretty and seemed to be an object demanding attention. The vertical lines and steps introduced in the clay due to impression by the angular 2" X 1" timber gave it a sense of instant forming – like viscid larva expressing its immediate and final moments of life before changing to become petrified for ever. The skull-like image of the clay model also possessed a sense of scale, almost architectural. Most important however was that it was personable and an image with human connotations, more so than any of my previous work. There was a sense of arrival and satisfaction in this; I felt good about it; perhaps it hinted at a direction connected more with *myself!*

Chapter 10

The Visual Adventure, concepts, and *black space*

It was 1961. 'I'm not showing in there with that!' said Mike Sandle very forcefully. He'd just hung one of his paintings in the smaller ground floor room of the Drian Gallery. Tom Hudson had persuaded Halima to put on an exhibition of our departments work – students work and one work each of the members of the teaching staff. The exhibition was to be called The Visual Adventure – it would be a further step in promoting the new ideas about art education.

Having got the work down to London we were hanging it ready for an invitation opening the following Tuesday. The staff had been given one room in which to show their own work – we were in process of arranging it. Mine was to be the only free standing piece – a sculpture. This unfortunately had proved to be the problem. Mike Sandle was not alone in his objection – the others were also complaining that it devalued their paintings, original and interesting as these certainly were. As soon as I'd positioned the sculpture on a

119

plinth just off centre in the room, there'd been an outcry. It was not a very big room the painters insisted and the thing on the plinth presented too strong an image – diminishing the look of the paintings. I suppose having lived with the work for too long when making it, I'd lost sight of the way they were seeing it. Looking at it now, standing there on the plinth, I was forced to admit it did tend to dominate.

Made of iron, beaten and welded into a helmet-like shell and raised up on a short tapered column, it measured only thirty inches high, yet, if anything possessed *presence* then this work certainly did. I'd begun it after casting the previous series of hammer works in cement-fondu. Sick of the mess of mixing up bowl after bowl of plaster followed by cement I'd decided to build a sculpture directly in a permanent material – I'd use my old friend iron. There'd be no boring processes afterwards of transferring the finished clay model into some other long lasting material. Taking a plaster mould from clay and then filling the mould – with cement for instance, was not only laborious, it took a great deal of time – longer to do in fact than working on the original image. So that having decided to work directly in iron whatever object turned up would be a finished one, complete in itself.

But there had been another cause which triggered the idea of using iron directly – a sign perhaps that the previous years of working in conceptual darkness were about to initiate a significant pay-off. Earlier that week the Related Studies department had shown 'Ivan the Terrible', a renowned Russian film. Its director, Sergei Eisenstein, had filmed it in stark black and white creating a remarkable experience for his audience. One shot filling the entire cinema screen was breathtaking, revealing the regimented, closely packed, stationary ranks of a vast army. A fear inducing picture, the line after line of ghost-like warriors standing shoulder to shoulder, were clad in full length white cloaks falling from shoulder to ground. Yet even more sinister were the inverted bucket-shaped helmets completely obscuring the occupants. What fascinated me was a symbol on the front of each soldier's helmet formed by two small holes at eye level divided by a narrow vertical slot. The cut out circles and slot were ultimately black – a black contrived by the total absence of light within the inverted helmet; no small feature of any person or existence was visible.

The strength of the image on the screen took time to register until it resolved itself in the form of a sudden idea to do with the introversion of light and space. The two being synonymous, or so I thought, the sheer blackness of the negatively formed symbols – row upon row of them, was something I would think of in future as images formed by *black space*. The metaphor offered a symbolic opposite to the visible world and things seen. Yet, I did not exactly intend it to imply a meaningless emptiness – imaginatively it could hint at the unseen, or things unknowable inhabiting unlit, enclosed space – space without light, ergo – *black-space*. Perhaps it was too negative an idea – reflecting the many undesirable, undisclosed things which inhabit human minds – including my own by God! There were vast unknown spatial regions within the intricate convolutions of the not yet fully explored (though often exploited) brains of men – and women of course. I well knew some of the unpleasant things existing in the worrying *black-spaces* where ignorance lurked within me – naive ignorance which desperately sought illumination.

Years later, teaching in Wolverhampton I came across the language of Cybernetics and the conjectured artificial model miming a human brain and represented by a *black-box*. In systems theory the metaphor of a *black-box* allows unsatisfactory *input* to be fed into its imagined system and so become inexplicably changed – transformed by exactly unknowable means to become a desired *output*. It was a gratifying discovery which reinforced the notion of my *black-space* concept, reassuring me that I was not entirely daft.

The work causing the problem with my friends the painters in the Drian 1962 exhibition was called 'Helmet I'. Boldly standing on a white plinth in the gallery the iron sculpture was certainly influenced by the Eisenstein film. These many years later, simple as the work later appeared formally, it certainly was the result of the complex if muddled thought processes stirring up my mind at the time. A second contributory factor to my making 'Helmet 1' had been a shock realisation that the cement-fondu sculpture, the skull, was in truth, *fake* – a false thing. It's shape, bound and described by its surface appearance, its skin, was a pretence – it pretended by visual means to be the outside of something else. What *was* inside it except a volumetric mass of hard cement, glass fibre and the iron bars of the armature – nothing else! The sculpture was a skin-deep illusion in the form of Art – honestly fashioned but which I began to realise was untrue; it masqueraded by imitation – the outer appearance suggesting a real inside which was not! Its sculptured image implied a mythical content, yet, there was no truth in it of any kind. This new work – Helmet I, 1961, the one the painters were objecting to had both an outside and an actual inside in the sense that it could be seen to exist, was real and accessible. And although the work was still largely a pretend object in the form of Art, it did embody a sense of the basic idea implicit in the newly evolved concept I recently formulated – the phenomenon of *black space*. I felt reassured on this account – with the helmet thing at least you got what you saw; it was honest, for nothing was hidden inside or out the object.

*

There was a quickening sense of excitement in the Drian on the opening night of the Leicester Polytechnic exhibition. There was also the usual sense of satisfaction and expectancy that comes after hanging the last painting or placing the last sculpture in a gallery ready for the exhibition's opening. The final worry after attempting to get everything just right and looking good is to do with the quality of the art work itself, which makes for the success or failure of any show. The work in this present exhibition would not fail on any count.

That Tuesday evening, around 7.30pm, the gallery was full of interesting people, some casually, some fashionably clad; the majority were young – the women looked particularly beautiful. Many of those who turned up were involved in art education or themselves artists – glasses of white or red wine were filled, emptied, and refilled at an alarming rate. Painters and sculptors in the early Sixties lived during the *heyday* of what was probably the most exciting time for both art and artists in the twentieth century – sadly, it appeared or seemed to last little more than a decade.

I have written before that Private gallery openings were popular and welcome events partly due to the generally lavish supply of drinks at the time. Openings were also an excuse and an occasion for the meeting up of the various groups of artist cliques and the multitudes of both artists and friends London seemed to support. It became the fashion, and openings were invariably on Tuesday evenings – for the many play-hard art people to visit one, two, even three galleries in a single night.

Numbers of gallery goers would race round London, passing on from one exhibition to another not only for free drinks on offer but also to be seen and meet up with like people; and of course – to see what new work particular artists were showing. Needless to say, after two, three, or more galleries had been visited the alcoholic effects of free drink became pretty evident – encouraging ongoing pubbing and late partying where sexual and social freedom might have been the final antidote wrapping up the grim, not long ago wartime decades. It was all quite mad but with a happy, infatuated kind of Sixties madness. They were delightful years, irretrievable in kind and vital when most times – which were without gloom, seemed full of hope, promise, and when illusions proved to be worth the payment they invariably demanded. It was impossible to be a part of that historically great decade and not be caught up in the excitement and glamour of what appeared to be a glorious, perpetual event.

In tune with these times the opening night of the The Visual Adventure at the Drian – successful in an educational sense also turned out to be good for me. Towards the end of the evening, after alcohol had already heightened the view of life for most us, I was chatting to people from College when Halima approached – beaming, she said she wished to buy the Helmet sculpture for the Gallery.

*

About the time of making that first Helmet I became friendly with Michael Tyzack and his lovely wife Patzy; they lived in a North London. A painter, Mike commuted to Leicester teaching part-time each week. Knowing that I visited London frequently the couple offered me a comfortable couch whenever I wished to stay. Their flat turned out to be a place of refuge. Any confusion of spirit due to life's ups and downs – and it was a period of many self-inflicted downs, appeared to fade away the moment I climbed the small flight of steps and entered the door of their North London flat.

Staying with the Mike and Patzy offered an insight into a way of life more sedate and cultured than I ever previously known or imagined – and there also was beautiful music. It was where I first heard Bach's Overture to Suite no. 2 when sipping a pre-dinner drink. The music helped weave a magic spell – momentarily obliterating other serious matters which were not at all magical. But then, it was the joy of being with two lovely people in calm considered surroundings; of listening to unique music; of being there and seeing and hearing the gentle stillness of the ticking of the French clock under its domed glass on the mantel shelf; of sensing the anticipated meal at the polished, round mahogany table laid sparsely yet perfectly – awaiting people to sit, to eat, and to talk. All of these things were offerings without discord.

Some weeks later when Mike was exhibiting work in a show of Hard Edge painters in the Bear Lane – an Oxford gallery, I was invited to the private view along with other artists and friends; there was to be a party afterwards in someone's house. I remember little of the opening because openings were always occasions I found difficult. One reason for this was that I was never particularly clever at the art of making conversation or small talk; added to this and, which made things doubly worse, was a congenital deafness in one ear so that hearing apart from talking was always a problem.

But what I do remember about the opening was that the supply of drinks was unusually liberal so that by the time everyone had loaded in to cars to head for the distant party, then if not tipsy they were pretty happy. It was before the more sensible approach to drink driving took effect.

The party was in what I took to be a serious art-collector's house. The decor was off white, the furniture comfortable and pleasantly tasteful, and the pictures on the walls numerous and well chosen. Driven there by some unknown friendly person, on arrival I found the two rooms and kitchen to be full of chattering people holding full glasses and well on the way to becoming even happily higher on alcohol. It looked like being the kind of party fast heading towards one of the unrestrained gatherings artists and their followers insist on enjoying. The average age of those present I guessed, apart from a couple of attractive girls probably under twenty, would be around forty/fifty – saving one or two balding or greying heads. Roger Hilton and Terry Frost were there as were a few other known artists I had come to know by sight over the last two or three years – and by now who probably knew me in some slight, distant way.

Hilton, looking happy, tiny and bespectacled seemed well on the way to the even happier place where an over indulgence in alcohol can take one; he was well protected from any bodily harm by an attractive, caring woman – his mistress I was told. Others similarly enjoying the generous hospitality of the house were soon dancing. For some reason I myself was by no means over the limit, although the glitzy occasion and drink had helped overcome my normal reticence. Rather than puddle my wits on this particular night the little drink I'd had seemed instead to have made them more sensibly active and also more voluble.

This being so I was soon in earnest conversation with a small, older, blue suited collar and tie gentleman. Behind his glasses he appeared to be listening seriously to what I had to say. Seated on a leather backless bench in the middle of the crowded noisy room we were attempting to make ourselves heard discussing the merits of art in provincial cities – particularly in Leeds the city of my origin and a place my companion seemed to know extraordinarily well.

Comparing painting and sculpture as it might be exhibited and understood by people in the North, we were expressing contrary but not seriously argumentative points of view to do with whether the importance of the Arts were generally more fully appreciated in London than Leeds. It turned out that the man opposite had lived in Leeds for some years; he seemed to have had a lot to do with art whilst there but didn't disclose exactly why or how. We talked with great interest and enjoyment for some time, until my glass being empty I excused myself to seek a refill and asked if he wished for one, but no! By the time I returned he was otherwise closely engaged – dancing with a beautiful tall girl in a bright red dress. Their disparity of size, age, and clothes made them an odd couple; factors which, I thought, would probably become the dominant forces in any likely sexual battle ahead – silently I wished the old chap good luck.

The party over, given a lift back to town by one of the other Oxford exhibiting painters – Malcolm Hughes, someone I barely knew, he asked me quite casually, 'Do you know that chap very well you were having the long conversation with at the party? What on earth were you talking about all that time? Do you know who he is?'

'I've never met him before,' I replied, wondering why on earth he was so obviously inquisitive. 'We were just talking about the town up North where he once lived, Leeds apparently. It's where I come from. We were just talking about art and art galleries,' I added.

'Well!' I was informed with the faint suggestion of a suspicion that I should have or must have known who the chap was, '...it was Sir John Rothenstein, Director of Tate.'

My first thought was – 'Oh, so what!' The name of the Tate Gallery did not mean all that much to me just then – so that it never occurred to me that there was anything special about having a conversation with someone at a party. But on reflection I suppose if someone had told me who he was, the conversation I'd certainly enjoyed with the older man would never have taken place – because no doubt I'd probably have seized-up!

Next, Hughes told me that Rothenstein was once Director of Leeds City Art Gallery, which of course explained his knowledge of Leeds and its people. But that was at a time before my advent into this present, new and exciting world took place.

Perhaps this meeting had a connection – although I do not think so and would never find out – with a telegram I received while in College a week or two later. A kind, thoughtful message it came from London sent by Mike and Patzy Tyzack – it congratulated me on having a work bought by the Tate Gallery, of which I knew nothing until that moment. My immediate reaction was one of appreciation that my friends had taken the trouble to send the telegram – it almost equalled the satisfaction I felt in the Tate Gallery having acquired the work. Perhaps at that time – 1962, I did not sufficiently value whatever distinction the Tate's purchase was supposed to give me. Anyway, hadn't I already sold the sculpture to Halima at the Drian.

Of course it was Helmet I that the Tate bought from the Drian. I never found what they paid for it but for some very questionable reasons it was to be the only work of mine they ever did buy; particularly questionable when later Herbert Read and Roland Penrose of the I.C.A. particularly recommended that Halima send two later sculptures of mine to be exhibited in an exhibition of English sculpture in Germany – Profile 111, in Bochum. But to cap my rather cool response on the day of the Tyzack's telegram I learned there'd been a brief, two paragraph comment in the Times about the Tate buying the sculpture. Following some lines telling readers about the Tate Gallery acquiring another Paolozzi sculpture, I read, 'Another purchase was 'Helmet' by a sculptor not previously represented in the gallery, Alurence Burt.' The ghastly typographical error could not have been bettered (or worsened) and took some time to live down among my various friends and others who were not!

The telegram from Mike and Patzy arrived in Leicester Polytechnic during a working day. In the staff refectory later, at teatime just before evening sessions began, I was sitting with half a dozen other staff, all painters, when one of them said something congratulatory about the importance of the Tate buying a work. Other good wishes followed about the sculpture going into the National collection – with one sad exception. There was one final comment – dropped like a bombshell, it came with the words, 'Well, anybody can weld a few bits of metal together, can't they?' The abrupt silence at the table was pretty obvious.

*

A whiff of professional success or not, life went on with no noticeable difference of which I was aware; nor did I feel or worry that there was any desire or expectancy that things should differ, or change. It was a busy informative teaching and learning period during which one continued to evolve by sharing the urgency to learn of a hundred or more imaginative young minds, and by a constant contact with the already learned, mature minds of the artists working in the department.

Tom Hudson was an unmatchable boss in that he loved art, enjoyed the company of artists, and lived art education. Head of Department for the first time he enjoyed the golden opportunity such a position offered. Education at that time was encouraged and financially urged on by the socially minded forward looking Government of the Sixties. Able to act out the role of introducing completely new methods in teaching art, Tom used his effective power to do so well! He was also in a position to offer employment to practising artists, employing only those he knew to be totally committed vocationally. Reasonably paid teaching offered them the wherewithal to live and the opportunity to carry on with their own painting and sculpture.

*

Self-imposed personal problems aside, life continued to be a full-time occupation fashioned around the creative people I worked with. We shared a commitment to create meaningful art whether it comprised the beautiful or spelled out something more intense; my own work, successful or not invariably attempted to incline towards the latter.

At home I fulfilled my role as best I could, leading what seemed to be a double life. My wife only distantly involved with the college and its people, built up a circle of neighbourhood friends as I became more and more patterned by the kind of people I necessarily associated with. If a gap in our relationship opened up and it became impossible to retrieve what was lost, then the fault lay with me.

The children seemed to be as accepting as children can be of their school days, and there were weekend treats like the cinema, picnics, trips up North to see grandparents, and occasional holidays. There were no disagreements where they were concerned for we were naturally loving parents – attempting to cope with a changed and still changing life situation for which we were ill equipped to survive, and lacked the necessary wisdom to do so. A demanding over-commitment to art and regrettably to myself, along with an ever quickening series of inescapable events was at the heart of the problem.

Chapter 11
The Old Rectory at Kibworth

That Summer I had another visitation – Mike Chiltern and his partner Joy Bates arrived down in my studio. The latter had recently moved into the painters flat upstairs. Right now both she and Mike seemed excited about something or other. It turned out that Joy, looking for a more convenient place for them all to live and at the same time better studio space, had noticed a 'To Let' ad, in the Leicester Mercury. It described an empty Georgian rectory available to rent for a few years prior to what now would seem to be a sheer act of vandalism – its demolition. She had driven the ten miles out of town to view the place. Isolated within its own spacious grounds it stood at the edge of a pretty, once Norman village called Kibworth. The new owners were only waiting for the moment when they would be allowed to reduce the lovely old red-brick building to rubble in order to build commonplace little houses on its once venerated land. Because therefore they were not in the least concerned as to the upkeep of the distinguished old Georgian house and grounds, the rent, should the artists desire to occupy it, would be a mere six pounds a week, plus rates.

There were three floors of relatively vast rooms, and slightly separate to the house stood two, single-room cottages – once for servants probably. Also, in the partly wooded grounds were stables, cow sheds and other outbuildings. Scribbled in faint, timeworn pencil, on the back of the door of what must have once been a cow-shed were the dates of birth of variously named beasts – Georgian beasts we liked to think. The view from the upper windows at the front of the house beyond a well kept lawn, overlooked a wide landscape of green fields, hawthorn hedges and scattered trees. In the far distance, trains on their way North puffed sedately across the horizon like tiny crawling toys trailing cotton wool clouds of steam behind them – appearing at one side of the horizon they disappeared at the other.

After much discussion with my wife who was at first hesitant about the move, together with the three painters and Joy we eventually agreed that the Rectory would be an incredible house and environ in which to live and work. Apart from the romantic aspects of the idea we joked about the possibility of Georgian ghosts and the many holy and historic vibes we might absorb being there. Apart from ample living accommodation we artists would each occupy a good sized studio and have ample storage space, all of us would be surrounded by beautiful English countryside.

As regards getting into College the village was on a good bus route, and between us we would have both a car and my van for transport. We would manage nicely providing everyone mucked in with the upkeep and helped with the expense of the place. The Rectory was undoubtedly suited for what it was to become – a commune of artists consisting of Mike Sandle, Terry Setch, Mike Chiltern, and Joy, and myself and Jean together with Peter and Paul our two sons respectively 10 and 11 years old.

It was generally agreed that myself and my family should occupy the top floor which was self contained apart from the lack of a water closet. My studio would be the old panelled library on the ground floor; I was also allotted one of the empty cobweb ridden servant's cottages just outside – to use as a store or workshop. The three painters shared out the various other huge rooms suitable for use as studios. They and Joy intended to share housekeeping, and the spacious kitchen on the ground floor would be theirs. In time two more artists would eventually arrive to join us in the Rectory. In the eyes of the staid Kibworth villagers the old house must have become a true Bohemian establishment – it no doubt added a sense of excitement to their old world pastoral existence. The early 1960s were still a time before England's ancient villages were invaded by the newly rich escaping from the busier cities. In due course, although the Rectory and and its lovely grounds showed obvious signs of wear and tear – the place soon worked remarkably well as a thriving creative community.

Peter, my older son was soon settled in and attending Kibworth Grammar School, an establishment equally historical in line with the Rectory, while Paul our youngest child attended the village school. Out of school both were experiencing the less conditioned lifestyle offered by my artist friends. They were also coming to terms with village life and getting to know the surrounding countryside. The roomy old house itself they concluded, although *spooky* after dark disappointingly lacked any visible or invisible signs of ghosts. Jean adapted well to the situation, became popular in the Rectory and in the village, and at the same time kept in touch with friends she'd made living back in Dulverton Road. Settled in, all of us found that life in Kibworth Rectory was rarely, if ever, dull.

*

Although welcoming a more spacious and ideally placed studio in the Rectory library, I found it a sad affair when packing up my tools and equipment in readiness to leave the cellars. The verse of Whitman's poem – 'I need no assurances...' scribbled on the back of a door was a nostalgic reminder of uneasy struggles juggling and attempting to resolve complicated ideas. After all, I had worked in the cellars for a very important two years of my life – during which time I'd dealt with many anxious questions involved in the ups and downs of creative thinking. The often lonely silence in the cellars had helped me take a few of the first tentative steps in forming the concepts and direction of some of the work I would in create in future. Those two years had also firmly established in my mind the *rightness* of the way of life and the profession I had finally chosen. No doubt opting out of the background I was brought up in was a selfish choice in respect of my family – yet it was due to an vocational commitment which finally therefore made any other option virtually unacceptable.

Before the actual move into Kibworth Rectory, having made and sold Helmet I, it encouraged me to continue working on similar lines and introducing wherever possible the phenomenon *black space*. During the following months I built a second, bigger helmet work – a variation of course but similar in general style; I also constructed a much smaller one in hard and soft-soldered brass.

A month into beating out the sheet iron and welding together the pieces making up the bigger sculpture, the idea came to me that the image I was building, constructed on a heroic scale, might serve as a unique form of cathedral. Constructed amid natural surroundings, high on remote moorland maybe – it would be a place of pilgrimage. The new sculpture measured about three feet front to back and resembled an iron shell more representative of a human skull than being imitative of Helmet I. Its front view or face, was cut into or cut away in the form of a symbolic cross, one arm of which extended into a circle; these symbols, piercing the iron shell, when seen externally appeared as *black space*. A second cross was cut out of the right side of the skull-like shape, and opposite to this a rectangular opening enabled the sculpture's interior and formal construction to be viewed from inside. Seen from the inside the symbolic cross shapes slashing or piercing the shell, reversed the concept of *black-space* – by becoming instead symbols of light.

Finishing the work I envisaged a mass of people gathered together within such a vast cathedral like space the work suggested. The rectangular opening in the sculpture at one side was barely, but just big enough to admit a head. So that curious one day as to what it would sound like inside, decant recorder in one hand preceding, I very carefully edged my head inside the metal shape. The plaintive notes of the descant resonating within the hollow space I immediately christened the the work – Temple.

Completed, I drove the sculpture up to Leeds for an exhibition in the University, and afterwards down to the Drian in London together with the smaller brass helmet. This last work, although conceived seriously, by the time it was completed I silently labelled it Don Quixote – simply because as it evolved its image came more to resemble (so I imagined) a ridiculous, peculiar helmeted man on an equally peculiar ridiculous, tiny horse. This same kind of ridicule also happened with other works in progress when, disillusioned with the way they were turning out I likened them to some common object – even a cabbage on one occasion. The effect of such an indignity applied to any partly finished creative work was fatal, destroying any further serious appreciation the poor thing or image might have deserved.

Driving down to London with the two works, I arrived late afternoon, carried them into the Drian, and heard Halima talking to someone behind the office curtain. Coming out she welcomed me with a lovely smile and watched with interest as I placed the Temple on a white box-plinth. The smaller Don Quixote work I shoved on a lower stand and then excused myself saying I wished to find a sandwich and cup of tea nearby. Although appearing to be delighted with the sculptures she seemed preoccupied, her attention directed to whoever lurked behind the office curtain so that I left her to it – mentioning that I would be back in half an hour or so.

Returning, I waited, knowing that Halima must have heard my arrival. Coming out from behind the office curtain this time she was accompanied by small man aged anywhere between fifty and seventy. He nodded a greeting, smiled and held out his hand while speaking quickly in what I took to be French. Interpreting, Halima introduced him simply as Lacasse, a painter friend, he was one of the lesser known Cubist painters. Unfortunately, unless Halima interpreted or we used appropriate gestures we were unable to talk together. He was a pleasant lively man and somehow managed to explain that he had, or once had, a studio on the same street as

Picasso. Afterwards, Halima gave me a small book illustrating paintings by Lacasse done during the Cubist period. These many years later, less self-involved than then, I would like to have known Lacasse better – which demonstrates the kind of wishful thinking one regrettably applies to many of the interesting people one unthinkingly allowed escape.

But there was good news coming. It was translated to me that Lacasse very much admired both sculptures and wished to buy them. Taken aback, I must have grinned and looked happy, nodding my head in a show of appreciation – both for the fact that he liked the work and also for the more practical reason that he was going to buy them. After a glass of sherry, some polite but difficult conversation translated via Halima, and many sincere goodbyes, I left the Drian.

Driving north, back to Leicester later, a healthy cheque tucked away in my inside pocket, the earlier sense of exhilaration at selling the works left me. The feeling was replaced by one of regret at parting with the sculptures so soon after their completion; I felt that I had parted with new found friends – unearthed so to speak during the struggle to conceive and drag the images out of the depths of my mind and imagination in order that they might exist in the phenomenal world; they were part of me and I had known them all too briefly; now they were off to Paris and I would probably never see them again. I never did – and Temple together with other sculptures of mine made all those years ago now lay in a museum's cellar in Warsaw, rusting away I'd heard, uncared for. But what then is the object of making sculpture over and above the artist's driving *need* to create? The two helmet works must have communicated in some moving way to the French painter, Lacasse – he'd wanted to possess them so there was nothing for me to gripe about really; I'd taken slides and photographs so that sight of the objects was not completely lost.

But this was all in the past. Since moving into the Rectory, each busy day seemed to take on an enhanced meaning. I imagine it was due to a more focused relationship living alongside other artists who worked no more than a few steps beyond my studio door. Each of them, I knew, would be exploring their own sensitive and unique world – aspiring like myself to create images which attempt to express the virtually inexpressible.

Most times I found it stimulating to wander into another artist's studio with a mug of coffee in my hand, to chat and to see how their work was progressing. – not too frequently of course. I had found it disconcerting at first when people came in to see *me* too often, particularly if they offered forceful suggestions as to how a work in process would be better done this way or that – done *their* way in fact! Yet, it proved helpful in having people around who were seriously involved in Art beyond a mere passing interest, who questioned ideas, and who even took out time to talk about intellectual subjects known to them but not yet to me! And there were parties and picnics. Occasionally it was a bind when one wished for uninterrupted privacy in the studio, but on the whole, it was an advantage having other people around with similar aspirations and as profound a belief in Art as I myself. That all were younger and therefore newer to life than me also seemed to help. Fresher in spirit perhaps, they generated an extra sense of urgency and excitement, as though believing that all of life was a positive trip into an – anything's-possible future. The Rectory certainly became a place of extreme contrast to the way it must have been a century and more ago. During that historical period it was probably a safe, sin free parish and a wealthy living for some incumbent vicar who overlooked the villagers morality *and* their eventual mortality. Now, in 1963, Kibworth village had become an extraordinary place where interesting unordinary people lived – and where unconditioned, uncontrived events merely happened.

Settled into the new routine, adapting to a new studio, I was soon involved in new work. Another, final, more robust helmet sculpture came into being; less humanoid and more machine like, someone remarked that it resembled a Teutonic war-machine. My initial worry when beginning to work in the old library was to do with the ear-splitting row which arose when beating and hammering out iron; the racket may at least have informed the painters that someone in the Rectory was working, encouraging them to do the same perhaps? No one ever actually complained but the noise did on one occasion bring one of the latest arrivals in the Rectory to my studio, curious to see exactly what the row was.

One of these was a fourth painter, Victor Newsome, recently back from his time as a Rome Scholar. He was someone I knew casually as being one of the more committed students of painting in Leeds College of Art when I worked there. I recall meeting him at a party where we compared our personal situations; I think that we were both at the beginning of a very eventful time in our lives coming up in the not too distant future. This was back in 1957-8 and long before I met up with my friends in the Rectory.

Now having moved in he brought with him an Italian wife who was a sculptor – Christina Bertoni. Victor was something of a perfectionist and immediately on settling, apart from his painting he appeared to commit himself and

Christina to a way of life the pastoral situation seemed to demand. Within the grounds of the Rectory amid a glade of mature trees stood a small, open sided brick outhouse or shelter. One of the first tasks Victor undertook – to supplement his fuel supply was to collect up the numerous fallen branches lying around. These, he systematically sawed into short logs exactly equal in length – stacking them meticulously in a perfectly ordered pattern, filling the open sided outhouse space with regimented exactness. The image of the freshly cut logs was not only visually effective and satisfying, it was in some ways a work of art – a sculpture.

Victor and Cristina also brought in mini-hens – bantams, and shortly afterwards a proud chicken-size cock appeared to give the bantams a hard time. The cock – crowing loudly well before dawn each morning became a much hated creature by the Rectory inhabitants. The bantams and their bigger sire were free daily to strut around the small grass close overlooked by Victor and Christina's living room – it lay between the ground floor kitchen window and my store place, the empty servants cottage. The introduction of the bantams and the overbearing cock into the grounds of the Rectory created a scene echoing time/space reversed.

To add to their degree of self-sufficiency Victor and his wife also bred Angora rabbits; these were kept in cages in the empty side of the hut containing Victor's sawn up logs; unhappily, marauding rats and foxes occasionally killed or stole a rabbit. But that apart, I was impressed for ever with an extremely horrific visual recollection of the beautiful whiter than white rabbits.

This came about one evening when, after dark, I had occasion to call downstairs to speak to Victor about something or other. His rooms necessitated my going outside to get to them, and I remember that night being a particularly dark winter's night. Having knocked, on opening the door into the long narrow living room I was confronted by a dreamlike scene which might have been conjured up by Hieronymus Bosch. The walls and paintwork of the Newsomes brightly lit room were painted a brilliant white – which seemed to bounce from the sanded and highly varnished floorboards glistening like water and reflecting the unshaded light bulbs overhead. The fact of suddenly entering the room immediately out of a pitch black night must certainly have heightened the surreal shock. Generally a bit squeamish I stood in the open doorway subjected to a vivid impression not easily forgotten. Victor, who had shouted, 'Come in!' in answer to my knock was seated back to me, crouched over, busily occupied in carrying out some attention absorbing task on the floor.

In retrospect, I think it was the whole visual dimension of the room which got to me not just the flayed, spread-eagled snow-white furred and bloodied skin of the glassy-eyed rabbit – being ripped off like a tightly fitting glove from the once living, now raw exposed pink and red flesh; the whole bloody image of the flayed creature set down against the glittering pine floorboards was like a scene out of a horror movie.

That earlier memory of Victor visiting my studio, curious as to the racket coming from it I also remember quite well. I was busily engaged in the noisy process of grinding up the iron surface of the new helmet sculpture preparatory to adding a few finishing touches of colour. On Victor's entry, switching off the disc sander, ready to enjoy his visit while hoping he wouldn't stay too long, I watched silently as he circled slowly round the now silvery iron object, examining it from every possible angle and eventually expressing his approval.

Next however to my dismay, wishing no doubt to be helpful, smiling, he took the sander from me saying, 'Can I have a go...?' and commenced to attack the iron surface, grinding it oblivious to the sanctity of my feelings as the creator and therefore carer of every minute mark or single blemish on the precious surface of the art work. Confused as to what to do, after a couple of minutes, desperate to stop him politely and without a loss of face or hurt on either side, I took over – gently intruding on his grasp of the sander, tentatively edging aside the friendly and willing helper.

Another vivid memory of life in the Rectory was by way of the other three painters and Joy. Needing to see them for some reason one day, I knocked at their kitchen door and walked in to find no one there. Joy, brought up in open countryside and therefore countrywise, helped by Mike Chiltern, Sandle, and Terry Setch, decided to adopt a self-sufficiency regime. Exploring surrounding fields and woods they collected mushrooms, other more dubious fungi, nettles, and other similar foods which were the free gifts of Nature. I thought that if they wished to risk eating such food all very well – but *not so* the kind of prepared fare I discovered to my horror in the otherwise empty pantry.

It was Mike Chiltern I think who acquired a high powered air-rifle so that there on the well-scrubbed deal table was the ghastly harvest it had reaped. Arranged in an iron roasting tray was a row of plucked, pathetic looking miniature blood-red carcasses; the tiny drum stick legs of each, tied to the spiritless redraw bodies with string – pointed heavenwards. They could only be the feather bare corpses of wild birds, artistically aligned in the tray in diminishing size

– from crows down to blackbirds, to song thrush and to sparrows! Once happily free to sing, flit and fly, they were now deprived of life and feathers – awaiting roasting in order to satisfy the hungry but not all *that* hungry stomachs of the downstairs lot. Perhaps I overreacted, yet, beautiful wild birds treated like this looked bad enough to me, but what I really dreaded was my children catching sight of the tray of pitiful dead creatures. To make matters worse a vile smell emanated from the them – permeating the whole Rectory even before they were roasting. The stink became something much worse when they were in the oven; Joy told me it came from the carrion eaters – the crows.

*

But on the whole the Rectory was a lively, never-the-same-two-days-running place in which to live and work. My studio space was ample and I enjoyed having my family upstairs – Jean made our rooms on the top floor comfortable and looked after us well. The worst aspect of being up top was carrying coals and wood to feed the big, open fireplace. However, there was the reward of having climbed the stairs entering rooms which were warm and welcoming – perhaps this was due to the Rectory's age and the taint of goodness associated with what it once stood for two hundred years ago. Our living room was vast, offering a stupendous view of unspoiled, open rural landscape. Peter and Paul visited my studio occasionally, and although not knowing exactly what I was about, found the mechanics of whatever was in progress of great interest.

Of the new helmet sculpture – I had ground up most of its surface to a bright iron finish so that the welding marks which might have added visual interest to its surface construction became of secondary importance. I also added colour here and there to the inside and to the outside of it – with a total unconcern for whether Halima would like it or not. Once it was finished I felt that this final helmet work really belonged to the Time/Space era of the twentieth century, and christened it Astro Helmet IV. In addition to the element of *black space* apparent in the sculpture – a result once more of cutting a cross and other symbols through the shell, I built in other symbolic patterns such as five keyholes one above the other, burned roughly through the iron with the acetylene torch to expose the blackness inside. The keyholes – with a little imagination suggested the five senses. Intimations of the 6th sense and/or Psi I left to the input of whoever might be looking at the sculpture; perhaps it's presence was particularly suggested by the various symbols it carried. As always, thinking along these lines helped bring a degree of purpose to the act of image-making, and adding strength to the self-conviction needed to reinforce the make-believe yet seriously intentioned underlying concept – Art.

Downstairs in the studio – beginning work most mornings was a wilful struggle. The first two-hours of each new day were often spent attempting to solve the riddle of some seemingly insoluble *formal* problem to do with the shape of whatever sculpture was in the making – these being works of a unique nature rather then wholly representative or imitative of existing life-forms or any mundane thing. The mind processes involved looking for a formal answer to enhance an imagined image must, I think, be similar to the problem of solving a lesser yet ultimately important Zen Koan. I think so – because after hours, days sometimes of worried and concentrated efforts of mind trying out various solutions, a probable answer would eventually arrive in a flash

– the insight, or so it seemed, coming completely out of the blue. I eventually convinced myself that there was a muse, a creative angel, or whatever Psi or spiritual being fits such a description, hovering in space – peering over my shoulder. I think I have already mentioned my belief that Psi is a subtle form of energy which some objects and even people seem to transmit; and which can actually effect an observer or even a whole audience should the art-form be at that level of output. A critic of that time wrote about one of my sculptures and described it as, '... *A space helmet which is at the same time an alien temple... suggestive of a 'device' and of an organic entity. (The sculptures actually seem to be observing you.)'.* Psi?

At about this time one particularly interesting incident occurred when I accepted an invite to lunch from Herbert Read. The lunch was at his lovely house, Stonegrave in North Yorkshire. Read knew of me from my previous time in Leeds and had included a photograph of the Tate's Helmet 1, in his publication – Contemporary British Art, Pelican, 1964. Never having met him I was naturally apprehensive about meeting such a great man.

I drove up to his house on a brilliantly sunny day and was straight away shown into a dining room empty of people but with a long table glittering and laid for lunch. While examining various pictures hung around the room a woman I later knew to be Read's daughter entered. Welcoming me she led me over to a small table of various bottles, asking what would I like, 'Beer!' I said, and stood beside her as she took up an opener and prised off the crinkly bottle top. The beer was either very warm or had recently been shaken, because out spewed a jet of froth which, to my great horror drenched a framed but un-glassed collage on the wall above, 'Oh!' she said, 'It's a Kurt Schwitters,' and picking up a handy cloth, added, 'There, that'll improve it!' smiling at me as she casually wiped the beer off the picture's paper surface.

Afterwards, I remember very little of the meal excepting that I probably behaved with my usual boring reticence of the time. Yet later, Herbert Read – the poet and compassionate first world war soldier, gentleman and scholar, took me into his study to admire a number of tiny Eskimo carvings he'd collected.

But to return to Astro Helmet IV – the last work of that particular group. I finally took it down to the Drian together with a newly made vertical, wing-like sculpture which resembled an astronautical thing; the two works were intended for showing in an exhibition of contemporary British sculpture soon to open in the Drian. Halima was pleased with both, but I did not learn until too late that Herbert Read together with the English surreal painter Roland Penrose, Director of the I.C.A. at the time, chose the two sculptures along with other works by British artists to represent Britain in an exhibition in Germany – 'Profile III', 1964. Halima Nalecz for some unknown reason failed to tell me of this and the first I knew of it was some months later when, calling in at the Drian I was presented with the sorry looking sight of both sculptures dull and dead looking – their previous ground-iron and vital appearance was gone, instead they were orange-red with early rust. Made out of iron and meant as gallery or inside sculptures they were never intended for exhibition in the open air. Placed outside at the mercy of the elements their exposure in Germany had taken its toll.

After efforts to de-rust and revive the helmet sculpture and bring it back to life, I returned it to the Drian never to clap eyes on it again because Halima, in the 1970s I believe, donated this work and others to the Polish National Collection in Warsaw. To my knowledge none of these works of mine remain in this country – with the exception of the 'Helmet 1' in store at the Tate.

But before that time, later in the Sixties, I did see a photograph of my Astro Helmet reproduced in the foremost glossy art magazine Studio International; the picture represented my work and also showed examples of the work of three other practising sculptors. The photographs were included in an article questioning why each of the sculptors mentioned were excluded from a very important exhibition of Contemporary Sculpture in Great Britain presently mounted by the Tate Gallery. I found it difficult to understand my particular exclusion when only the previous year the Tate had purchased that first helmet sculpture for its collection. The article, written by Charles Spencer – eminent art critic who was to become editor of the publication Art and Artists – asked the direct question of why these few, nationally named sculptors, were left out of the Tate exhibition.

As far as I was concerned I thought the probable explanation a pretty bad one if there was any truth in it, because it did not appear to be based on any reasonable evaluation or true assessment of works of art. The causes for non-inclusion of the artists in question seemed to lie with the sculptors rather than in the sculpture they fashioned. I concluded that the obvious reason for my exclusion, and it might easily apply to at least one of the others, was that the selection of work would have been largely chosen by the newly appointed director of the Tate Gallery – Norman Reid. If this was the case then the objection to my work and to that of the other artists was certainly not based upon any aesthetic value, but more probably – considering the old-boy Royal College network of the time on nepotistic friendship or else on 'who do I know merit!'. We of the left out – *and it did hurt,* all came up by the *back door* and not via colleges of art; we therefore lacked the necessary old-boy credentials and any very influential patrons of the Arts.

In the important sense of keeping up elite standards, we were outsiders, hard-working and self-taught rather than having gone through the *establishment* process of becoming *artistic* artists. Unhappily, as in any professional specialised system – background counts, makes a difference because the point in this particular success pyramid often seemed to be guarded by a one or two failed artists-cum-organisers rather than creative doers – who guard and protect the favoured and chosen elite. With exceptions of course, such establishment high-risers are rarely creative doers, but seem instead to be persons who enjoy the questionable privilege of judgement and the compensating negative satisfaction that such power can afford.

If, with the other left-out sculptors, my dismissal as an artist unworthy of inclusion in the Tate exhibition gave me a brief spell of paranoia and bitterness, it was not for very long – for although the success of inclusion in such an exhibition might have meant the reward of a more well established reputation and resulting financial gain, in the end these things could not be of ultimate importance.

I think that what most mattered to me was that there were people who supposedly guarded our cultural heritage but who were selective where truth entered in – they sadly practised a form of falsely applied elitism.

Chapter 12
Comings and goings

Around 1963 it felt extremely dangerous tearing up the A1 in heavy rain. Travelling North my head was strained out of the driver's window of a recently purchased second-hand, black Morris Minor; it was well after dark during term time on a Friday November night. Battered, wet and cold by facing onrushing wind and rain, my head was stuck uncomfortably out of the open window because of the dire necessity to see ahead and so avoid crashing into the close dazzling headlights of the endless stream of traffic rushing threateningly towards me – the aged car's single wiper was not working very well, nor was there a windscreen washer. Occasionally I contorted further out – stretching my arm round to wipe splashed up mud from the bit of windscreen within reach of my outstretched fingers.

I was not alone but accompanied by my friend the Greek Cypriot painter Stass Paraskos. He taught part time in Leicester and we both travelled down from Leeds each week where my family and I were living once more. Therefore, although lecturing full-time I was also commuting; the journey up had become a regular Friday night event. Our shared life had not worked out too well in the Rectory and it had seemed safer for the family's peace of mind to return them to home ground. Conveniently, the Victorian house we bought was right next to our old one; empty and up for sale it did in some measure ease their return by settling them back in a familiar neighbourhood among friends and relatives. In terms of my work as an artist the change came as a retrograde step, further emphasised each weekend when passing the once familiar garage at the end of the now next door garden – which was the concrete block garage I once built to use as a second small studio. Driving up from Leicester every weekend I found it increasingly difficult to escape the sense of moving backwards in time, back to take up a life discarded three years ago as though the ongoing events of the intervening years never actually happened. I found a desperate need to actualise them in my mind, dwell upon the many happenings and the numerous people involved – doing so in order to recognise as fact that the people were real and the events had actually taken place.

I was obviously changed as a person, unavoidably, and was still changing, both inside and out. My understanding and attitude to life was vastly altered and in some ways not for the better. All the insights, the triumphs – if that is what they were – seemed to be fast disappearing, drifting off like imagined episodes in a once exciting now fast dulling dream.

The many life changing happenings over the last few years appeared to have undergone a reverse in Time. After spending those many years in industry and the army making and mending things like a tinker, luck or fate had offered up an entirely new kind of life and now came this reversal, and a virtually uncertain future.

*

Teaching weekdays in Leicester I missed the family and home life quite badly. Having vacated the top floor of the Rectory there being little alternative but to do so, I moved my bed and few necessary belongings down into one end of the old library – my studio. It was a long panelled room lit by fair-sized Georgian windows – looking out on to open countryside from one aspect, and from the other onto a pleasant wooded drive leading down to the Rectory's front door.

It proved to be an unpleasant change of place. Worst were the welding fumes when working on metal sculptures which, together with the metallic smell of iron clung to my every day clothes, my bedclothes, and just about everything else. Even though my understanding friends the painters were close by nothing dispelled the dismay and sense of emptiness awaiting me when arriving back from College most evenings.

Entering the old library, studio and bedroom all in one – the crumpled bed, littered clothes, scattered books, records, food, and all the other requirements necessary for daily survival seemed entirely alien to the welding plant, tools, modelling stands and the variety of sheet iron, rods and similar stuff at the far end of the room. This untidy conglomeration made the old library an unfriendly place in which to live, work and eat – never mind attempt to sleep.

Beginning this writing I quickly realised the futility of getting down in true words even a small part of the story I would like to tell. It would take as long as a whole lifetime again to do justice to the intricate patterns of happy *ups* followed by the greater number of psyche destructive *downs* which I, like all humans experience over the passage of their *never* uninteresting life. The dull realisation also struck me that I could not possibly write down what really happened during the more exacting times of personal trauma and which – exposed, might cruelly effect others. Nor would I wish to cold-bloodedly reveal the magical intimacies encapsulated like rare jewels in shared moments with another which, brief as they are, persuade us to forgive Life when it is no longer magical. The obvious question arising is – why bother getting a life down on paper at all? Well, for me, it passes a lonely less active time on, assists catharsis, and anyway – sharing experience is a common human need and desire; I always found it helpful when reading of other peoples lives – particularly in difficult times. In such circumstances once someone passed me Fitzgerald's 'Crack Up', which depressing as it is, at least allowed me the recognition of an all too human state of mind and provided a timely element of reassurance.

*

My teaching time in Leicester continued without interruption, helping occupy my days. The newly devised Basic Course was going well – and when I was able to put personal problems aside I continued to enjoy the intellectual stimulation of the teaching and the camaraderie working alongside fellow artists. Also there were those satisfying days teaching when student skills improved and one saw original work appear. And other peak moments when observing a student's sudden formal break through after tutors had plugged away for weeks attempting to crack a young mind-barrier.

Many years on a mature woman travelled down to where I eventually ended up teaching – which was in beautiful

Falmouth School of Art, Cornwall, She had come especially to see me she said when led into one of the sculpture studios. An ex-Basic Course student from the early 1960s in Leicester it was at first impossible to place her among the hundreds of students I'd known over many years. *Until* that is she described an occasion when working late one evening. Attempting to trip my memory she told me that it was about eight o'clock when no more than half a dozen students had chosen to say behind to continue working – the main studio was a vast room accommodating fifty or more trestle tables. She described the moment I arrived at her work place to find her in abject tears. At this – a vague memory of the incident came back and I suddenly recognised the girl in the face of the woman opposite me. Maybe I remembered because of the distress that took place so many years ago.

The seventeen year old, or she may have been sixteen, had quietly sobbed out that she could not continue the course because she sometimes failed to understand what the tutors were talking about. Apparently I calmed her, reassuring her that her work was quite good enough and that she *would* understand in the end – after all, the course was only halfway through. Finally, attempting to take her mind off work I asked -

'What do you like doing most of all?'

'Playing the piano. I love music,' she'd said, the tears drying up and her expression brightening. My recollection of the incident coming back more clearly I vaguely recalled saying something like, 'I wouldn't worry about this...', and gestured towards her work on the table, '... if I could play the piano!' And I think I then added something like, 'I'm sure you'll be fine!'

That had been sum of it! Apparently, the moment's

attention, a small kindness, or whatever it might have been – doing my job in fact, turned life around for her in a matter of moments. Becoming a successful fabric-designer and eventually running her own business she had sheltered the memory all those many years.

Teaching art, when I came to the end of it – left me with one sure spark of wisdom which is to do with the purpose of all teaching really. Spelled out, I realised that it was/is, comparatively easy to pass on factual knowledge of whatever skill is in question, and although it might be difficult to convey the concepts underlying a work of art, the greatest imperative in teaching is to make people *believe* in themselves, in which case creativity will out!

One passing memory revived recalls others, and a humorous incident from that same teaching period comes to mind. A not yet wise student needed a replica human ear for a sculpture he was assembling. He persuaded another student to take a cast of his own ear – not the volunteer's ear but that of the student needing the replica. It meant covering the ear with plaster in order to obtain a mould which, when removed could itself be filled with plaster – thus, when removed from the mould there would be the anticipated replica.

Accordingly, an unduly thick mould was cast over the student's liberally Vaselined ear. Fortunately someone had had the common sense to seal off the ear-canal with waxed cotton wool – otherwise, no further evidence of common sense came to light throughout the whole process. The mechanics of removing a hardened plaster-mould from the intricate undercuttings of a human ear had not been thought out, or not even seriously considered. The heavy, single block of plaster with the delicate negative shape inside it naturally refused to part from the side of the poor chap's now sore and worried head – unless, that is, the actual ear came away with it. Needless to say, no tutor had been in sight when the original process of taking a mould took place.

The upshot was that the self-chosen victim walked unhappily around the studios supporting with one hand a fair slab of heavy damp plaster, each movement of it dragging painfully at the delicate shape of his entombed ear. Using the other hand to support the opposite elbow he walked panic-stricken round the studios, yelling loudly for help; various ribald solutions were offered and someone, giggling, suggested a dash to the A & E department of the city's hospital.

The situation was saved by Vin Baldwin, a sculptor teaching with us, who bravely took up chisel and mallet to painstakingly attack the mould amid loud cheers of encouragement from the student-pack who plainly ignored the pained cries of, 'Get the fucking thing off!' from the distressed student.

I continued working and sleeping in the old library. Finishing work at College late evenings, not looking forward to the drive back to the Rectory, I would often delay it by nights spent drinking with friends, cinema-going, or grasping at whatever diversion might offer relief from arriving at the studio to a dishevelled and lonely bed.

*

With the end of the Helmet series my immediate interest in *black space* was temporarily left behind. I mentioned earlier that the ideas giving rise to its use was of great help much later on when I came across the precise language of Systems' terminology – the *black-box* concept served as a symbolic model for studying the mechanics of the brain. I learned all of this later in 1968 when invited to lecture at Wolverhampton College by Ron Dutton, sculptor and medallist. The painter Roy Ascott was Head of Painting at the time and seriously involved in applying the creative ideas stemming from Cybernetics in art-form. So that my thought-up idea of *black-space* preceding my time at Wolverhampton ceased to be of immediate importance. Yet, in essence it would reappear in minor guise in later works.

But analytically onward – my essential progress as an artist, or image-maker seemed to follow a pattern of concentrating for a period of time on one particular idea or image – and working with that in mind to produce one, two, or more sculptures. After that point, hopefully, some new formal or purposeful direction might arise by indirectly evolving out of the old. I firmly believed that the sequential search and the creative fulfilment of each idea as it came along would leave behind a vestige of moved-on and moved-up understanding. I believe I have already implied that I never found that making art was an easy option; and that the finished work – the sculpture or whatever turned up, standing boldly in reality, *never* actually achieved the satisfactory clarity of expression or meaning originally intended and most laboriously sought.

Perhaps to labour the point if I have not already done so – then having given up the traditional aesthetic of the art object echoing the naturally beautiful, my particular interest lay in the strength of image conveying its true intention – this, rather than opting for a too fetching image verging on the nicely acceptable.

I had long realised that the art I produced would never be in any way great or world-shattering, but neither would it be mediocre or ineffective. If it raised questions, good! If it lifted the spectator's mind above the mundane, good! If it first attracted interest by its manner of making and not merely by formal interest and invention, then good! What more could one ask for or do? For a work to be totally ignored would be fatal because even a minimal amount of appreciation is vital for any artist – otherwise he, she, would probably end up madly biting their respective nails owing to the sheer frustration of failing to communicate with even one person. If all this sounds a bit over the top then...

*

To return to the late Spring of 1963, not intending them to be taken as intensely serious works, I welded up two wing-like sculptures. One of which I mentioned previously resembled an astronautical device; the other, smaller, about three feet high, stood like the plumed crest on a Roman or Hellenic helmet. Although both when completed were attractive yet strong images, the idea behind their basic shapes arrived from another very ordinary source.

In a café close to College one afternoon tea-break, chatting about the course work with Brian Fielding, a friend and a painter, having eaten a delightful chocolate cup-cake I was was doodling with its empty case. Listening and responding to Brian, at one point I'd flattened the soft silver foil out into a circle, folded it in half and absent-mindedly pressed in adjustments to its shape. During a lull in the conversation, happening to glance down at the tiny silver thing in my hands I immediately fell in love with it – picturing in my mind the miniature object as an enlarged entity.

Back in the studio, all else forgotten, excited by thoughts of the new thing I was about to create it proceeded to materialise. The shapes, cut out of 20G sheet iron, welded up to three feet in height (and gallery sculpture was not necessarily monumental) each side was a segment of not quite a semi-circle and made up of four pieces. Welded together the four roughly ground welds formed the linear symbol of a cross and became significantly symbolic. From the front the two sides were connected by a tapering piece welded at right angles to the radii of the segments – starting six-inches in width at the centre it rose pointing and sloping backwards, narrowing to one inch at the tip of the form; similarly a piece tapered again from the centre, sloping down and angling back to narrow almost to a point at its base – the lower end of the segment of the circle. Back view, the circular edge of each side remained slightly apart, leaving a thin, say a one inch line of *black space* circling high between them – gradually narrowing to come together at the top of the curve and together at its base. The object, standing on a plinth soared up vertically and geometrically and also satisfyingly sculptural.

Secured to a heavy iron base-plate at its lowest point, the work gave out a sense of the heroic. Seen from the front, in a small oval inset in the centre I slotted the metal through to create the symbol of a small, *black-space* cross and finally added five short brush strokes of bright crimson enamel below. The brilliant colour contrasted beautifully with the ground silvery armour-like, tooled iron surface.

Completed, I drove with the sculpture up North for it to be shown in a open exhibition held annually in Bradford Art Gallery. Each year a selected number of reputable artists were invited to exhibit a work. Quite out of the blue that year a letter arrived from this Northern gallery inviting me to send something in.

Later, when the exhibition opened, at home for the

weekend, I took the children over to see it. The sculpture looked well – mounted commandingly on a high plinth in the main room. I had called it, topically – Device for an Astronaut. It received reasonable mentions in the Art columns of the local press and a few visitors to the exhibition certainly appeared to have shared this approval. I knew of this for certain when, after the show ended, having collected and driven the work back down to the Rectory I carried it in. While lifting it out of the van I was aware of an odd rattle. Once inside the studio, turning the thing up-side down, out fell a meagre shower of pennies – the big copper kind from the 'olden days' before the degenerate era of new-pence took over. It looked very much as though the slot of the black cross cut into the front, slashed beneath with brilliant red, converted the sculpture into an expensive art money-box for generous though sardonic gallery goers. At least, I thought, the work elicited an active form of art appreciation from a number of spectators; I could also claim it as an early example of audience participation – a psychic suggestion of things to come? Apart from that sign the story of the pennies made a good anecdote to tell in future whenever lecturing and showing my work.

*

It was around this point that I got caught up in an unstoppable emotional slipstream, becoming hopelessly entangled in a maze of unhealthy romantic dream-days of the kind one might read about in a dramatically unfolding novel – each turning page blanking out any semblance of reality and sadly harming others; the others being my family.

The immediacy of what came about swept what guilt I might have felt into an unused corner of my mind, hiding it away – temporarily of course! I fobbed myself off with the thought that although what was done was in no way excusable, yet I had done my utmost to ease the separation. The pretence, though guilt never remained quietly below the surface, led me mistakenly to convince myself that everything would work out all right in the end.

Meantime, before that impossibility could finally *not* happen there was this wonderful deluded, idyllic role of artist and lover to fulfil – so my emotionally soaked senses informed me – denying any sane perception of what was really happening. I saw true facts in a half-light as things to be put aside and out of mind during the ardent hours conjured up by an impossible to sustain romantic attachment which, although loving, given time, would change to become a self-destructive obsession.

*

Until then, although almost drowning so to speak, avoiding real issues, I escaped by working on in the library studio, constructing a final sculpture in there. Welded up in sheet iron and brass I called it The Wall, completing it before at last abandoning the Rectory. Five or more feet wide, similar in height, its shape resembled the peeled off bottom-half of an onion skin. The slighter lower curve was secured to heavy, half inch iron plate, the curving top remaining open. The shape was made by welding together consecutive iron plates, side by side and row upon row; growing them upwards and adjusting the rectangular proportions of each according to formal need – the method suggested natural growth. Sheltered within the resulting curved space I carefully arranged various minor forms. Some were of brass consisting of unused small shapes left around the studio having been discarded as unsuitable when made for earlier sculptures. One, consisting of a curve formed in brass was pierced by a hole which might well have been an eye; it parodied a human face in profile. Another small brass oval form placed within a heavy six inches iron ring was symbolic of a brain. At the top of the iron wall I opened up the shape of a cross and circle. These, together with the other small images gave the work reasonable import and significance. The Wall was eventually given picture space in Art International – although I doubt if anyone realised the intention behind the work and its title.

As with most of my works an eventual history, perhaps only meaningful to myself attached to it; in this case it was certainly a strangely coincidental one. The title, The Wall, was derived from a book I had just read called that. Written by John Hersey if my memory serves me correctly it was a history-based novel graphically describing the terrible suffering in the Nazi-created Jewish Ghetto in Warsaw during the last World War. What I read was beyond belief in terms of how evil human beings can be in inflicting such cruelty on other helpless humans. Naming the sculpture was the only measure of sympathy for the Jewish peoples suffering I could offer – an ineffectual gesture towards something I could otherwise do nothing about.

By a remarkable coincidence many years later, for no directly connected reason as far as I ever discovered, The Wall was one of the works donated by Halima Nalecz to the Polish National Collection. I suspect that no other person except myself ever knew at the time, or even now – the unhappy connection between The Wall and the history of Warsaw.

*

Out of necessity I decided it was time that I packed up at the Rectory and left. I shifted my studio equipment, materials, bed and belongings to the deserted ground floor of an old brick factory building in Leicester. The sculptor Vin Baldwin rented me the place. He lived on the rejuvenated upper floor of the building with his wife Pat and their two children.

It was late October when I moved in – hoping to live there and get on with some work. But both the move and the idea of working in the place turned out to be wishful thinking. There was no form of heating except one of those round cast iron coke stoves to be found in factory or workshops in pre-war times – this one had seen better days. It gave out lots of smoke suggestive of fire yet transmitted almost no heat, and the place was freezing cold. Electric fires and paraffin stoves also seemed more than useless in what seemed like a vast empty, inhospitable space.

What I clearly remember about the fiasco of attempting to survive let alone live there, was the utter sense of abject dejection it imposed on its occupant – me! My means of conquering this depth of feeling was by blasting out music on a recorder, the solitary notes echoing round the peeling whitewashed brick walls in some kind of sympathy – not empathy for that would have been too much! It sounded as though the building itself regretted better days. Unable to stand the desolation any longer I impulsively and abruptly abandoned the place – and rather than attempt to remove cumbersome equipment, like tools and materials comprising sheets of metal, iron rods and such like, I simply gave the lot to Vin – the act reflected my state of mind.

A next almost equally bad choice of living space involved a worn bed-sitter not far from Leicester railway station. Its only saving grace was that it *was* close to the station when

I needed to escape after fulfilling my teaching quota and travelling either to London or most times back up to Leeds. Renting the place meant sharing a shabby kitchen and a never quite clean bathroom – still, I consoled myself, it was only intended for sleeping in three or four nights mid-week; the rent was as much as I could then afford.

The problem was that word about my convenient bed-sitter got around and the place soon became a casual doss-house for part-timers commuting on the nights when I was not there. I learned in time that they also used it for numerous illicit assignations. I seriously discovered this one Sunday evening after driving down from Leeds in order to teach on Monday morning. Retiring after a usual pub nightcap I unearthed from my tangle of ill-used bed clothes a black bra. It looked to be the biggest bra I had ever set eyes on and of almost gargantuan proportion. Next day in College, by discreet inquiry I understood it belonged to a recently employed model in the department. Her breasts had apparently fascinated one of the more adventurous London painters – up teaching he had found them irresistible as did she his determined intention to more fully appreciate them.

Chapter 13
Interlude

The house was beyond a wood which was all that remained of a once vast English forest. The city over the years gradually engulfed the forest – destroying it. I left the suburbs behind and walked to the house along the stony clay path between the remaining broad leaf trees...

...the woods were lush with that darker kind of grass stronger and more virile than meadow grass. The wood was an intercourse – a fellowship of trees of ancient origin. A fairy tale house stood upon a hillside at the far edge of the wood. The hill was made of flowers, yellow flowers which touched upon the old grey stones. The house must have known how beautiful it was for countless years. On that night within the grey stone house where the daffodils grew he was exultant like a rampant bloody stag reaching the ultimate cleft, disappearing within its confines; it would be profane to disclose its uniqueness. He entered the apple a grub, a larvae awaiting metamorphosis, devouring its succulence, drinking of the sweetness of the

fluids of love – each crevasse exploding in a violet surge, propagating the race and committing his seed to the womb – that receptacle for the extravagance of Man...

*

I was at the centre of a group, increasingly aware that I was the cause of these people coming together. Whilst happy, if that is what I felt my mood to be in sharing this new world, I was also keenly aware that its peaceful continuity seemed to be at the mercy of a series of uncertain events. These alternated from light to dark, changing from moment to moment like reflections in a bright mirror poised to shatter at the whim of a wrongly spoken word, an apparent unwelcome turn of mind, or a mood wrecked by an unsought for lucid flash of reality.

Our separate worlds, joined were too intense. What we achieved was based on a false premise of happiness bought out of unhappiness. The euphoria spawned by a mutual attraction went along with a demand for perfection – each from the other. It depended upon the shared delusion of an impossible ideal of romantic and sexual love. Unfortunately, as people, we were too seriously minded and mistakenly and hopelessly intent on achieving near to perfection in the new life on which we had embarked. It was an attempt at a life of being together, *if* we could, in green and idyllic surrounding *when* we could, and loving *when* we could; all of this ventured in the midst of insoluble material problems and the volatile emotional insecurity our obsessive attraction and vastly differing psyches generated.

Of the many squalls to follow I was able to track down the cause of my partner's irritation. It happened whenever a chink in my naive intellectual armour momentarily exposed a shade of ignorance, exhibiting a pettiness of character which she wished and thought ought not to be there; it marked an imperfection in what she wanted me to be and a truth she appeared unable to bear.

But the weekend my friends were staying with us in the grey stone house I recall well for an odd reason. Strolling in the wood on a lovely summer Sunday morning we were enjoying a pre-lunch ramble. What followed was a recurrence of something which had occurred more than once recently. This was a strange feeling of viewing myself and what was happening around me as though from another place – a distance; this other place gave me clearer, more than an acute perception of the people, of myself, and of the immediate situation we collectively inhabited.

Leaving the woods behind, we were edging down the valley slope towards the beck below. It was a narrow beck flowing between grassy banks where water persistently carved its way over a crossing of time-sculptured stepping stones. Still pools here and there held quickly fleeing red-breasted fish if disturbed, and in shallower water shy, whiskered catfish could be found beneath carefully lifted up stones. Coming down the hill, the children, excited, bounded and raced here and there, climbing to perch as pretend king-of-the-castle on one or other of the embedded granite boulders scattered about the hillside. The two painters were in heavy conversation, swapping London Art gossip I suspected. The three women were evidently talking about the men, nodding frequently in the direction of the others or myself whilst edging carefully sideways down the slope of velvet smooth grass – each one of them looking beautiful. It seemed to be a very special day – one I would not easily forget.

*

There was the usual uplift to my feelings when I saw her step down onto the platform and walk slowly towards me, smiling. Yet I sensed doubt in the smile and wondered if like myself she was wondering what on earth she was doing on this strange railway station meeting someone not too long ago a stranger. Perhaps she felt as I did – that what we were doing was completely out of context with our other, comparatively safe lives.

I pictured an unusual looking lovely woman approaching, not exactly a stranger, far from it in the sense of physical intimacy, but neither was she a person I seemed to know a great deal about. Intuitively I felt that she was less than happy – yet she shared my compulsion that we each love the other. Perhaps both of us were seeking proof to satisfy the very human need arising out of a mutual loneliness – not the loneliness of isolation but more a desperate wish to be comforted and loved at a deeper level – deeper than that on which people share no more than a harmony of temperament. Or it may have been that we each sought our spiritual nature – hoping to find a particle of this captured within the other, and which might disclose some profound meaning for the singular and often discordant lives we complex beings separately lead.

Other such thoughts, less resolved than these written down here entered my mind as I watched her step towards me. There was also a momentary disturbed feeling that this woman, this person, had nothing at all to do with me. I sensed that here and now was a moment of opportunity for backing off, of persuading her to return on the next train. But by that time it was too late, she was up to me and we were embracing, it was much too late. Whatever happened in the future was inevitable – it would!

*

I was not yet used to the idea of living back in the Rectory. Working in the tiny outside servant's cottage which was once a part of my previous occupancy but then used as a store, it did not feel at all like old times. So much had changed, not at the Rectory which was more or less the same, but in myself and circumstances.

I stood contemplating the thirty-six inches circle of block-board out of which – near to the perimeter in each approximate quarter of the circle, carefully designed spaces were cut out. Into one of these I intended to place a wooden hand – once part of a lay-figure; it would be fixed in the space on the same plane as the circle, the fingers open and relaxed outwards towards the perimeter. The cut-out shape, formally designed around the hand, would add a negative interest to the image of the work as a whole. Opposed to the hand – across the circle I planned to inset a sculptured symbol of a heart – once again in an appropriately designed space. At right-angles to the hand and heart or midway between them would be a fertility symbol comprising two 1 ½ half inch wooden lathe-turned balls or spheres separated by a thin lath about seven inches long. The item in the remaining quarter circle was a vertical row of five horizontal keyhole openings of a size proportional to the other images. The whole was a wooden pattern made ready to be sandcast in aluminium. Back from the foundry and finished, the work was meant to stand vertically on a plinth – literally in space supported there firmly by a non-intrusive aluminium base; it should present a strong image in any London gallery.

Months had gone by without my being involved in any creative work of my own, so that I was particularly excited about this new thing. There was a second reason for my great interest in this very obviously far removed image compared to anything I'd come up with in the past. The reason, I imagined, for such a revolutionary change was due to my association with the painters working in the Rectory and the constant talk and swapping about of ideas. Their influence, I fully believed, had helped free me from the limiting academic *musts* I'd been stuck with which limited the concepts and form of traditional sculpture. However, I would learn in time that probably there were much more subtle sources, or forces at work defining the nature of the symbols appearing in the seeming unique image I was in process of creating. The true or probable fact of this source was to be pointed out to me by an unknown woman looking at the finished work when it eventually appeared on exhibition in London. She casually informed me exactly what the image represented, *where* it came from, and *what* kind of truth it intimated.

*

After approaching my painter friends who were still in residence in the Rectory, I rented a fair sized first-floor room as living accommodation. I realised only later on, when it was all over, that she had been incredibly brave in order to risk coming down with her two children to live among this colony of near enough itinerant artists. On the surface I suppose the Rectory and its band of creatively intent individuals represented a vague Utopia and way of life far removed from the ordinary. Such as it seemed, it might well inspire and attract anyone of quixotic inclinations – and she most certainly possessed those. It seems in retrospect that we were both emotionally blinded as to a reckoning of whatever might transpire from out of the euphoria of such a compulsive desire to be together. If selfish it was a brave although foolhardy attempt to make something out of less than little in the way of either material means or plain common sense.

She had done the best she could with the room we occupied. A double sheet hanging from the ceiling became a room divider with beds arranged either side for the children and us. The dining and all-purpose table was placed in front of a window where one might see the distant steam trains still chugging across the horizon. She otherwise beautified the room using the natural gift she had for doing such things. The surrounding countryside of yet unspoiled meadows grew an abundance of wild flowers and some few of these adorned the room most days that Summer.

The cottage studio was ample as a space to work in. It looked out upon the small, grassed close where Victor's bantams still roamed. Although there was electricity in the cottage the lighting was not good – there was only one small window but it being Summer I compensated for this lack by keeping the door wide open.

Alone, working in there, I felt more secure than out of it – unoccupied and when not making art. In the tiny, quite gloomy cottage, surrounded by bits and pieces of images and ideas in progress, I felt kinship and a sense of real oneness with the littered workbench and tables, the strewn chaos of tools and colourful symbols in process of creation – a crimson heart, various sculptured hands; one a silhouette in block-board painted green, a more real lay-hand, and my own once cast in plaster and graphited; a fertility symbol and innumerable other *things* also lay scattered – imaginable debris awaiting origination.

Inside this tiny cottage with the outside and mundane temporarily put away there was a sense of release and joy in the creative process – I sometimes felt privileged to be part of it. The interior of this tiny room must be like the inside of my brain I fancied – often messy and unwise but with an essential purpose underlying the apparent disorder. I had thought on numerous occasions that the appearance of my studio or workplace, or anyone's for that matter, was often far more interesting than a work of the artist's on exhibition – viewed in its individual separateness. A studio stimulated *progressive creativity* where new things were happening and coming into being – yet nothing was finite or sealed in – thereby allowing opportunity for ideas to evolve and unique images to appear...and maybe, just maybe, something meaningful might emerge out of the apparent chaos?

As well as the circle of block board with the built in symbols which I hoped could be successfully cast in metal, I was also working on a female torso. This began as found-object made of shell-plaster and bought from a shop which sold window display fittings. The torso had been used to show-off female apparel. One of the painters called into College to tell us that the shop was selling-up. I dashed to see what was on offer – the headless blue figure, thighs ending just above the knee, boldly standing behind the plate glass window looked to me like a sculpture already made. I'd bought it for under two-pounds and with it two wooden lay-figure hands costing next to nothing – paltry sums for the pleasure of owning the fascinating objects received in return. Now the torso stood in the cottage – raised to person height, sturdy and secure upon the tubular base of an old office chair. Carving a short wooden pillar I'd secured it between the tubular base and the torso and then added plaster to reshape and sensually beautify the torso's hips.

Next, taking a keyhole saw I carefully cut through the plaster shell around the line of a rectangle I'd drawn around the left breast. The breast could then be lifted away or replaced at choice – by using the simple mechanism of a turned, half inch wooden screw fixed immediately below the breast-piece; the screw was big enough to be easily manipulated with one's fingers. A pink Perspex heart and a second bright orange shape were loosely slotted over a small brass fertility symbol hidden within the space behind the removable breast piece.

Elsewhere, a *keep-off* orange spotted triangle overlaid the pubic mound – symbolically placed as warning. The torso's navel became a keyhole, and on the lower back in the subtle hollow where spine joins buttocks I inserted a second triangle of black Perspex. Bending to peer through a hole in the centre of this, one looked into an eye and at oneself peering back; it was contrived out of a silver Christmas tree ball and false eyelashes. All the way down the left side of the torso – at right-angles, a one inch fluorescent orange strip of Perspex echoed the curves of the torso, vividly contrasting its glazed cobalt blue surface finish.

Beneath the torso where the bottom of the thighs were secured to the tubular stand I shaped and inserted a flat one inch thick wooden base and screwed three cup-hooks into its edge immediately below the thighs. The breast-piece of the torso, unscrewed and removed, so exposing the brightly coloured Perspex shapes beneath, was meant to be hung on one hook; a second hook was for a block-board, painted green hand cut in silhouette; the third supported an old circular cast-iron weight fortuitously pierced with a keyhole. The latter – lifted from its hook, allowed whoever wished to do so to peer through the keyhole in pretend-naughty secrecy at the colourful shapely blue torso and its gaudy array of sardonic sexual symbols. The image of the sculpture which evolved as it progressed in making was not intentionally contrived to shock – it just happened. I suspect the sexual irony expressed was directed more at my own maleness rather than intending any derogatory intention towards the opposite gender.

Catalogued as Blue Torso, Green Hand, when finally exhibited – aesthetically shocking as it was (and people in the Sixties *were* shockable) it offered the opportunity for a second visual experience to any brave gallery goer choosing not only to view it but to manipulate the simple parts hung upon the screw-hooks – or if it was not already removed then remove the left breast to discover the evocative forms inside. Appearing on Earth too early in Art-history time, the Blue Torso allowed a spectator the opportunity to become actively involved with the sculpture's materiality – to join in with it as in audience participation, and even on a physical level this was a relatively new concept for 1964 in the enlightened James Bond society of the delightful Sixties. One undiscerning, unenlightened critic of Modern art described the Blue Torso as a *vacuous image* – it was far from that from any high or low point of view. Whatever the source of its inspiration, the work was of imposing stature and great presence. It stood as a discordant image bordering upon the ugly but also stood as a unique twentieth century humanoid experience. It appeared out of emptiness – I was merely being honestly intuitive in making it and un-bothered as to *why* I was doing so. But there it stood, unblushing and shameless! What could I do except bravely exhibit the thing! Not unnaturally the painters, curious as to what I was doing, often appeared at the door of the studio while I was bringing this unquestionably unique object into sculptural life. I suspect they probably thought me quite mad – it is likely that I was at the time in an indirect, not dangerous and certainly not uninteresting way; but they being the good friends they were refrained from telling me so.

What was of great importance to me at the time was that I enjoyed creating the Blue Torso; it proved to be a one off and a special creative experience during which I felt a total sense of liberation from all the inhibiting restrictions I previously observed when making art; the only clear concept in my mind was – *if the image worked then to hell with the rules* – I was free of them. I was also aware that the colourful images conjured up were inherently *true* to me at the time of their conception and therefore probably helpful – this was the value of the work; if others wished to look at the thing, or did not, so *be* it, they could take it or leave it!

About this time the painters had organised a collective exhibition for all of us living in the Rectory with the addition of Tom Hudson our collective boss – although the work we would be showing had nothing to do with the College. Consisting of the work of seven artists, my self included, we would be exhibiting in Grabowski's, a slightly more up-market gallery in London. It was impossible for me to back out of the exhibition at this late date even if I wanted to – and I did, because owing to my recent upheavals there were only the two new works I could show. Also worrying was the critical reaction to the new sculptures, that is if they could even be described as sculpture – objects or images would be a more apt description because they were extremely unlike anything I had previously exhibited in London. Well... I would just have to face the music when the time came – I'd faced much worse situations and felt convinced that there were still more desperate confrontations yet to come – which proved to be a very correct assumption.

*

The foundry had not made a particularly good job of casting the flat, three-feet in diameter block-board circle. Fortunately, the heart, hand, and fertility symbol were well reproduced. The flat bed of sand impressed with the circular pattern appeared to have got disturbed in the moulding box. The molten aluminium – flowing into the mould formed ledges on the surface which, when I came to clean the casting up, needed heavy grinding in order to bring the surfaces back towards something like their original flatness.

Still, when this had been done, the symbols pegged in place and the base attached, seeing the work standing upright on the bench for the first time I was pleased with the strength of the image it presented. Light coming through the sculptural and sympathetic spaces surrounding the diverse symbols emphasised their solidity and shape. Altogether, it was a commanding art-work – one not to be ignored; also, as far as the coming exhibition was concerned it did represent a work closer to what might be accepted as conventional sculpture, that is, in comparison to the shock image of its companion – the Blue Torso.

Carrying the aluminium sculpture which I christened 'Circle, Hand and Heart' outside one Summer evening I mounted it on a high white plinth. Upright, sited flat against the background of green trees, blue sky, and billowing white clouds, it looked good – the silvery, ground aluminium surface became alive in the evening sunshine and reflected the surrounding naturally beautiful things of Earth. Momentarily excited by what I had brought to completion I dashed into the Rectory and upstairs, calling my partner to, 'Come and see...!'

Racing back down I stood waiting, contemplating the work against the background landscape. The shining circle of aluminium embodying the four emotive symbols gave off a timeless, archaic feeling. It was not a perfect image, but who besides myself would notice the flaws the maker's eye could see.

Coming close up beside me she said, 'It's really beautiful. How clever you are. It's like something for magic!' Then, 'Look...!' she cried with excitement, and grabbing up the strutting sire of the hens pecking nearby – the brilliant red-combed cockerel, she thrust it out and up against against the silvery moon-like disc. The act imbued the work with extra meaning so that in the mellowing evening sunlight the whole scene looked truly occult, her black hair and gypsy mien helping transform her for an instant into someone or something medieval.

*

What happened happened so relatively quickly that it could have been the kind of dream in which one is totally powerless to prevent the action taking place. She had told me that her ex-husband was driving down to see the children next day, Saturday. I worked out afterwards, when it was all too late, that it must have been *she* who had telephoned to ask him to come down. We'd had a particularly bad row the night before I went for a walk when he appeared in order that the two of them might spend time alone with their children. Arriving back at the Rectory later I saw that they were all outside, the children being helped into their father's car. At the same time I noticed suitcases strapped on the roof-rack which had not been there on the car's arrival. I wondered what was happening, assuming that the children were probably off to stay with their father for a short time. She, was hovering around, indecisive, glancing over to where I stood waiting for the car to be driven away and for her to come across – all had been forgiven earlier that morning.

She did come to me, a serious expression on her face, kissed me on the cheek in an odd way, walked back to the car, its engine idling. She was about to say goodbye to her husband and the children, I thought, but no, she'd climbed into the car and it had driven away.

Too shocked to take in exactly what was happening, all that I later recalled was a glimpse of her unhappy face framed in the rear window as the car disappeared down the tree lined drive and out of sight...

*

According to pattern I did as many abandoned, immature lovers probably did – revelled in disgusting self-pity in the sheer disbelief that what seemed like one's whole world could collapse within the short space of an hour.

Long after the event I am able to understand that my lifelong propensity to emotionally dramatise situations was at that time at its peak. A character flaw? Yet in a different sense it is unquestionably that level of experiencing which might rightly or wrongly gear ones life to express the deepest of feelings in material form – like Art maybe? In retrospect of course my feelings were selfish – which I can now put down to an early naiveté or a late growing-up!

Back from the village pub later that same day, not too far gone – which might have been better, sitting in the tiny cottage studio I listened to music, music which helped an emotional need to intensify memories of the grey stone house. A badly scratched record of a Chaconne by Vitali contrived to bring back most vividly all the things I knew were devastatingly lost; there had been some very special times, both beautiful and rare.

Feeling the need to escape these present surroundings I realised that it was much too late to do so that day. Looking round the darkening Georgian cottage which had served me well as a studio for a brief eventful period, I became dimly aware of the images occupying the historic old space it contained. The aluminium circle embodying the symbols of heart and hand stood there looking strange and mysterious in the half-light. In front of the tiny blackened fireplace stood the incongruous Blue Torso, almost completed, only lacking its final glaze. Well…perhaps this blue figure, majestic in sculptural sexuality was my Pygmalion.

Recently, I had come to realise that a perceptive other person could tell me things about myself I never previously considered. One art critic, writing about these latest works when they were finally exhibited wrote that the sculptures were: '…*a complex of symbols that have a profound meaning for the artist himself. The image, bound up as it is with his individual and unique emotional experience, inevitably takes on a hallucinatory quality.*' The critic continued '…*he secures his identity in an environment of shifting emotions and values…*'

At the time, when I read the words I knew that they were all completely and obviously true; but for the present, undergoing the effects of a lover's unforeseen and abrupt departure I was despairing of the future; if it came to that – *was* there a future…

*

Having failed to sleep I was up and about early next morning, my mind in no way clear. There were unavoidable decisions to be made which I felt incapable of making. Memories of my own family were also reoccurring; I knew that I must act quickly and get out! – away from the Rectory and this part of my life. All I had succeeded in doing here was to bring unhappiness to the people I professed to love.

Sitting down in the painters' kitchen, offered breakfast I politely refused. What was I going to do, I was asked, and reminded that the group exhibition was to take place in two weeks time, there was no escaping the fact that I must exhibit; they would get my two works down to the gallery in London when the time came.

Fortunately, not long ago I had acquired an old Bedford van sufficiently roomy to take sculpture, and now if it came to a pinch, to take myself and my belongings. Hastily packing my few clothes, my books, the record player, records, camera and slides of work, blankets and a pillow – all my worldly goods, I shoved them in the van. Closing the cottage door, after a final look at the two sculptures standing there, I felt unhappy to be abandoning them so soon – life appeared to have become a sad, never ending process of leaving places, people, and all manner of things behind me, and now it was happening once more. As to where I intended going I had no idea, it was only important to get away from where I had stupidly hurt people.

The others stood outside the old red-brick house as I finally slammed the van's rear doors. I was to take care and not to worry about the exhibition – they would get the work down there. With a final wave I was off down the drive feeling like there was no top or bottom to existence, no solids, no remaining supports on which to lean to come to rest. Heading down the M1, for in what other direction could I possibly travel, the roar of the engine and a need to concentrate on the streams of fast traffic helped delay the greater anxiety of mind I knew was steadily approaching. There was no clear idea as to where in London I was heading, except it must be North of the river. There would be safety in the familiar and in knowing there were friends not too far away. I would not inflict my present mood upon them until it eased off. For the time being this van would be my refuge.

Chapter 14

London

That first night in London was spent in the back of the van. I'd parked in a quiet street near Chalk Farm. The van was not a good place in which to sleep. It wasn't altogether the actual discomfort, although it had been pretty cold it was not that – it was the stark dreariness of the whole sordid situation. The street lamps shone nightmare fashion through the rear windows, filling the van with a bleak, chilling, half-light.

Arriving in London I'd headed for a familiar area, allowing myself that degree of comfort. I could quite easily have gone to stay with a Eric Brown – a painter friend living not far from where I was parked, but chose not to do so. We had shared years of nights pubbing together and I'd stayed with him often when in London – or rather with *them,* for he shared a flat with a fabric designer, Karen Moller, who also taught in Leicester. I would see them tomorrow perhaps. Later, when things got decidedly worse it was Karen who passed me a copy of Fitzgerald's 'Crack Up'. Regardless of its grimness the story helped by showing me that my state of mind was by no means unique – it is only causes that differ.

I spent most of the following day plucking up sufficient courage to knock at the doors of the many Victorian houses standing at that time in Chalk Farm – inquiring for a room to rent. It was late afternoon before I finally landed one in a terrace of smaller, less opulent dwellings.

The single room was not quite as tenant-exhausted as the awful bedsitter I'd rented in Leicester where I'd unearthed that gigantic bra. Although the cold impersonality of the place was equally as bad it was at least, cleaner.

Proportionally the room was long, high and narrow in width – six feet maybe. The door, when it was opened, banged hard up against the side of the single iron bedstead. Pushed up into the left hand corner of the room, behind the door, the bed took up most of the space. Less than three feet away, against the opposite wall, was an old, two-ring gas cooker with a tiny, tiny oven. A little further along a once elegant but now cracked Victorian hand basin sported worn brass taps; a battered hot water geyser overhung the sink accompanied by the inevitable coin meter. To one side of it on the faded, flowered wallpaper was screwed an ageing mirror.

From the door to the tall sash widow at the far end of the room the narrow walkway was a short five paces. A shallow wardrobe and tiny chest of drawers were squeezed in at the end of the bed. Across from these a few inches away from the sink stood a small square, cup-ringed table accompanied by one hard chair; there was no armchair.

The only saving grace of the bed-sitter was the tall window overlooking a long, overgrown and unkempt London garden. Happily, the garden possessed a black and white cat which often sunned itself not far from the window, so that with the window wide open I never felt completely alone. The cat would not come to me – completely ignoring my, 'Puss-puss-pussy', and other such noises humans usually make to attract tame animal life. Merely glancing up, disdainfully, it often stretched out lengthways – abnormally elongated and half twisted over, washing a held-up paw or stretching half-up to get to a rigid, skywards pointing back leg. At times, stopping suddenly mid-wash, the cat stared at me in a vastly *I am me* superior kind of way, its pink tongue still and stupidly lolled out, the half lick-washed leg remaining cocked in mid-air.

There was a further shock over and above the meanness of the room I was to occupy; this came when I saw the bathroom. It was sanitary but all but bare, and almost deprived of any sign of human habitation – apart that is from the existence of the absolute necessaries.

These consisted of a huge, unboxed Victorian cast-iron bath – its enamel badly repainted an off-white, its outer shape a dull, cold green. The bath was sinisterly overlooked by an enormous, antiquated, possibly lethal gas geezer; a nearby slot meter which probably ate up shillings like chocolate drops was the only decoration on the wall; the remaining items in the bathroom was a W.C., a scraggy wooden stained lavatory brush, and a roll of shiny brown toilet-paper. The room itself was half-tiled in white, the rest painted the same cold, depressing green as the outside of the bath; patchy brown linoleum covered the floor.

I hated the place on sight but there was no immediate alternative – and whatever else the 'Let' provided safety for the time being and a place to stay; it also gave me an address. I had read recently that people without an address were generally described as – persons of no fixed abode, and were invariably those who ended up in deep *stuck* – to use an apt Sixties expression.

Sitting at the window each and every day of that first week after a daily trip out shopping down England's Lane for bread, cigarettes, and other bodily needs, I wrote her page after page of letters. Also helping save my state of mind were the lovely midsummer days of bright sunshine. And the cat continued to visit the garden, staring at me between bouts of washing, helping console my need for *any* form of companionship.

I found out in months to come that all the letters I wrote in that lonely room were kept – there were many! Contained in a clear plastic satchel they hung from a velvet cord around her neck. It may have proved something to other people seeing them, in that they stood as convincing proof that she was loved. Later the letters were burned, flung into a fire in a sad, angry gesture!

My mood became increasingly emotional; imagination distorted both past and present, constructing an untrue sense of reality – what appeared to be real was not! Each day at the window I wrote ten, twenty, thirty pages; in time I forgot exactly what it was I wrote about but it must have been in serious, regretful language – the stuff of unhappy romances.

*

Some how or other that first week passed by. I had seen friends, called at the Drian to see Halima, and been in touch by telephone with the painters in the Rectory – having promised to let them know how I was making out. I had done so, assuring them that all was well, inquiring at the same time if the Blue Torso and my other exhibit, Circle, Hand and Heart were safe – and were the arrangements for our forthcoming exhibition in Grabowski's going well?

Sunday morning, about nine, I walked over to Haverstock Hill and to the row of shops opposite Bellsize Park tube. During the week, having explored the district afresh for decent, inexpensive cafés in which to eat, I'd discovered one. More like a transport caf' it was not an establishment I would have expected to find in a slightly *posher* London district – it may have been called Jimmy's although I am no longer sure. But it was where I intended eating Sunday breakfast-cum-lunch.

Below the café was an interesting modern bookshop – its window full of shiny new paperbacks covering a range of subjects. Delaying breakfast I went inside and casually looked round the shelves, pausing at a section marked up 'Psychology'. Whether it was an intuitive or an intentionally conscious decision to find something to help me I cannot be sure. Maybe it was, maybe not, but either way it was certainly the first decisive step in a search for a few basic truths about myself. It *was* – could I have known it, the beginning of a search which would take many years before I came even near to whatever that truth might be.

For the time being I chose to pick out two books. The first was a paperback concerned with the human psyche written by an eminent English psychologist. The language it used was very new and strange – I remember pausing concerned over over such odd words as *anima* and *animus*. The second book I straight away decided to buy – skimming the pages it appeared to be written by an extremely wise and feeling person called Erich Fromm. Its simple title 'The Art of Loving' seemed more than appropriate for me at that particular moment. Buying both books, determined to come to some understanding of my innumerable problems – the causes of which I was fast suspecting lay at my own door, I walked on up to the café.

Its narrow, lengthy interior reeked of tobacco smoke and fried bacon. On one side of the room steaming urns or water boilers for making tea and coffee took up half the serving counter. The place was not very well lit and painted out in dark greens and browns. The tables and chairs were an odd assembly and solidly functional. It was a café without contrived character – although its very drabness gave it that. Unpretentious, it was a comfortable place for lone, homeless men such as my present self to frequent in order to enjoy a reasonably substantial meal at a price they, we, could afford. Looking around I saw that there were a half-dozen sitting alone customers – one or two of them were reading a Sunday paper; the others I presumed were much like my myself, quite alone, keeping their own company and immersed in whatever gloomy thoughts they were thinking.

Over a plate of bacon, egg, tinned tomatoes and fried bread, sipping a mug of hot strong brown tea, I gave the other customers up and concentrated on my food and the newly acquired books. The one by the Englishman seemed to read as straight psychology but did tell me things I hadn't known previously – I would read this book carefully, later. The other was written in less clinical and much more human language, saying things I could well understand and which might very well apply to my own wrong doings, and hopefully just a few right ones – that is, if I could differentiate which actions were which in terms of right or wrong behaviour. On an introductory page to the text I read a quotation I took to be by some historical figure called Paracelsus; much later on, finding the name mentioned again by another well known writer, I sought out who Paracelsus was. Before that however, in the café that Sunday morning I felt the quotation deserved my very serious consideration because it read - *'He who knows nothing, loves nothing...But he who understands, also loves, notices, sees...'* Minimal words for what I realised, in time, were particularly important observations. Another brief opening sentence in the text also posed a very worrying question, *'Is love an art? Then it requires knowledge and effort...'*. I forthwith decided that the Paracelsus quotation together with this question asked by Fromm himself, hit my personal dilemma smack on its head! Continuing to read, I began to suspect, in fact know, that I had never *really* loved anyone else very much at all – in the true sense of the word. Instead, naive and unaware I had self-loved much too much. Eventually, by the time I reached the last page of Fromm's book I knew without doubt that I had got everything wrong about love and loving.

*

Habit seemed to ease the mental severity of living in the fourteen by six-feet bed-sitter; or was it that I'd become accustomed to the false sense of security the place offered? On and off I was spending time wondering what the future held in store for me... It was fortunate that all that had happened did so during the Summer vacation when colleges were empty of students. The few weeks ahead free from teaching would allow ample space to sort something out. Just now I was marking-time – living from day to day, playing a visiting game, over careful that I didn't turn up at my various friends often enough to bore them, or else allow my emotional plight to surface overmuch when I did see them.

I had learned a few hard psychological facts from the two books I'd bought and read more than once, and learned also from others borrowed – but to no immediate avail; it would take time, lots of time, months, even years had I but known it, before whatever I was taking in worked through into my more everyday awareness. Right now I felt a desperate and urgent desire to talk to someone who might possess enough knowledge and understanding to provide some helpful advice. By now, far beyond the self-conscious or paranoid anxiety of feeling afraid to take a step out of line when need applied, I looked up the telephone number of the man who had written the first of the two original books I'd bought – the more specific one about psychology. Rightly, I'd guessed he probably lived in London.

After making sure I'd ample coins for a longish call I squeezed into a phone box at the bottom of Primrose Hill. It was Sunday morning and more than likely the psychologist chap might be at home. Having looked up the number, plucking up courage, knowing it was an odd thing I was about to do, I dialled, only to achieve a dismal anticlimax to what I considered a bold effort – the man was away somewhere up North, lecturing. It was his wife apparently who'd answered the phone – she was apologetic but that was the limit of the information she offered. Nevertheless, leaving the phone-box I felt a sense of relief that at least I'd made the attempt – it might have worked, and wasn't it a damn sight better than sitting on my backside in that poky little room doing nothing at all?

The following morning immediate decisions were more or less taken from me when two letters arrived. One envelope was half A4 size and fatter than normal and felt soft and bulky. Inside it there were no written words but it contained a more imperative message – dictated in a symbolic language clearly interpretable. Tearing open the envelope I discovered a familiar violet pillow-slip redolent of a special scent – and secretly concealed within its folds, a small clinical thermometer. Who but *she* could devise such an eloquent and expressive sign to summon a lover.

Opening the second letter, cheered up in spirit by the preceding one, I abruptly knew for fact that Life manifests its reversals so quickly that our double ended psyche reverts from glad to sad in less than the time it takes to spin a coin. This letter bore the unhappy news that my mother had died. Cared for in hospital for months her illness was such that when I visited her not too long ago she'd failed to know me. But whatever the sad news taking me North on the day of the funeral – I felt a great sense of release to be out of that dreary room for a few days.

*

The funeral as I fully expected it to be was a traumatic event. Although my wife and children were not there my brothers, their wives and numerous children were present. Proud of me in the past I wondered what their thoughts were now? I had very much wanted to see them, some I had not seen for years. The family had more or less broken up after my father's death, and when I, the youngest of the brood and last of the sons left home it left my mother quite alone. Visiting the hospital in Leeds to see her that last time, the marks of loneliness and illness were deeply etched into her sad old face.

The crematorium, though no better nor worse than any other I had been in was grim – the grimness projected there by my own mind no doubt. The sight of the coffin soon to be consumed by fire summoned up the constant image I kept of Mam's lovely, younger face; I found it impossible to stem the sudden flood of tears.

Thinking back to the occasion, on reflection I felt that I cried not only for the my mother and for her death – but for all my family present, and particularly so for those other lives not far away which I had affected so cruelly recently.

As the old priest intoned the funeral service, gazing at the flower laden coffin I seemed to see Mam actually standing there beside it, really there – lovely and looking as she had once looked, her hand resting upon the coffin within which rested her life exhausted body; she appeared transformed, gently smiling as if to tell me that all was well now, that there would be no more suffering to endure.

The beautiful biblical words of the service were being said, '...and our tears shall cease to fall...dust to dust, ashes to ashes...' The violet curtain swished impassively across, hiding the coffin – it was finished!

Eventually, on returning to my bed-sitter I attempted once more something I had tried to do for the last few weeks. Having no other creative outlet apart from letter writing I had written things down about any event or happening which had affected me at more than a mundane level. Such efforts were intended as a semblance of poetry I suppose? Once involved, I persisted – writing and rewriting the words and phrases over and over again until I felt that what was written down was sufficiently moving – creating a response of feeling as near as I could get to the original experience. In the case of Mam's funeral it read – *'It is sad that I did not see you again / until you lay within the long wood beneath the curtained arch. / The intonation hung over my years away – a silver web of Time. / It was not you Mother, still and enclosed beneath the lily and the lavender. / I stood with others, yet alone, and you beheld us as you stood / in radiant light and beautiful beyond the silver web / which gently sprang to my imaginings. / Peace now, and to the clay this lifeless thing which lies in there / and purified by suffering go! / Go Mother! In glory, go...!'*

I felt that the words did attempt to express my feelings, standing there at the end of my mother's lonely life. I hoped that they expressed an essence of her goodness yet also her undoubted suffering in mind and body. And if whatever remained of her soul or spirit – should it not quite have left Earth yet, may she forgive us all for our selfish and unforgivable neglect.

I would never be adept at this new discipline but it did help, these attempts to write about extremely moving events in a poetic way – the strength of feeling being *used* rather than letting it slip away to vanish into the ultimately forgotten past. I also realised that attempting to use words contrarily or out of their normal order whilst retaining the intended context, was practically the same process as modelling a sculpture or composing a painting. Working on an original clay model for instance one added a bit here or there while paring others bits away – it was a matter of altering and shaping the form until the image worked as a harmonic whole, visually expressing as near to damn-it what you had hoped to say in the first place! The reward for the effort was an emotional charge – a spin-off which lifted one's spirits and perhaps anyone else's who might experience the creator's intention.

*

Before returning to London – directly after the funeral, calming myself down I'd gone to meet my children. I took them to lunch in a good Yorkshire fish and chip restaurant – one which I knew they liked. I spoke to them about their grandmother but they had never known her for any consistent length of time sufficient to generate a serious fondness; and she was old which can also be off-putting to children.

I told them about the sculptures I had made recently, describing them in simple terms, talking about how they were made and what kind of materials I'd used. I inquired about their mother, their maternal grandparents, and the schools they were attending at which they appeared to be reasonably happy. I was glad to get the impression that apart from any long-term damaging effect my leaving might have had, they were settled not too unhappily into a new life on familiar ground. Our meeting had not been too bad; there was the usual regretful parting but it was nothing like as tearful as those of earlier days.

Holding back in respect of the funeral which had taken place that day, and also to punish myself for the real guilt I felt, I slept in the van that night, uncomfortably in a drive-in local car-park; I'd brought blankets half expecting that I might need them. Awake early morning – after shaving at a cold tap in the park's ageing white-tiled Victorian Gents, I drove off to find a café serving breakfast and afterwards drove up to the grey stone house – which looked as beautiful as ever...

*

'It's a mandala!' declared the woman, 'A Jungian mandala,' she affirmed, slowly walking round the aluminium sculpture embodying the four obviously symbolic forms. The work's title – Circle, Hand and Heart, in the Grabowski exhibition catalogue and its dramatic appearance standing boldly on a high plinth in the gallery, must have made it an obviously recognisable image to this perceptive woman. After taking in her comments I later searched out the word *mandala* in a dictionary of psychology – the definition pretty well determined the actual content of the image and its source. As well as the original meaning of the word mandala as explained in the Penguin Dictionary of Psychology and connected with mystical things in the East, it also stated that, '...*In Jungian theory it is the symbolic representation of the striving for unity of the self.*'.

If that did not directly explain my recent and present state of mind and determined search for self-knowledge what else would? Not altogether understanding the various implications of what I read at the time, I *was* aware – that whilst my mind was not disturbed in a crazy sort of way I *was* quite emotionally disturbed and pretty confused. But at least I knew of the fact and also knew that I certainly had these problems – which must have helped restrain or override other more telling symptoms. The other factor in my favour, I decided, was the attempts to do something about myself – even if so far I'd only read a few books on psychology.

*

When the Grabowski exhibition – The Inner Image, finally closed down, none of the artists myself included had sold a single work. Going along with the others to collect the sculptures and paintings from the gallery, I was about to remove the mandala work – I now thought of the sculpture as that, when Grabowski himself quietly took me to one side. He said that he liked the aluminium piece and wished to buy it, offering what I took to be an almost insulting small sum of money. Not in a particularly peaceful state of mind I recall angrily and abruptly saying, '*No, thank you, very much...!*' and immediately and impatiently heaving up the sculpture to carrying it out to the waiting van.

Later that evening after the pubs closed, together with a group of friends I moved on to someone's Camden Town house in order to continue what had turned out to be a pleasant evening party. Glass in hand I was approached by a young Canadian architect called Bob Oulston, a friend of Eric Brown and Karen Moller.

'I really liked that aluminium thing of yours,' he enthused, 'The one with the hand in it. If I wasn't so broke I'd buy it!'

'You really, really liked it?' I asked him, feeling slightly high on alcohol yet at the same time remaining antagonistic to an unfair world. He nodded with evident enthusiasm. 'It's yours then...!' I said to the astonished man. The gesture was, I suppose, an impulse resulting from the anger I'd felt that morning at the paltry value the gallery owner placed upon something which in every respect meant more to me than its mere worth in money. Giving the thing away was an impetuous response, but one I never seriously regretted. I might easily have done so the following day when offered a respectable price for the mandala by someone else who also admired it. I could well have done with the money, but no, it was gone and no longer mine; it now lived, wanted and appreciated, in a good home.

One further story attached itself to Circle, Hand and Heart; I only heard it two or three years into the future. Asked to lecture about my work to would-be teachers of art a slide of it came up on the screen. It looked exactly what it was – a good, simple, unique image. At this point it was my usual habit when showing slides of work – particularly the mandala, to inform the audience that in this case I had been asked by an important person in education in the Midlands to design a sculpture for placing outside a grammar school. Commissions were always an anathema to me – I hated and feared any request to produce a work of art on demand so to speak; I was never successful at that kind of task.

However, there was no way of avoiding the job I'd just been handed. The unwished for demand happened not too long before the Circle, Hand and Heart work was placed on exhibition; the sculpture at that moment was standing in my cottage studio – complete and readily available. I imagined that it would look both interesting and meaningful placed outside a school. I rang up the education chap and asked him to call at the Rectory.

'Well!' I told my audience of student teachers, he liked the sculpture very much but then came out with what to me was a most extraordinary request. It concerned the fertility symbol composed of the two 1½ inch spheres, or more starkly put and in line with this anecdote – balls, separated by the thin dividing line a few inches in length. Perhaps difficult to believe, the design of this particular symbol came completely out of the blue when I was making the work – it was never intended to be crudely representative of the sexual organs; its form I imagined was quietly symbolic. However, sexual *must-nots* and minds differed greatly in 1964 and what was actually said to me was, 'I think if it's to be situated outside a school would it be possible to have a third ball added to the other two?'

Reduced to silence I finally responded with a regrettable, 'No...! Sorry, but no! I couldn't possibly consider doing so.'. And that, as far as I was concerned was the end of the commission I told my listeners in the lecture theatre.

But it was *not* the end of the story, because at that moment someone at the back of the darkened lecture theatre stood up and politely stated that he'd heard a sequel to the story of the fertility symbol on the sculpture and would I, the lecturer, like to hear it. The speaker it turned out had been an art student in the county when the proposed commission incident took place. The story had apparently done the county teaching rounds and he'd heard it from one of his lecturers. The punch line was connected with the fact that the sculpture was to be paid for by a charitable *endowment* fund. Apparently informed of this fact prior to the naive request for a third ball to be added to the existing two, the embellished tale recorded that my gently derisive reply to the educational chap was supposed to have been, '*Sorry, I'm afraid that would be carrying endowment too far...!*'

It was a good anecdote to tell in a lecture but I realised on hearing it that dubious reputations can arrive in many ways – *and* it seemed from all directions. In this particular case it stemmed falsely from a comment I had not but certainly wished I had made!

Chapter 15
The Mews

A gloomy day, it was pouring with rain. I was back writing at my bedsit window. Regardless of the occasional raindrop splashing in through the open the window I looked out for the cat. She, it *was* a she, had responded to saucers of milk on the window sill, although any thought of stroking her silky black and white fur was out of the question – she fled if I intimated in the slightest way any sign of a direct approach.

Up North, the day after the funeral, my visit to the grey stone house brought about an emotional reunion. There was forgiveness, pledges and passion, *and* stress. Afterwards, fearful of shattering our love-healed truce we each behaved timidly both in word and act, speaking of causes and where each of us felt the failure lay on our part.

It was at this point she told me gently in an inoffensive way that I seemed to possess one of the biggest inferiority complexes she'd come across. Some of it she put down to modesty, not false modesty, I was not that dishonest she said

– it might be more in the nature of being too bloody over sensitive for words.

I knew that all the conclusions she came up with bore a likely element of truth in them, but the eternal question came up once again – how does one change oneself?

Her confessions were of a more recent nature – about the unhappiness of living down in the Rectory. She felt the others had not liked her, and perhaps this was true. Also, there had been a shortage of money which didn't help matters, it only added insecurity to every other problem. Apart from that she'd felt isolated and friendless; whereas I had my work she had no other interest to fill her days. When the last row blew-up it was just too much. Seeing things in this light it was impossible to blame her but more my unseeing self.

*

Following all the traumatic and disrupting events which had already taken place, others loomed – bringing further significant change to my present circumstances. Important among these was that Tom Hudson resigned his headship of the Basic Course in Leicester in order to move South – he was to become Director of Studies in Cardiff College of Art. It was no great surprise therefore when he asked me to apply for a post about to be advertised in this same college.

What was on offer was a Principal Lectureship in Fine Art. The problem as I immediately saw it was that largely self-taught I lacked what others applying for this comparatively lucrative and valued post would not lack – academic qualifications. All that I might put forward as equivalent in worth to a diploma, a degree or suchlike, was my previous teaching experience together with whatever professional reputation I had so far gained as a sculptor. This absence of any even vaguely certificated recognition of my educational standards gave me a bad time when filling out the complicated job-application. I could only enter in my years of evening classes, my time as a studio assistant and the part time lectureship at Leeds College of Art. Of course this had been followed by the Grade B post in Leicester – but that was still only a minor lectureship as things go. On the positive side, supporting my ability to fulfil whatever the job required were the art and educational exhibitions I had either exhibited in or helped organise. These were listed on my CV along with every other single thing I could dig up which had been to do with Art or Art Education. There were also my *brag-book*s containing photographic records of work together with write-ups and newspaper cuttings should critics have mentioned my name. Most important were the notices concerning the sculpture 'Helmet 1' bought by the Tate Gallery in 1963 – this had done much to boost my professional reputation. Finally, I had a number of flattering references to show the Cardiff Education people – these were from reputable artists and professional people. Seen from this distance in Time, had I been less timid I would have thought that all that was ample and the evidence spoke for itself, however, I did not! But that is how I saw the situation at the time, because the person writing about the past – here and now, is certainly not the same one who was applying for such a prestigious lecturing post in 1964. Thank God we become more self-assured with age – but until then my earlier life was certainly ruled by anxiety and a fear of this, that, and just about everything – being older is better!

*

When the letter arrived from Cardiff calling me for interview I smartened myself up, bought new trousers, a jacket, shoes and a shirt and tie, and on the appointed day travelled down by train. I dreaded the interview after receiving a warning in advance from Tom Hudson that it might prove difficult; in actual fact it was worse than he imagined.

It took place in the imposing and majestic County Hall in the centre of the city. There were three other applicants short-listed who were already in the waiting room when I was shown in. I suspected that two of them immediately gave up the ghost of any slight hope of getting the job when mutual introductions had taken place – it seemed they were well aware of my long standing connection with Tom. Knowing how the appointment system in education worked I am sure they fully expected the appointment to go to me – it was only I who doubted that outcome. Educationally, everyone there appeared to be way above my lowly head and what was in it! Sitting waiting, self-conscious, never a good speaker, I felt certain I would fluff the whole interview. The only bit of common sense I had come up with in recent months was the irrefutable conclusion that nothing in life is ever sure!

Anyway, right from the start I had dreaded the idea of applying for such an high grade lectureship which was only one down in scale from a vice-principal – I would be an imposter, a fake, the job demanding a level of intellect and other skills I felt I could never possibly fulfil or live up to. Working with Tom over the previous ten years I was automatically sheltered and secure beneath his intellectual wing. I had given much back in return, but right at that moment facts did nothing to help change my belief in a favourable outcome from this present situation. Basically my fear was, I suppose – that never having stood in a position which relied for its success entirely upon my own intellect, but right now – I must!

These were my thoughts as I sat like a sacrificial lamb awaiting slaughter. Over the last decade I had absorbed and learned much and made a willing imaginative contribution to help bring about the right way forward for Art Education. On the other hand I had never offered up deep conceptual ideas in written form about Art, except when composing paragraphs about my work for inclusion in exhibition catalogues. Had I ever presumed to write about Art and the implications involved in teaching it, then I might have felt less nervous and more self-confident – waiting to be grilled for a choice post in Higher Education, but again, I had not, and here I was – in a few minutes to be called to be put on the inquisitional spot!

My name *was* called. Walking through the impressive mahogany double doors held open for me I was confronted by a row of twelve, even more, important looking personages closely packed behind and round both ends of a very long polished oak table. Centrally, across in front of them, some three-feet away from the table stood a single lonely, very upright hard-back chair. On the table, exactly opposite the chair, facing me when I was politely asked to sit, was a small white card. Folded it stood tentlike, its typewritten surface angled towards me. Above this seeming innocuous but sinister looking missive I saw a long row of curious faces intently examining me – not all of them unkindly; but no matter, I knew that they were assembled to put me through my paces – including the two business-like middle-aged women among them.

During what seemed to me to be the ultimate in pregnant pauses before the questioning began, feeling like a unique item stared at in a shop window – attempting to still my close to shaking body the curious simile of a turned out strawberry jelly trying its hardest not to wobble flashed into my mind (thank God for imagination). The ridiculous image fast dissipated when I sensibly recalled the important reason of why I was sitting before this row of influential people. The event *was* important – not only for myself but also for Tom *and* for the pride of the city this present board of citizens represented.

Afterwards I was told that one of the women on the interviewing committee was a local councillor – I could well believe it! Apparently she wanted the appointment I was being interviewed for for her well qualified artist son; understandably she gave me a hard time during the interview, doing her best to reduce my stature in a mild yet devious and subtle manner.

The nasty little typed card in front of me bore three tricky questions relating to Art Education. God knows how I succeeded in answering them when asked to do so – but I must have done so in some fashion or other.

Later, waiting in the ante-room until all four of us applicants had been interviewed, we each experienced the nerve-racking ordeal known to all who have waited in similar trying circumstances. After an abnormal delay the usual form of procedure followed – one of the interviewing body came out, called my name, smiled at me, and politely asked would I come back into the committee room, please? The atmosphere in the room was changed, the people were mostly smiling though I sensed they were worried as to whether they had done the right thing. However, they did congratulate me on becoming their Principal Lecturer in Fine Art and said without reservation that they were very happy to have me with them. Perhaps it is worth mentioning here that the college had fallen short and failed in two aspects of Fine Art when inspected by a National Committee. Therefore, afterwards, they were unable to award the usual National Diploma in Design to students of Sculpture and Ceramics. This is not to suggest that the respective departments lacked committed artists and lecturers, or that the skills and expertise needed to teach these disciplines were lacking – quite the opposite. The problem lay in a need to imaginatively update their existing outlook.

I suppose once back on the train to London I should have felt elated – far from it, there was no obvious sense of personal success. Instead, my thoughts naturally and quickly turned away to face the whole dilemma of my present life crisis. This new job posed all sorts of problems and innumerable questions – there were few ready-made answers forthcoming. First of all I was going to have to live permanently in Cardiff – this was something of a shock but it went without saying – it was a must! Before that time I would need to commute and search for a place in the city to live. The question was – would I be living alone? The new lectureship would pull in extra cash, yet not all that much, and my family remaining up in Leeds would continue to need financial support. And what about creative work – when was I going to get round to making sculpture again? The new job would inevitably demand more teaching time and a far greater level of commitment and personal responsibility than I had ever previously known.

Buying my ticket at Paddington, rattling along on the tube to Chalk Farm, I felt that day by day life was becoming inordinately and increasingly complex, the mounting number of problems appeared to be insoluble and finally inescapable. The first thing I must do was to get out of that damned bedsitter. I'd start first thing in the morning – looking for somewhere better, although it would still be a temporary move.

Coincidental and with what seemed timely good luck I was saved the bother of a search. Eric Brown told me that Robin and Carol Page – Robin taught part-time with us in Leicester, were about to leave a squat; I could take it over and might safely live there for some time. They'd actually heard that it might be months before the place was due for demolition. The squat was the end dwelling in an otherwise abandoned Victorian mews not far from Chalk Farm. It was one-sided house in the sense that the long row of dwellings with living accommodation above and a single car garage below – once a stable, faced a six-feet high soot-blackened wall which hid behind it a cluster of busy overground railway lines. The squat was ideal – in good order and remarkably – the electricity, water and gas services remained on – why this should be no one ever discovered. The row of tiny dwellings were now standing empty – all but the one occupied by Robin and Carol who were about to pack up and travel North. In one respect Robin and I were virtually changing places, he would be heading for my old stamping ground to take up a lectureship in Leeds College of Art.

Given the good news I walked round to see the couple. Greeted like a long lost friend the welcome extended to a plate of bacon, egg, and sundry other things set down before me, because they said, it looked like I hadn't seen a square meal in days. Sitting there eating, I realised that the place was all but perfect for my present needs. Once I was living there there would be no one around to interfere – and the place was actually free.

Entering by a door at the side of the single garage, a climb up a short flight of steps brought one to the living space situated directly above. The steps led into a narrow passage-way. On the left side of this were three tiny bed or living rooms and on the right a bathroom, a bog, and the kitchen – all equally tiny but adequate. I chose the first of the rooms for sleeping and in which to live. It was the one my friends had occupied and was directly opposite both kitchen and bathroom.

The three rooms were probably intended originally to house a cabby or a servant coachman and his family – each measured less than ten feet square. In the one I intended using Robin had left behind his discarded furniture, which, battered as it was, would do quite well for me. It consisted of an almost floor level bed, a propped up old table, three rickety dining-chairs, a threadbare floor covering, and a torn chintz curtain which drawn, barely covered the window – although of course, there would certainly be no passers by to look up and peer in. In the kitchen there were were various pots, pans and other utensils left behind – it was all adequate and like a gift from God.

One item so far unmentioned in my future living space was a more complicated piece of furniture – a tall coat, glove and umbrella stand which also bore a convenient mirror. The stand was pushed into the corner to the left of the window, standing at right-angles to it – the window overlooked the cobbled alleyway of the deserted mews. The glove and umbrella stand contained two extraordinary surprises – surreal in fact! These were exposed when one lifted the lids of the small glove compartments at either side of the shelf beneath the mirror. Each contained a made-to-measure, fitted bird's nest cunningly fashioned out of straw – and nestling within each were three, speckled brown, hen's eggs. They were evidence of Robin's recent occupation – a left-over creative gesture and a gift.

I was also delighted with the very small arched Victorian iron fireplace in the middle of the wall quite close to the umbrella stand. To the left of the fireplace and lengthways against the wall opposite the window – pushed into the corner was a single, almost floor level iron bedstead complete with mattress and tattered sheets. The door, opening into the room was at the end of the bed, faced the window and the rickety assembly of two chairs and table hard up in the right hand corner. The walls were papered with a once-blue forget-me-not flowered wallpaper now faded and timeworn. From a normal point of view it was a sad room, but then, looking round contentedly I thought, 'Yes! God must have sent me the place!'

*

I said an unacknowledged fond goodbye to my friend the cat who was absent when I cleared out of the bedsitter. And much as on occasions I'd hated the room I left it with some feeling of affection – in that it had guarded me safely through a particularly difficult time.

Moving into the Mews I propped up my few books on one end of the narrow mantel piece, placed the record player in a corner, made up the bed, organised provisions and then what? Time stretched endlessly ahead – there were some weeks of the Summer vacation left before I was due to take up my new appointment. Although badly missing out on creative work I was grateful for the independence the squat provided – as well as allowing me to be close to my friends and live not too far away from a good pub – the Steels. That being said – I felt a proportionate sense of isolation when stepping outside after dark, and even in daylight when glancing up the alley and seeing the long row of deserted dwelling places – once homes for a neighbourhood of hard working families but now an almost forgotten part of London life – its history in fact! The once inhabited places awaited a thankless fate – a destructive reduction to old bricks and mortar. Late at night, returning to my squat, the desolation seemed to follow me in. Coming back from the pub and friends was most times to enter a rejected world – empty of people.

I had books of course, *and* music, both were time-passing friends; although music represented a danger dependent on one's immediate thoughts and its seductive power to invert the mind instead of spiritually lifting it. On and off I continued reading psychology, attempting to discover what made me tick as a sensible yet alternately stupid human being. I soon found out that my kind of mind would never be capable of taking in and remembering a great deal of concrete or factual information. It somehow still fails to be interested in remembering indirect or never useful facts and items of no practical use – preferring instead to use any available brain-space for simple ongoing questions about living such as why do this and not that. My psyche, apart from being an emotional heavy, otherwise appears to be a selective instrument – only picking up information about material matters it considers really important to my daily survival. Wishfully however – any information coming through via the senses should also be advantageous to creative thinking. Unfortunately it does not always work like that! Computed out, what's gone into the complex grey matter within my head prints out turbulent mind-maps – which create emotional havoc within and consequently chaos without – for other people quite often!

*

Visiting the Belsize Park bookshop again, occasionally since my invaluable introduction to psychology and a fried breakfast at Jimmy's caf', I occasionally bought other books. Of these one was a slim volume of very loaded poetry; there was little in the lines or the spaces between them that I could fully, or even nearly understand. I'd read glowing reports somewhere about Eliot's Waste Land – it was said to be great poetry. So – curious as to what great poetry was I'd bought the slim paperback. Reading the first page I quickly knew that what I read *was* special – the trouble was, I failed to grasp its intrinsic meaning. It would take a very long time indeed before my appreciation reached that level of poetic comprehension – or longer still in time before I fully grasped the genius of the beautiful and spiritual words of Burnt Norton – the first of Elliot's Quartets.

Until then, this admission of my past ignorance regarding the absolute meaning of words brings to mind an angry exchange when someone once cried out in protest at my careless and indiscriminate use of them. During a particularly desperate argument I was blasted with a close-up shout of, '*Words mean things...!*' The effect of the truth within the raw statement was invaluable – in that the shock of it triggered off a marvellous crumb of desire for the need to *really* understand – which remains with me to this day.

*

After a week of literally marking time, dejectedly, I decided to ring the grey stone house to see if she had returned from wherever it seemed she had been. If she was back, although my finances were becoming more and more limited, I would go up to see my children and then on to her; both intentions were marked with uncertainty.

Chapter 16

Cardiff

When September came and the new academic year began I travelled by train from Paddington to Cardiff on Monday mornings. I usually went across with Norman, a close friend and painter teaching for three days a week; he'd also taught with us up in Leicester.

Initially I experienced a few awkward moments in the new job. As within any established system such as a college of art and its staff there were the usual internal hang-ups and resentments clogging the works. Taking up a very senior appointment in the lecturing hierarchy in Cardiff College – which placed me over and above all the lecturers who had been there for many years, proved both embarrassing and difficult. I was not in a very reasonable mood to accept some of the obvious resentment at the idea of another stranger along with Tom – brought in to liven up the existing teaching standards.

Nevertheless, on my first day there, nervous but resolved, determined to face the music if there was to be any, I braved the staff room for morning coffee. Naturally reticent, I overcame this initial blip and began the process of attempting to form working relationships. My problem was the idea of *me* having authority over practically everyone; I found it was not easily acceptable and in some ways objectionable. On that very first day of my humble career as a studio assistant back in Leeds I remember thinking that life certainly presents us with odd turnabouts. Now – here in this new college I was in a reverse situation feeling no or little difference and certainly no sense of superiority considering my altered status.

Things settled down and it soon became obvious – I believe, that I shared every student's natural enthusiasm for the visual arts along with a great desire to be or to become an artist. This was the real reason students were at college I often pointed out to staff – hoping they would show the same level of commitment as their students and this would be apparent. In time it also became obvious by example that better teaching was done not from on high but from a standpoint where teacher and taught were setting out together on a mutual quest – each learning by exploring both old and new ways of using a variety of media in order to create unique and emotive visual images. It was important therefore that students needed to feel unconditionally free to express the concepts and ideas belonging *their* generation – should they wish to do so.

Part of my time was spent alongside the existing Head of Sculpture, Frank Roper, who was also a successful ecclesiastical sculptor. He proved to be an invaluable friend in the not too distant future. Other help apart from the staff of lecturers was provided by three studio assistants – Joe, Winston, and Don. They, realising that I was unlikely ever to talk down to them, gave me not only every assistance but also their friendship. Don would eventually point out a new dimension in the direction my self-imposed psycho-search might take.

*

Outside of teaching life became somewhat dire. My mind in unoccupied moments turned North towards the grey stone house. I felt compelled to ring there often – feeding the phone box coin after coin. The calls were invariably unsatisfactory and emotionally emptying. During the Summer we had driven down to see what she thought of Cardiff in order to decide whether to join me there. She enjoyed the trip and did not seem averse to the city – as a result there'd been vague suggestions that when I began commuting to teach in Cardiff I might keep an eye open for a suitable place for us to live. However, whilst not wishing to doubt the idea or admit it to myself, I felt there was little positive intention of her joining me – I was too much of a risk, which was probably true. In emotional limbo, my day by day existence became a perpetual struggle to keep up appearances. During the four days I travelled up from London to teach, the task of finding a bed each night when College closed around 8.00pm or sometimes 9.00pm, presented innumerable difficulties. The cost of a hotel or a regular bed and breakfast place was financially out of the question. Norman, travelling down with me each week was in the same boat. If no one offered us a bed or a floor and sleeping bag for the night our last resort was to walk and to keep on walking the streets of the city's B&B district until we found one vacant. Late after dark it was a foot-sore, thankless end-of-the-world kind of task.

One particular night that sticks in my mind was when, around ten-thirty, having knocked at countless doors for what seemed hours, we at last found an available room. Being November it was freezing cold – proverbial brass monkey weather. The room we were shown into seemed even chillier in appearance and temperature than the black night we'd left outside. A small attic with sloping eaves, the place was three or four floors up – reached by treading one barely lit stairway after another. The attic itself was lit by a single 60 watt bare bulb. Painted and papered in cold depressing greens the nightmarish garret reminded me in a way of the bathroom at my grim London bed-sitter.

That night we had little option but to take the place. Although at first, on asking for a room, we were almost turned away. The woman answering the doorbell, staring out into the darkness suspected us of being something we were not! Hesitating when we asked for beds she then said, 'Well, yes...there's an attic, but I've never let *two* men up there before, not together anyway!'.

However, after further eyeing us up and down standing there shivering, she must have decided that we were innocent and not what she had wrongly imagined us to be – quite obviously we were very weary and so she had relented. 'Come on then, but no funny business mind...!' she said, beckoning us to follow her, leading us up to the top floor of the house – demanding cash in advance. It was a nasty experience and did little to enhance my own present, jaded view of life.

But all these various anxieties in Cardiff were left behind, to be momentarily forgotten when each Friday afternoon came round during those first weeks. Fridays became special days when, about four o'clock it was marvellous beyond belief to escape and slip away from College where for the last week, each day – hour after hour, I had been compelled to act out my comparatively important role. The relief of arriving at Paddington Station was virtually life saving.

*

One alleviating factor in this new job was a group of seven or eight students who moved down with us from Leicester to continue their studies. Interesting students, Tom had persuaded them to study for their diploma – soon to become a B.A. in Fine Art, in Cardiff College. The plan was that this imported few, the pick of their year in Leicester, already accustomed to the ways taught by Tom's Leicester staff, would influence and help set the standard of work and ideas to be expected in the Cardiff College of Art of the future. This they did – influencing any new intake of students, and indirectly, the existing students and staff. Having myself taught the group of Leicester people for a year or more they had also become friends. Teaching Art during the Sixties I worked out – must be entirely different to teaching purely academic subjects to young people in universities or similar educational institutions. Art students – apart from learning necessary techniques, attending lectures on subjects to do with the the Arts and other related topics, were very much left to their own devices. They were often given an opportunity to re-discover their individual uniqueness; in other words – to dig deep and find themselves as all artists inevitably *must*.

Daily tuition was generally carried out on a system of advice and tuition given by lecturers and visiting artists walking round the studios or workshops – commenting as need required on the progress of a student's work. In addition, weekly or monthly group tutorials took place when a student's paintings, sculptures, or other art work would be discussed – collectively by the student and any tutors present. Ultimately however – what seemed to work most successfully was that more serious teaching took place on a one to one basis. Naturally, a particular student's work might prove to be of greater interest to a tutor whose own work was sympathetic to the content and imagery of the student's work. Discussion would first of all hover around the formal aspects of the work in progress. But of equal if not greater importance was the more delicate questioning into the personal whys and wherefores' of the particular student's subject matter which are the essential source or sources predetermining an artist's or any aspiring artist's content and imagery. Therefore the one-to-one conversation between tutor and student might often deal with deeply held personal feelings and beliefs related to the sometimes introvert images overtly displayed on the canvas, paper, or appearing in three dimensional form. One result of such tutorials, apart from the better and more understood art which arrived was that quite often lasting friendships were created.

This opportunity for complete freedom, self-inquiry and uninhibited creative expression in art education was a change which occurred during the post-war years of the 1940s European war. The later requirements for a student entering art education specified a higher academic record – unless there were obvious signs of exceptional ability. The generally higher intelligence rating of students coming into art eventually produced more intellectually mature people – graduates. Whether they finally became practising artists or not, is perhaps, of lesser importance than the fact that they would become more mature members of a fast evolving technological society.

I fully appreciated my student friends from Leicester;. one or two remain friends these many years on. At the time we shared the common goal of working together practising Art; they being young, wished above all to create great Art. Back in Leicester they had shown interest in seeing someone like myself exhibiting work as a sculptor; they had also seen examples of my work – some of it actually made in the studios they themselves occupied. In many respects I often felt myself to be one of *them* rather than representing what I actually was in the College regime. This did not mean neglecting my teaching role in any way – it was just that I did not see myself in a superior light nor in a lesser one. I was just a person whose job it was to help and discuss things when the need arose. I took this commitment seriously – juggling the system the best for each and all of us.

*

Leaving Cardiff behind and arriving at Paddington early evening – exactly as I had done each Friday for the last few weeks, I took the Northern Line to Chalk Farm. A short walk – collecting bread and other provisions on the way, eventually brought me to the Mews. I knew that later there would be the pub and friends I hadn't seen all week to look forward to, and the sweet freedom of the weekend. Thinking like this helped combat the emptiness of the squat when clattering up the stairs each time. The fact that she had come down to stay overnight on more than one occasion did nothing to prevent the same feelings arising when I returned every Friday – whether she was or was not there. Regardless – seeing the place for the first time, I knew, that in an odd kind of way she liked the idea of my being there – squatting; not for the first time the situation I was living in appealed to the romantic side of her nature. On the rare occasions of staying with me in the Mews she inevitably stamped her presence on the place – in a way strengthening the feeling of her absence all the more. Her brief visits were most times gratifying in helping rekindle our feelings. On the other hand – because of the shortness of the time we had to spend together and my suspicion of the unlikely chance of an *ever-and-ever-after* future, the visits left both myself and probably her more irresolute than confused.

One visit had been beautiful beyond imagining. I had arrived back that special Friday – surprised and unexpectedly delighted to find her there. She must have arrived early because the fire was already lit and warming the tiny bed-living-room. Across the passage in the kitchen a pasta was steaming and almost ready to serve. The table – lovingly set as gracefully as it could be under such sparse circumstances, awaited us. A slender glass vase she must have brought down contained a single red rose. A white candle newly lit stood on a saucer – helped by a second on the mantelpiece, together they gently illuminated the scene. A bottle of red wine, uncorked, stood next to two empty glasses, and close by a bowl of ripe cherries. Candle and firelight flames filled the room with a warm benevolent glow, sparkling and glittering on the glassware.

When I first climbed the stairs to discover her there her familiar scent flooded over me so that the unexpectedness of her visit became an enchantment – an intimation of earthly paradise.

In early morning light, awake, side by side, squashed together in the narrow bed against the wall, she laid her forearm and hand flat against the faded forget-me-not wallpaper, her elbow resting on the bed. The image of the hand I had embodied in the mandala sculpture stole into my mind. Wishing in some vague way to immortalise her presence in the room for when she was gone, I picked up a discarded green felt-tip laying on the floor nearby and drew around her arm and outspread fingers – her hand was there on the wall, for ever, and for whenever I came into the room.

Later I thought – that when she and I were no longer there her hand would continue to exude our intense presence until the time the place ceased to exist. Many months later I drew a picture of the place under darker circumstances.

Around the room there were also other evidences of her here and there – love tokens pinned over the fireplace, two sculptured shapes, one in golden bronze, the other in silvery aluminium lay near the bed – iconic reminders of the mandala. Above the bed, high upon the wall, two crinkled paper roses, one red, one pale blue, lay imprisoned in the shiny chrome cage of a lettuce-shaker – looking not at all incongruous, its image retained significant memories of events special to the two of us. A left-behind feminine adornment – a yellow flowered dress hung empty and forlorn from a nail in the wall beside the bed; on the floor beneath the window her records together with mine lay scattered around the open player. The most evocative of these, a Vivaldi conjured up echoes of time spent in the grey stone house – a heavy inducement to melancholy.

*

On the train to Paddington I felt composed for the first time in months. I had finally decided the step I must take in order to achieve the longed for peace of mind; I was quite determined – there was to be no turning back, I'd

218

had enough and wished to be done with it all. Arriving at the decision brought an unbelievable sense of calm which spread throughout my mind. The idea had been tumbling around inside me for some weeks. Before leaving College today – it was Friday, strangely happy, peaceful and resolved. I'd gone from one student cubicle to another for a brief chat with those I felt were my young old friends. I now felt for certain that the past was irrevocably concluded! There'd been an unpleasant parting between us the last weekend we'd shared. The following Friday, leaving college early, I'd picked up toothbrush and razor and headed North by train, determined to sort things out once an for all. A long journey – the train arrived in Leeds very late. I spent the night in a bed and breakfast not far from my old home and on Saturday morning took my children out to lunch.

Glad to see me they appeared to have settled back into their new life; it was apparent they had come to terms with my desertion – for that is what it was I'd told myself more and more frequently lately – *desertion!* Poor young buggers! If they were well used to my absence by now – good, that was something to be thankful for.

After leaving them I walked over to the house beyond the wood. Its trees, stripped of leaves were black, claw-like and unfriendly. Not having slept much in the strange bed I was over-tired, dispirited, and churning over in a muddled mind the contrast between now and the very first time I had come this way – recalling my mad dash to get to see her. Then, the trees were ripe with green foliage and I'd burst out of the shelter of the wooded path into the open – coming upon the house seen against a gentle slope of yellow flowers and a bluer than blue sky.

Ringing up from the far away city where I now taught

had become a horror of misunderstandings – which arose at each real or my imagined negative inflexion in her voice. Telephones I decided were the death of relationships – empathy was non-existent without the evidence of body language. Most often I left the phone box in a worse state of mind than entering it. What had noticeably changed over the last few days was her voice – it had become unusually casual.

Yet only the week before our last and not unusual disagreement we'd spent a great weekend in London. Getting a red bus to the cinema down Tottenham Court Road we saw Jules et Jim and Ingmar Bergman's Seventh Seal in one go! Seen one after the other the films left us both starry eyed and aesthetically high. Leaving the cinema, madly searching out a music shop we bought a Satie record, caught a bus to Regent's Park and strolled the rest of the way over to the Mews. Later that night we met up with my friends and other acquaintances in the Richard Steele's for a drink and weekly get-together.

All seemed well, but doubts about the question of *what next* for us were never absent from my mind – a mind speeding towards some kind of unhappy impasse. I needed answers in the context of plans for our future together – the inconceivable future? I had no doubt that she was similarly troubled. These thoughts, and a concern for what I felt to be the drop in temperature of our telephone conversations decided me to travel up and talk things out – finally!

Through the iron gate at the front of the house, up the three stone steps – along the short stone path, I knocked at the door and waited. No one came and I thought how stupid of me not to have given her a ring first. About to go for a short walk – deciding that she was probably out shopping, I heard the sound of the bedroom window sliding up – it was directly over the door. Stepping back, I looked up to see her head appear – she stared down at me, her face expressionless.

'Wait a minute...!' she called, disappearing back into the bedroom – she would be coming down?

I heard the key turn in the lock and the rattle of a bolt being drawn – the door swung open and I was met by the blandly smiling face of a lesser acquaintance from the pub in London. The man had obviously slipped on shirt and trousers not a moment ago. Turning, I walked away...

*

It was all in the past, the irrevocable past. And now here I was, back at Paddington. Winter sunshine brightened the busy station and the people thronging it – I half wished I was one of them, but no! The trouble was – too many out of the ordinary good and bad things had happened to me over the last few years, and lately – more bad things, which, as usual I'd brought about myself. Well...I'd asked for it. The thought reinforced my purpose!

Once in the mews, I tided up, prepared what seemed necessary, made the coffee, and finally, putting on the Vivaldi lay down on the bed – the lines of the green hand on the forget-me-not wallpaper beside me were soon to be unseen...

Chapter 17

New End, Hampstead

There were noises – the hiss of curtain rings dragged along a rail, the chink and clink of bottles clashed together, someone calling, 'Nurse...!', a responding patter of feet, and, 'Coming...'.

My mouth tasted like the contents of a cesspit or some other equivalent ghastly thing – repulsive, sore, foul and medical tasting, it was ulcerated; I could feel tiny blisters or lumps on the tip of my tongue and lips. It was also very, very dry. My mind and vision blurred...a cup or glass was held to my mouth and a gentle female voice told me to sip – it was water, which helped the dryness but failed to cure the overall sense of acute discomfort. I think I must have faded in-and-out of consciousness.

Awake, or it seemed like I was awake – surrounded by people in beds. Everywhere and everything looked brilliantly white and the brightness hurt my eyes. An unusual hospital ward it was circular – my bed touched against an outer curving wall which circled around a central one way across from where I lay. The patients over there were feet first towards me.

Someone eased me up on the pillows until I was half up, half down. Puddle and light headed it was not at all like being drunk and might well have been part of a dream – a dream I did not care for very much. I wished morning would hurry up and come soon and the dream end. Curiously though, I sensed that it *was* morning and that my eyes *were* open and I *was* awake – yet the dream persisted. Convinced that what was happening was real I was also anxiously half aware that...*my wife was out in the corridor, I could hear her raised voice. Restrained from getting in to see me she was protesting. I was afraid – not of actually seeing her but for her – she should not be here and would only become more hurt...*

In my delusion – *across the ward someone in a bed was reading a newspaper – held up, its stark black headlines, magnified, spelled out my name and I knew without doubt that it told everyone everything about me and what I'd done. People in the ward in the other beds were staring, shouting – pointing at me...I shouted something back but could not tell what it was that I shouted. Calling loudly to an old man across the ward I asked him something – what? Hearing my own voice I saw the man shout back in response but all I hear was babble of nonsense...*

Disturbed, I slid down under the bedclothes, my eyes tightly shut! I needed to hide...*in front of me amid the blackness a vast cinema screen unfolded; made up of interlocking pieces resembling a gigantic jigsaw puzzle. The horizontal and downwards rows ranged in tone from black to grey to white – the startling thing was that here and there a piece of the puzzle revolved, spun – slowly, momentarily exposing the face of one of my children. The faces appeared at random intervals*

– each jigsaw piece would suddenly unlock then interlock back in with a click, hiding once more the face of the particular child. The process went on and on – repetitively, relentlessly. I felt impassive and unaffected by it, although there was an overriding compulsion insisting that I watch... I was a captive spectator, observing – hearing the click-clack and rattle as random pieces slowly paused to expose a child's face, then spun back in to await its turn next time round...

The illusion left a stark black and white image – like a photographic memory permanently etched somewhere deep within my drugged brain.

*

'Come on now, sit up, open your mouth, I want to have a good look at you.' It was a white capped, blue uniformed sister. Certainly awake now but not entirely clear in mind – although the jigsaw thing had gone away, I did as she asked and accepted a thermometer in my ill-tasting mouth. 'You've given yourself a lot of trouble,' she said, sympathetically. 'The doctors are coming to see you soon. Don't go to sleep again,' and patting down my pillows left.

Screens were pulled round the bed. Two extremely young doctors arrived led by an older man I took to be a consultant. Reading my case notes the latter felt my pulse, looked me in the face, pulled my chin down, saw the ulcers in my mouth and angrily told the attendant doctors to do something about them – *and* quickly! Next, after brief whispered words to his young colleagues and a curt but friendly nod to me, he disappeared.

The two doctors, probably straight out of medical school, took over where the consultant left off. The more nervous looking of the two, a stethoscope pressed to my naked back, spoke over my shoulder, worriedly exclaiming, 'There's a bit of an irregular bump here...! Come and listen, will you?'

'You bloody fool!' his colleague almost shouted back and proceeded quietly but forcefully to lecture him about the stupidity of allowing one's patient to hear such a diagnosis. He himself then checked my heart and giving me what I considered to be something more than a merely sympathetic look said, 'Don't worry, it's fine, it really is, don't worry about it...'

'Can I smoke?' I managed to croak out as they were about to leave. Looking doubtfully at one another they then nodded, yes, certainly, of course I could smoke!

The idea of the desperately needed cigarette did little to calm a mounting anxiety – *was* there really a bumpy noise, an irregularity of heartbeat? Remaining in drugged confusion, not yet positively conscious about my virtual presence – my reading of the situation worsened and was made even worse when two unsmiling nurses arrived. Not speaking, avoiding my gaze, they removed the screens, then stared at me in what I imagined to be a odd way before and hurriedly going off...

Worried – having lit up, I quite seriously wondered – *was this it, had* they found my heart to be fatally bumping and thumping when it shouldn't have... Had it gone seriously wrong? This fag they'd said it was all right to smoke – was it allowed because *my time was up?* If so, 'Bugger it!' I said aloud. Wondering – if what I imagined to be true was about to happen, well...under the circumstances and considering my recent actions perhaps I should not have cared all that much, but suddenly – *I did!*

*

Later – not having departed this life after all – recalling my daft imagination working overtime I enjoyed the joke at my own expense. They had checked my heart on several occasions since that loudly spoken silly diagnosis and found it to be a good strong heart – otherwise I would not have been here – 'right now!' they told me.

Unfortunately however, medical complications had set in – a thrombosis occurring in one leg meant that I would need to spend endless time laid up in hospital – the consequences could be dangerous otherwise and the illness *was* quite painful. Cross at the idea I could not honestly complain because it was all, entirely, my own fault.

After what seemed to endless weeks in bed I felt thoroughly bored; there was little apart from overmuch reading and radio to alleviate the boredom. Beyond a daily hospital routine not much else happened, and very little of what did was self determined – except for things like shaving, writing letters, reading, and performing the usual natural offices. One raw hospital determined event was the daily penicillin dart – literally thrown at my naked, right buttock which was often badly aimed by the yet inexpert student nurses. There were also the doses of countless pills – possibly as many as twenty or even more. They were evil looking things – the pills, reminding me of the vivid blue copper sulphate I'd sometimes used to patinate bronze.

Nights were worst after more pills had been dished out from the medicine trolley – sometimes by a sarcastic older staff-nurse who, one night early in my stay, commented, 'Mustn't leave the trolley near you, dear, must we?'

But each night, knowing that sleep would be almost non-existent owing to the forever aching leg, the dread of more interminable semi-darkness and compulsive attention paid to my ceaselessly chattering mind was an unpleasant prospect. My thoughts – bent on unending adverse reflections and self-recrimination were most of all to do with my family; alternatively the negative inner meanderings invariably ended up with often repeated simple but nonsensical, unanswerable questions such as – why had I done *this* and not *that?*

But anything that broke the habitual monotony of hospital nights was welcome. Last week they'd brought in an attempted suicide; it was a ward accustomed to this kind of self-injury. Settled in the bed next to mine he looked to be a middle-aged nondescript man not altogether happy or sensible in mind. His worldly belongings apart from tattered trousers, shirt and shoes, were an old belted-raincoat and a battered brown cardboard suitcase; a nurse packed the things and pushed the case under his bed.

During the following night the man, only half asleep, murmured incoherently on and off. In the early hours of the morning, awake between intermittent dozes, I became aware of noises and signs of activity coming from the suicide's bed. In the dim light of the darkened ward I saw the man leaning over, half out of bed, desperately feeling underneath it – for his suitcase I realised.

Gathering that something must be wrong I called loudly as I dared, 'Nurse...!' so as not to wake the whole ward. The night nurse failed to appear. By now I saw the chap had climbed completely out and was crouched down searching the suitcase case while muttering to himself. There was nothing else for it I would have to get out myself. Grasping the man gently but forcefully by the arm I persuaded him back into bed, at which point the night nurse came on the scene, crossly asking me what I thought I was doing – on that leg! Informed, she went round to the far side of the other chaps bed, saw the suitcase pulled out and razor blades strewn about the floor.

'A good job you saw him,' she whispered. 'That's what he was after, he'd already cut his wrists when they brought him in.' She then surprised me with a brisk telling off for getting out of bed and shortly afterwards, a finger to her pursed lips, brought over a cup of tea.

No matter, the incident – sad as it proved to be, broke the back of a long night. They'd taken my unhappy neighbour away next day; God knows to where, but I sincerely hoped that life would pick up for the poor man. There had been quite a few visitors to see me – artist friends, their wives, and other male and female acquaintances. Several attractive women were among them – a fact which failing to go unnoticed was invariably remarked upon by other, envious male patients; pointed comments also came from some of the younger nurses. These kind angels of varied race, creed and colour, although reserved, became in time a little more communicative – as might well be expected when called upon to perform a bed-bath on me, or propel the occasionally misdirected penicillin dart into my backside. This last caring ministration was usually, if the nurse could speak good English, supported by the telling of outworn nurse-to-male-patient jokes. These supposedly, would be told to quell the patient's immediate pain of a punctured bottom, and at the same time allay any possible embarrassment the nurse or the victim might feel when baring the normally unexposed expanse of male flesh.

Later, when about to leave the hospital, a tiny oriental nurse, giggling, dashed over to cheekily present me with a medical finger-poke and quickly sped away to rejoin a group of her similarly giggling colleagues. Assuming that the rubber item was intended to resemble something else she was familiar with, I took the gift as a not altogether unkind, unspoken comment on the size of my John Thomas – which indeed seemed to have shrunk to juvenile proportion when I was very ill.

But time dragged... There seemed to be no apparent end in sight to my stay in hospital. Fed-up, I had been on the point of discharging myself more than once – until a doctor alarmed me with talk of blood clots floating about in the body and hence to one's brain.

Almost worse than nights were evenings, before lights-out. After tea or cocoa and biscuit were brought round and when visitors were gone, if no one had been to see me I easily became maudlin, sometimes slipping into the ultimately selfish disease of feeling sorry for myself and ruminating uselessly on the past. I'd been fortunate in experiencing unique and beautiful times, which could not by any devious face-saving reflections serve as an excuse for the fact that they cruelly affected others. But there was nothing I could immediately do about that, nor were there any steps I might take to expiate even a little of the vast load of accumulated guilt I'd evidently shouldered.

I was left to accept the fact that I react – and probably always will, to events at a more susceptible than normal level, which, on the minus side can lead one into great emotional difficulties. Opposite to that I felt incredibly fortunate in acknowledging a capacity to feel great affection for others. Fromm's book The Art of Loving had caused me to question what this really meant – it offered an altogether clearer, perhaps truer perspective on such feelings.

But the most important insight gained was – although

having little control of the ever changing patterns of the life of which I am part, I generally tend to be *aware*, perceiving, registering and storing up memories of events, people and places; this does not necessarily occur consciously – it just happens. It might well compensate for an inability to retain, or bother, to fill my mind with indirectly useful facts.

Immobile in my hospital bed I knew that I would not wish my psyche to behave in any other way whether it causes me pain or pleasure. Anything, I thought, is preferable to a mind mechanically responding or failing to respond with feeling to life's mundane events or its strange complexities – in which case I would be a person appearing to be awake yet asleep – daydreaming, somewhere in the past or in the yet unlived future. On the other hand I also realised that I would never be the kind of cool, laid-back person who knew exactly what sensible thing to do and what equally un-sensible thing *not to do* in any given behavioural situation.

On balance I would not like to be that kind of person. How could one move on, learn – break out of ones inherited shell of ignorance and evolve by stubbornly refusing to question any doubtful truth, or be too fearful to take a chance in case of making a mistake. Most people I thought, at sometime or other envied another person, occasionally wishing they were them, but in the end knew I would not want to be anyone else but me! And while deeply regretting my unwise and apparently wrong actions, I knew that if they were to be of value rather than a waste of the mental suffering they'd caused – to myself or others, then eventually they must be used in some way. The medium of Art offers one such way – maybe it was the only real recompense I could make, and if there was an element of delusion or conceit in thinking this – so...?

Stuck here in hospital was a further form of retribution – wasn't it? I now felt only sadness. The healing of any ill regard I might have retained for the person I had lost was because of sense of indebtedness felt for the gift of poetry she had offered. Never mind that something precious had been taken away – the actual manner in which it had happened, ended, seemed in retrospect in keeping with the extremes of experience such affairs demand in order to remain memorable. And if I tend to idealise and transform things that happen into something resembling *romance* – then it is in my nature to do so, without regret for approaching life from a perceived view which often mistakes absolute reality for the half-truth I wish to see. I find a need to continue accepting events and things in this more intense, more beautiful yet perhaps unreal light. What are idealistic beliefs or religions anyway I questioned, but blind faith or a belief in some ethereal, spiritual non-existence.

Love, for instance, does not die I concluded. Instead it's memory may mature to become a more lasting thing and not merely the pale recollection of a tenuous excitement of the emotions – sexual or otherwise, which cannot always sustain long bonding between two people.

I was glad that my feelings for the women I had loved were resolved without bitterness. In time they would merge into an indestructible sincerity of affection which had nothing to do with mere sentiment.

There would be one other memory to add to my store of inquisitional bedtime thinking when I left this hospital. It was also to do with those late evenings of lying in a hospital ward feeling disconsolate and wondering what the future might hold. Once a week, around nine o'clock, a particular programme came over the ward radio just before lights-out.

It was a BBC musical offering and the introductory theme was pure Handel; it was music vast in space and spirit with a capacity to lift the mind above and beyond the trivia we each of us represent in whatever great spiritual plan exists. I learned eventually that the particular music was an aria from Xerxes.

*

It was time to leave. After six weeks of interminable, boring hospitalised bed-rest, much against the doctor's advice I finally decided I'd had enough and discharged myself. Norman had volunteered to pick me up, or more to the point – come to carry me off in a taxi. Arriving, he was accompanied by Helga, a young silversmith and designer who had taught with us in Leicester and once fashioned a ring for me to give to a special person.

Dressed and ready to go when they turned up I walked with the help of a stick – the injections in my backside had temporarily injured the hip muscles. Glad at last to be leaving the hospital – as I crossed the ward to greet my friends, thoughts of the many anxieties and problems I had caused everyone crossed my mind, and also the knowledge of the evident kindness people were capable of when occasion arose, enabling them to *give!* This applied very much to the people in the hospital here, including the young nurse who dashed across to present me with the gift I mentioned previously, and which now – measured in real terms was no longer appropriate.

The room in the mews was never mentioned to me again and I never returned to it. There was no nostalgic desire to do so, it was behind me and in the past. My few belongings, collected by some kind friends when I was admitted to hospital were stored at Eric Brown's, and my old van it appeared was safely parked nearby.

*

Recovery was slow but happened. The next problem was the future! There was no doubt I would need a kick-start in order to resume where I had left off when I broke the pattern of conventional life. It meant taking up my job again over in Wales. I must go back to Cardiff College and *stay* back in Cardiff – return there as though nothing at all had happened in London save the dissembled illness I'd suffered. There was no alternative – my salary had continued to be paid during my stay in hospital. Apart from that, I thought it was high time I stopped being such a bloody nuisance to people and to myself.

The thoughts of the effort needed to face both people and place was more than off-putting. Yet, on the plus side there would sculptures to be made. Images, though vague, were already forming in my mind. I suspected a vast charge of emotional source material was waiting to be unleashed; spewing it out by way of Art would be curative. The mid-life crisis, still present to a degree needed resolve; the dregs of it lingered on and would take time to disperse and never would entirely, I thought.

The seasonal break was over; College was two weeks into the Winter term – I would be needed. Setting off, I hoped that the going back was not going to be too difficult.

Chapter 18

Cardiff

Fortunately, the drive across from London was accomplished in remarkably fine, late January weather. Neither the old van or my not yet quite better leg played up on the journey. There'd even been a couple of hours of cold but bright wintry sunshine. These were all good omens I thought, guiding the loaded van through the iron gates into the small Art College yard in Cardiff. The building was one of the older red brick Victorian colleges of art situated not too far from the city centre. Parking, I noticed a student on his way out who seeing my arrival hurried in again – to break the news of my return I imagine. Probably, I was already something like notorious from the students point of view – although I had not yet spent a whole term there.

On the whole, fitting back into the working life of the college was not too bad; the anticipation of unwelcome events often makes things much worse than they eventually turn out to be. Everyone welcomed me, hoping I was better. My old students from Leicester were delighted to see me return – their apparent pleasure was worth a lot.

That first day back – intending to find a hotel or guest house from where to search for a more permanent residence, I was persuaded against doing so. Frank Roper, having discovered my need when asked if he knew of a good estate agent, insisted I stay with him until such times as I found a place of my own – it was a generous gesture. Lately I thought – help always seemed to be on hand and came from the most unexpected directions; I would never again take people for granted.

In the caring, restful home in which I was to live as a guest for a short time, my hosts Frank and Nora Roper could not have been more understanding. Coming from an extremely different situation and background compared to the secure life they led, I must have seemed an odd item – yet, my unreserved welcome was total. If I felt at all out of place it was due entirely to myself. The calm, organised household I entered provided exactly the kind of respite I needed before plunging back into the less sheltered life I was accustomed to. The Ropers were Christians – their natural kindness followed.

My stay there provided the space and time I needed to reflect and take stock of the present situation and my status both as an artist and a principal lecturer. Less than ten years ago I earned a living as a metalworker; it was now nineteen sixty-five, I was forty years of age and more than halfway there – *there* being the normally expected limit of one's living time on planet Earth. And, I considered – that at the rate I was using up life I was inclined to doubt my seeing in anything like another twenty never mind forty years. But I had returned to this kind city to make a new start I reminded myself, this line of thinking wouldn't help

– I desperately needed to settle down – to achieve some kind of normality in conventional terms.

Yet, what is normality? I was born into a vastly different parental, social background and habits compared to the people I associated with these last few years – was that normal? And diverging wildly off-beam, guessing at pre-birth causation I decided that I must have been sent out from a dissimilar pre-earth dispersal point to that of my parents and brothers – I was unlike them. Does this imply then that I believe in some ethereal spot in space or other subtle dimension where ones psyche and character traits are genetically imprinted before an individual arrives on Earth – in the flesh. This is a difficult idea to come to terms with whether true or false – yet, to a cave man television would be impossible and even a box of matches magic.

This line of thinking happened when I was wide awake in bed early one morning. Never a consistent thinker, ideas, often far-out, fly in from all directions – offering up difficult questions and sometimes shaping incredibly complicated answers. On this occasion I happened to be following a train of thought resulting from a poem written in the 1930s which I'd read in bed last night. 'Prayer Before Birth' by Louis MacNeice expresses grave concern for the unborn child about to be thrust out into the twentieth century. A century which promotes a civilisation less concerned with vulnerable individuals and more seriously involved with the advantages of technology and science for the *Big!* Extolling the Natural things of God's world, MacNeice's poem sounds out a prophetic warning aimed at the traumatic happenings and probable dangers of its time. Such warnings seem even more apt and appear to be actually happening in this third millennium.

Lying back, resisting getting out of bed – my mind continued to excavate at depths of predictive thinking and levels of inquiry I never knew existed. The lines of the poetry made me reconsider the prior nature of human beings – did we in fact exist as etheric some*things* or subtle actualities before the moment of conception within the womb?

Take a plant seed – after all, the *program* and therefore the *image* of the flower must exist somewhere even before the seed exists. The task of the seed is merely (merely...!) to produce the flower. Could there then be a creative *mind* with a capital 'M' somewhere – existing in Virtual space and capable of imagining, imaging the flower before setting in motion the process of its creation from start to finish. If one equates this Mind with the source of *information* implanted within a seed, then it follows that a kinetic image of the emerging, growing, blooming and decaying flower – induced by some incredible act, precedes even the actual seed. And where (and I cannot say on Earth) does the seed *a priori* come from – from out of an *infinite empty place!* Or does it? Whatever supernormal, seemingly magical phenomenon brings the seed into phenomenal existence, the information it contains directs the plant's life – processing it through its life cycle, informing each cell to multiply and shape the flower to the *predetermined* instruction. And like all animate life on Earth, the flower begins the process of decay immediately it reaches the fullness of its blossoming. Soon, languishing, it droops and finally dies – as do we humans.

Back to square one, I was stuck with the mad, imponderable question of – can anything come out of nothing? Which is an even more negative variation of the apocryphal chicken and the egg riddle because there's absolutely nothing in phenomenal existence for it to come from in the first place.

To return to the previous question of the seed and its programmed information, I read in later years that Buddhists believe that the precise moment, the millisecond (if the event *can* be counted in Earth Time) when a human's sperm fertilises the egg – then that is the moment when psyche actually sparks into conscious existence. The embryo then – if this event is true, is not as has been often suggested a mindless unfeeling thing.

Not for the first time I wondered *where* out of Earth does the impulse to trigger human consciousness and pass over the complex of necessary information come from simultaneous to the moment of biogenesis in the womb. I could never and still cannot seriously imagine that the creation of life on earth is due to the improbable existence and action of consciously intelligent chemicals.

All such questions just lead on to others in an endless chain of forever unresolved cause and effect. I gave the problem up and returned to the essence of the MacNeice poem – the plea within its demanding lines for a compassionate appreciation of the preciousness of human life. Surely the unborn child gestating within the womb is not something to be lightly given up, got rid off – wasted unwanted, aborted and discarded. Perhaps the causes which impelled the poet to write his unhappy poem are less connected to the pre-birth questions of humans and more to their questionable, mature actions. Basically one might guess MacNeice was contemplating the fact that we appear to have made a completely out of control mess of the world and continue to do so? Or it seems that a fair proportion of the male gender of the population seem dead set on instigating further wars – wars to be fought by bigger (certainly not better), bloodier weapons!

Contrary to the madness of man's often evil intent I thought of the innumerable acts of spiritually inspired compassion performed by men and women – often calling for heroic sacrifice. And didn't the curative sciences working to help humanity arise out of humans wishing to help other humans. And what about the inspirational languages of music, poetry, and the other God-sent arts seeking to imbue the lives of people with purpose and meaning – not kill them off by employing bombs of mass murder or a ghastly man-made lethal virus. Where then *is* a man's wisdom to be found – certainly not down the front of his trousers which often seems the contributory spot to bringing great sorrow and catastrophic suffering upon the world...

Enough I thought, mentally backing off, finding it a further problem to come to up with more hopeful signs of better things to come, But where then does any significant truth behind it all lie? Is it contained within the foetus newly brought forth in the flesh and therefore that much closer to the Original cause? And if so why do we miss it, ignore it – because as far as I could see as soon as a child is born into the light of day we bury any vestige of truth beneath a mountain of mental excrement imposed by sad, or angry power seeking men negatively inclined. Men, whose many sexual and egotistical aspects of character as often as not overrule their more natural and humane instincts – and I do not exclude myself!

I thought of a baby born with a beautiful empty and open mind – lovingly inquisitive, godly, and receptive like an immeasurable and immaculate sheet of white paper or vast, endless expanse of consummate white space awaiting the first meaningful mark or recorded thought-form. Were humans the original purposeful creation – the intended genesis of a race of self-conscious, wise and compassionate beings capable of approaching as near to perfection as any super-intelligent animals could? Then, I thought dejectedly, finally – look how we've ended up and what we've done to ourselves.

*

Work in Cardiff was going well at the College. Having regained a right to award a diploma in Sculpture, Tom asked me to do something about the ceramics department which had also failed its inspection. Although it was a well run department with a hard working staff and a committed head of ceramics, desperate remedies were needed to establish a new, more imaginative and modern course of study. Over several weeks I had asked for the shelves lining the walls of the ceramic studios to be cleared off – they were piled doubly high with examples of work of historic design. It was not as though they were bad ceramics – the problem was that the style had not moved with the times in any obvious way. They were heavy, solid, often dull pots – bowls, cups and vases all glazed in not unpleasant but sombre tones of browns and olive greens. Well made as pots go and of reasonable design, they lacked any imaginative suggestion of the exciting 1960s. I felt sure that Frank well knew what was wrong but was unhappily trapped in past-Time and set in his ways. He was at a complete loss as to how to change the situation and literally reinvent his department – and his life in fact!

Being cruel to be kind, bravely one Monday morning, having waited long enough – and the time was urgent, I banned students from the ceramics studios for the day. Finding a ladder I literally attacked the dusty pot-laden

240

shelves. Before the astonished eyes of the ceramic lecturers, saving just a few examples, I flung, or rather dropped the rest of the pots to the ground. Strangely the attack seemed to work – the heavy atmosphere of tradition dissipated when the very *pots of ages* crashed down from the shelves. Immediately the studios began to look bigger, emptier, healthier – opening up space for new imaginative adventures in ceramics. The row I half expected from Frank and other lecturers in the department who open mouthed had watched the destruction, never happened. Instead, I was surprised that after the initial shock was over there was an evident sense of relief – in that something had at last *actually happened!* But what must they do now they worried and wondered – so did I!

I could not immediately think of what to do – how does one go about changing a leopard's spots. It took me two days to work out exactly what must be done. In the meantime the ceramics lecturers carried on teaching in exactly the same old way with no apparent change in concept or tactics. What they did do was to cast many curious 'Ha-ha!' looks in my directions because the buck stopped with me – didn't it!

The final cure I decided and did was to take ten of the first year painting and sculpture students into the ceramics department, telling them that they might make *anything* even inconceivable in ceramics – anything that is excepting conventional pots. I gently told Frank that whatever these fine art students dreamed up on paper *must* be made in clay, fired, and coloured to any desired colour of the spectrum they desired. There was to be no argument or can't do's, no olive greens or rich browns – I wanted colour in its most colourful sense. I told the staff of the ceramics department that they *must* find a way to produce the fine art students ideas, far out in design as they might be and eventually *were*. They did exactly that and all was eventually well!

Returning on a visit to Cardiff College of Art a few years later (now a polytechnic), Frank, somewhat older and wiser, still head of a now very successful ceramics department, took me aside to offer a delayed, appreciative thank you by saying, 'By god, the day you did that was the best thing that ever happened to me...!' Meaning of course that the well intentioned destruction of outworn, fixed ideas is the only way to create new beginnings.

*

Outside of teaching, life, while not worsening was standing still in respect of emotional improvement or emerging signs of personal creativity in the way of Art. I was busy and preoccupied in establishing a new pattern of life – resurrecting or making better crashed inner states of mind and attempting to do right, safe things. For three or four weeks I had been occupying a first floor flat in a pleasant suburb of the city. An easy bus ride or walk into College it faced the wide open spaces of a grassy park and playing fields. Coming to me at a particular time of need it was a gift of a place. Thoughts of the Mews flashed across my mind as I unlocked the front door of the Victorian house for the first time and climbed a flight of stairs. Finding and renting the flat was the result of one more kindness offered by the Ropers who provided the name of a friend of theirs – an estate agent. As luck would have it that very day a place had just come up for letting at a rent I could safely afford. It was an exceptionally lucky find, for as well as pleasant external surroundings – inside, it could not have pleased me more. Opposite Roath Park, the flat, after an initial settling down period, was to allow me two safe and relatively happy years living there.

On first seeing it I discovered that after climbing the staircase, except for the dark passage leading from the kitchen to the front bedroom, everywhere but the small bathroom was emulsioned out an immaculate white. Let almost unfurnished the flat gave out good vibes and was, I think, an unexpected omen of good luck – it seemed like a lovely place in which I might choose to live. The kitchen at the back of the flat was sizeable and well lit by a French window which opened out onto an iron balcony. The balcony itself was connected to fire-escape steps which led from top to the bottom of the house, ending in a small backyard. A tall wooden gate opened out of the yard into a quiet alley-way and a drive-in entrance to a garage which came with the 2nd floor flat. The ground floor flat was occupied by the owners of the house – my would be landlord in fact. The top flat people were not yet known.

My inside kitchen door was on a small dark landing opposite the top of the entrance staircase. Facing this door, and turning sharp left – back towards the front of the house along the dark passage, one passed the bathroom, toilet and a small spare bedroom. The passage ended at three carpeted steps up to a door into the main room of the flat – a superb Victorian, well proportioned room with a high corniced ceiling. The front wall had two upright long windows – one wide the other narrow and both overlooked the front door porch and tiny garden. One of a long terrace of houses it faced a wide main road. Directly across this, beyond the pavement was open grass parkland and playing fields; young trees were spaced out on the edge of the grass a yard or so in from the paving stones.

I remember standing in this pleasant room for the first time feeling an enormous sense of surprise – thinking that as long as I paid the rent then this place it would belong to me, to me alone, to use however I chose to do so. Would I be happy here I not unnaturally wondered? I hoped that things would turn out well! Whatever might happen within these unspoiled white walls was bound to be better than the events of the last couple of years.

The flat needed furniture – fortunately both kitchen and the bigger front room were fitted with modern gas-fires. Somewhere in the neighbourhood I found a second-hand dealer in furniture and was shortly equipped with a low, almost ground level double-bed, a table for the front room which was to be my sitting room and bedroom, two chairs, and a red loose-cover arm-chair. I also bought a cheap bed for the smaller room and a narrow single for the kitchen – it would serve as a couch and for relaxation. Vague ideas also crossed my mind about letting the small bedroom off; also there would be people staying occasionally – my friends up from London, teaching; I really owed them and would be glad to give something back if only a bed for a couple of nights a week.

There was already a table in the kitchen and four dining chairs. Finally I needed one more most important item – a cooker. The one I found, when installed, achieved a small measure of fame among my friends because of its true World War One appearance. I noticed it put to one side in the furniture man's store – ready to be sold for scrap I was told. Taking an immediate fancy to it despite unbelieving grins from the dealer and his two strong men, I offered to pay the £1.50p for it providing they installed the thing. This they did, merely connecting it to the kitchen gas supply with a flexible rubber tube. Its primitive looking two gasrings and small oven worked well and my first cup of tea in the flat would forever be something special to remember.

Called the General, the cooker looked undeniably antique! Its black cast-iron body was totally undecorated and its oval gas-taps of yellow brass were even finger-worn. Only the oven door had been graced with enamel – bordered in green the centre panel was white with the title *General* blazoned across it in black script. The old cooker could quite easily have figured in a Charlie Chaplin film. I loved it, and probably the General helped add to my unsought but growing reputation as an odd loner. Having finally installed enough furniture in the various rooms I bought curtain material for the front windows. The curtains for the narrow window were to be red, for the wider, raw white canvas. They were cut and made with a bare minimum of sewing, the only stitching required was attaching curtain rings – Copydex served for the rest of the job. Finished and hung, they were perfect enough and suited the spacious, sparsely furnished white interior. When the curtains were drawn after dark, a bedside light switched on or candles lit, then the room mellowed and became mine in the sense that I felt secure within it it – and within myself for the first time in what seemed aeons.

The low, double-bed was covered by a remaining keepsake from the grey stone house. It had arrived at the old Rectory, passed on from there to Mews, and now it was here in this new dwelling, it was something she once gave to me because I admired it. Now, it served as a not entirely unhappy reminder of the more idyllic days we shared before the unhappy final scene was acted out.

The once given item was a double lambswool silk-edged

bed covering; dyed a gentle blue-violet there were pillow slips to match. Without top or bottom boards the bed was head up against the back wall facing the windows and the white canvas curtain. Within arms reach to the right, arranged on white-glossed shelves were my books, records, the record player, and a previously installed white telephone. The latter was of the old kind which pur-r-r-ed satisfyingly when one turned the dial and did the same on turning back – doing so automatically when one's finger was removed; it was a friendly telephone. Altogether, the room, with its minimal furnishings and without the visual noise of unnecessary clutter peacefully fulfilled my needs.

Yet, once moved in, living there did not prove to be all that easy. For the first and only time in forty years I was living completely alone. The years, months and days spent alone working in a studio did nothing like spell out or alleviate this new kind of aloneness. Working creatively is an important being alone time – requiring absolute contemplative solitude during which time ideas and hopefully unique images might appear. For months I had been without a studio or the right circumstances and requisite peace of mind conducive to even think of making Art. This situation looked to be changing and soon maybe, I really hoped that I would feel the old urgent need to do so. But until then the first weeks in the flat were quite difficult – the weekends especially so! The days Mondays to Fridays were fine – I was busy in College, and my London friends up teaching in Cardiff would be staying one or two nights.

The very first Friday after college closed until the following Monday, when saying goodbye to friends I would once have travelled back to London with, I became acutely aware of the weekend stretching ahead – empty of people.

Returning to the flat after shopping for food and cigarettes in the neighbourhood, I swept and tidied the rooms, made a hot drink, and sat down at the bare kitchen table to enjoy a smoke.

Sipping hot coffee I gradually became aware of the *silence* surrounding me – utter silence I could almost touch, almost *hear;* but the only real sound to be heard was of myself exhaling cigarette smoke into the still kitchen air.

The sense of isolation was severe, unexpected and surprising. By five o'clock on Saturday, bored, I knew it was too early for the pub, and anyway I couldn't spend all night sitting there, or here in the flat come to think of it – I'd go bonkers! Saving thoughts flooded in – what about a radio? That might help! Television was out of the question – too costly in my present circumstances. Wireless, better than a book would provide an actual company of voices.

Not far from a shopping centre and a suitable shop I hurried out before it might close. Arriving back at the flat, sitting in my kitchen or alternatively for the sake of change in my front room, I played with the newly purchased portable for a short time. Turning the long-wave dial I simulated travelling around the world – tuning in to various incomprehensible foreign languages countries until I felt it might be time to eat. Once more, feeling bored and also angry with myself I looked at my watch – it was barely a an hour since I'd gone out and bought the radio.

Damn! it then, I'd go and treat myself to a bloody good meal whether I could afford the expense or not – it was something to do...and I would be among people. But where would I find somewhere decent to eat in this largely unknown city. I ended up in the glitzy restaurant of probably the most expensive hotel in Cardiff. Feeling extremely conspicuous among the many other tables occupied by more than one person, by the time I had eaten and consumed a bottle of inexpensive red wine it was still only eight-thirty. After settling a shocking bill I walked towards my own new neighbourhood and into the local pub. A strong pint did the trick and back to the flat I literally fell into bed – realising that it was no later than nine-thirty.

*

Of course I survived that first weekend and others succeeding it. Minor things came along to help. the most life-changing of these, which in retrospect turned out to be a major rather than a minor event, was one of those casual *ships-that-pass-in-the-night* important kind of meetings which quite unexpectedly, and unspectacularly redirect one's life.

Conveniently there was a good shopping centre round the corner from the flat so that on this particular Saturday morning, having dumped a load of washing at the laundrette, waiting for it to be done I sat in a newly opened Espresso bar drinking an overpriced, heavily foamed and milked coffee. Across the far side of the café he noticed a vaguely recognisable face. I could not recall ever having spoken to the woman, and remembered only that she was American and a mature student studying at Cardiff College of Art. Tom Hudson's fame as a foremost lecturer in Art Education had spread overseas and students were appearing from the U.S.A. and she was one of them. I believe her name was Mary Magdelene.

Now, a coffee in front of her, she looked across and smiled faintly in mutual recognition. I nodded back, unsmiling probably, looking much too serious as I always did (so I am told) in those days. After a moment's hesitation

I made my way which for me was a brave move. Gesturing – I asked if I might I join her? She must be quite alone I imagined, crossing to her table. She was in a country strange to her never mind an unknown town. There was no ulterior motive in my joining her. Women just then were merely other people and of no other interest to me. I suppose I was much too wrapped up in my untold self-reflections.

We talked pleasantries at first; she seemed to be a wise person – younger than me, yet in a way, older. Naturally we got round to talking about Art, the College, and eventually she asked me about my work. The means, or media by which an artist was able to express him or her self came up. Here, I believe I said something quite casually like, 'If I could, I would write a book. Making sculpture is an incredibly slow and restrictive medium to say things in, it's so much less direct and to the point than words.'

Her response to this statement was, 'Well, *write* a book then! If I felt like that I'd just go and write one.'

I recall talking to her only ever once more. But her simple, direct and down to earth comment I will never forget.

Not that I would ever write a book! But that first negative thought did not deter me from immediately buying two sixpenny notebooks and almost filling the first in one session. The words poured out like when I had written long letter after long letter to the person in the grey stone house. Then, I wrote and wrote while sitting in my London bed-sitter window, stopping now and then to watch the cat's pink tongue busily washing a paw as it eyed me warily from the garden. I had not connected that kind of letter writing with book-writing, but I suppose in a way it was almost the same. What I now wrote in the first sixpenny notebook was a non-stop scribble – attempting to explain myself to my older son Peter, now too young to understand but perhaps in years to come he might? Not that that would undo what had been done.

Thinking back, it also made better sense in having another person in mind to write to, the words became real, and who else needed an explanation more? All heavy emotional stuff, the writing *did* act as a safety valve, releasing some of the choked-back feelings which might otherwise emerge as black thought. I also felt that what I was getting down was indirectly creative, it was actually *doing something* – not just moping time away.

Naturally I had dramatised everything – not intentionally, it just came out like that. Scribbling away without pause, getting down all that had happened, the words and sentences arrived of themselves, automatically! The narrative became a sombre, fairy-tale, told as I *imagined* it had been – how it *felt!* Re-reading it, it at least meant something to me, regardless of what others reading might think.

*

Passing a second hand junk-shop on my way back from college one early evening I stopped to look in the window. There, right in the middle, among innumerable cameras, musical instruments, old medals, binoculars, and other, bric-a-brac – almost as though fate had meant it to catch my eye, was a small, neat looking typewriter. Its pastel blue case was labelled Olivetti and it looked like a good, well designed machine – although I was quite ignorant as to the ins-and-outs of typing or the mechanics of typewriters. Having definitely come on to the idea of writing things down the sudden thought of typing out what I wrote was irresistible – I desperately wished for that little, magical looking machine.

Money was more than tight; I was living largely off beans on toast and envious of students sharing the local milk-bar near to College, watching them settle down to a glut of sausage, bacon, egg, chips, etc., etc. Nevertheless, I must have it – the typewriter. In the shop I asked the price and whether it was a reliable machine, did it work alright? 'It's fifteen quid and a good one,' the shopkeeper said. And, 'Bring it back if you've any trouble and you can have your money back!'

Planning to forgo the pub for a night or two I took the plunge and bought it. It was a decision I never regretted; the typewriter proved in time to be the most rewarding thing I ever gave myself. Seeing a poem I had struggled to write in my often illegible hand-writing, and comparing it to what it looked like in print – even if only in type-writing print, was fantastic. Watching it appear on the paper, right there in front of me, letter by letter and word by word, happening with immediacy as the keys were tapped and tapped again, was like composing sentences visually, so that as well as reading well, what I was saying looked good! Late one night, having over the past week achieved a fair two-finger typing speed, feeling solitary and rosily content after consuming half a bottle of cheap plonk by the light of a single candle at the side of my new friend – the typewriter, I allowed my mind free rein...

> ... *words are ambiguous comments – communications and directives never ultimately understood; they are sententious verbal descriptions of acts and emotions rarely true...!*

I had also bought myself a second-hand Oxford Concise Dictionary and was revelling in the intoxication of a new found pleasure in words...

... now, yesterday, tomorrow; is there no existence without tense? Is it important when, how, why, or in what period of time he, she, me, exist? I am, I will, are suppositions based upon historical sequences of events cultivated by a fear stemming from the imagination – you are, we are, are propositions arising out of Man's boredom, loneliness, and a dread of being meaningless... and yet, one may be moved by words – inwardly they formulate thoughts and become the end product of an impulse commencing from the deepness inside of us, progressing through numerous layers of consciousness – attempting to gain clarity of expression in a struggle to reach the maturity of sound and issue out from the mouth into Time and into the Past... words are the excreta of the brain, the product of our imaginary soul, they are illusory and most times deluding, they are just words! Although, if I could achieve anything, it would be by using words – to move people, to move them to drop tears as big as lemons, to move them in such a way that it was as if they sensed the vastness of the Macrocosm for the first time, the entirety of the Universe, and felt like gods astride a pinnacle of the highest mountain in the loneliest land, or as if they heard the most sublime music God could create...the silence of a whisper out of stillness – the sigh of a lover...

Chapter 19

Creativity

It was the Easter holidays. College was closed except for administrative staff, although I myself was free to go in and work there each day – even at weekends when no one else was in the building. At the moment, sitting on top of a double-decker bus, I was coming away from the house of Peter Jones of the Welsh Arts Council after accepting an invite for coffee.

By now, mentally more fully surfaced, I had at last begun work of my own; my studio was the College itself, and the tiny office first given me proved a welcome bolt-hole in which to escape if need arose.

Once upon a time I would have found it impossible to work without the privacy and solitude of my own studio – now, something had changed. Too early to say what, the upshot was that I did not altogether care what others might think or say about the ideas and images in my mind soon to appear – although I was not exactly clear in myself what these would be.

So far there was little positive to be seen except for a small, incomplete, box-like thing in iron. All that could be said for it was that I had contrived a way to construct the main form of a possible sculpture much more quickly than usual. This new shape, basically simple, proved easier to make and fitted in with the ideas and concepts vaguely forming in my mind. These, if maturing, would take nothing like the length of time a single helmet sculpture took to beat out and weld up in iron.

Sitting on top of the bus on my way back to the flat I was mind-doodling – a pastime I had indulged in quite often these last few weeks. By reason of the Easter holiday when both students and lecturers were away I'd spent too much time alone. Perhaps this was the reason for what happened on this present bus ride – because what did was quite significant and provided an insight I could almost call a revelation – to me anyway! It arose out of something so simple that attempting to describe it might made it seem like absolutely nothing at all.

The bus arrived at a Stop and the only two upstairs passengers besides myself clattered down the steps. As they stepped out onto the pavement at that precise moment the bus stop sign immediately outside my window suddenly zoomed into more than sharp focus, at the same time the bus appeared to become unnaturally still – as though poised in a momentary suspension of Time; the sign at the top of the stop's green metal pole obviously read BUS STOP but the letters, black upon white appeared to stand out three-dimensionally, and simultaneous to this stark image a clear insight occurred which I could not tell anyone about convincingly! It was a sheer intrusion into my mind completely out of nowhere – I was informed that – *this bus stop is of much greater importance and use to people than you are!* The simple mundane statement fed into my mind by some weird intuitive means was as direct and straightforward as that.

The incident and insight were an altogether-happening-at-once-event which came as an abrupt shock in terms of the absolute truth the words bore on examination. The intuitive communication stated without reservation that the Bus Stop was of more use than me – to people of course, but why? The answer was simply because it *helped* innumerable people *unconditionally* – day after day, year after year without the least confusion of purpose it stood there leading an uncomplicated inanimate existence, yet an invaluable one – halting buses and allowing people to get on or off, doing exactly what it was there for, expecting and asking for nothing in return – giving unquestioning service, It stated in the simplest possible terms exactly what it was doing – it was completely *honest,* and what you saw you got! If only I and everyone else were like that? The better part of my mind grasped the taken-for-granted roadside bus stop as a model – an example offering me a symbolic comparison between *its* valuable existence and my own. It was a shock revelation, unexplainable in sensible terms but a useful self-observation to be tucked away somewhere – a reference guide for the future.

*

I named the completed iron box Vanity Box, Green Hand. It was not altogether a cynical title meaningful only to me; I thought that if others responded to it from out of their own experience – that would be good, if not, well... Perhaps the unique image the object presented might at least be of some interest to those who took the trouble to look at twentieth century Art. The first piece of work I had produced for some time, it was to be the beginning of a prolific, creative period.

When finished, Vanity Box, Green Hand, proved to be a simple ten inches by eight by eight inches deep box, open at the top and made out of strong iron plate. I welded and ground the metal surface up so that its appearance was that of a near enough solid block of grey iron. The top ten by eight inch piece, not yet fixed, I cut short ways across, dividing it equally into two and piano-hinged these to the box's longwise opposite ends. Where these half-lids then swung down to meet in the centre – closing the box, I arranged an eighth-inch gap, and in addition, a little way in at either side of this top central line, cut a perfectly round hole, finger-size, which enabled the two halves, fingers inserted, to be lifted in unison – opening up the interior to disclose whatever contents might be within. Unopened, the top displayed a thin black line separating two black circles – the blackness being a left over effect from the *black space* concept of the Helmet sculptures. As before it drew attention to the absence of light within the enclosed interior, and to whatever inner mystery that might suggest and contain. The blackness of the negative shapes also imaged that of the fertility symbol used in the mandala work, giving the sculpture a more significant visual impact – at the same time it might just prick an observer's curiosity as to the hidden contents within and available to be viewed if he or she was not too timid to become involved with the art-work by opening Vanity Box, Green Hand.

The idea of allowing an onlooker to take part physically in the art-experience was one I originally offered in the Blue

Torso. A tactile involvement admittedly, but the images were strong enough and of sufficient visual interest to stimulate further curiosity, leading perhaps to a hands-on level of appreciation.

What I also did to add to the work's more outer sense of mystery was to solder near the top of the box, on one side, the small silhouette of a hand cut out of thin brass sheet; the fingers, outspread, reached over at right angles on top – towards a slim, emerald-green, life-size gloved hand – a woman's, secured to lie casually across one half of the hinged top.

The brilliant green glove was one of a pair bought in a sale at Liberty's when she and I were shopping once in London. Filling out the glove, giving it an appearance of reality, was a lay-figure hand similar to that used in the wooden pattern for casting the mandala sculpture – glove and hand were a perfect fit.

Finally, I lined the inside of the iron-box with red-velvet and welded up a slender metal stand so that the top of the box was at table height. The work was intended to contain and entomb a portion of the past, *times past,* hers and mine. What was really inside was a miniature junk shop consisting of romantic artefacts – a box of memories epitomised by a black silk red-tasselled slipper, a champagne cork and cage, cherry-stones, a sea-shell, and a bright crimson satin glove bought on the same Liberty shopping expedition as the green one adorning the box; in addition to these were two paper roses, one pink, one blue, a tiny bronze African sculpture she'd once given me, the ever so tiny pink head of a Victorian porcelain doll, and an ivory die; all of these and other wistfully enshrined entities manifested her intangible presence – resurrecting moments of passion, helping recall nostalgic, lapsed mind-pictures of both passive and intensely romantic occasions. Vanity Box, Green Hand became a time-capsule recording a deeply felt episode of human love – *her* scent and absent presence impregnated the *black space* of a once-upon-a-time-world.

Insignificant as it might have seemed as a work of art, the iron box was particularly important to me at that time; and what else could I have called it but Art? Certainly it expressed my feelings while making it, and although over personal in concept, knowing it might be regarded as self-indulgence rather than dealing with greater, more important subject matter, I did not really care! Trivial it might be in one sense, yet it *had* turned out to be a creative work as well as curative, both in the making of it and in allowing it to become what it was – a box of past-delights. The outcome was that I was back, once more – involved in creative work! And now other, yet unspecific ideas and images were crowding my mind – intimations of more important things than a decidedly unimportant self.

*

Thoroughly settled in my new home I had finally learned to appreciate its sense of peace and quiet seclusion when no one other person was present – which was most often. The green parkland opposite my window was a continual delight. I kept the flat fanatically ordered and clean, feeling more secure and in control that way. The General, my ancient cooker, had introduced an element of originality in the kitchen-come-living room, and books and other odds and ends were bringing a more lived in feeling to the place. The mantel-shelf was acquiring a collection of small, interesting object matter – at one end the built-up block of empty, shiny, silver twenty-packets grew each day as I smoked my way through endless cigarettes. There was also a recorder and a cheap but excellent Chinese mouth-organ on which I could play only fragments of tunes; although more than fond of music my musical memory was practically non-existent.

I bought the mouth organ after listening to a November Armistice Day programme on the radio. The background music was the melancholy dirge of Its a Long, Long Trail of Winding played on a mouth organ. The lonely sound of it expressed an ultimate hopelessness that moved me to unmasculine tears for the poor despairing men who'd suffered in that horrific Great War of pure, bloody minded murder, and which in the end – proved nothing except for showing the unexampled courage of millions of individuals and the callous stupidity of a very few others.

Over the weeks I got to know the people in the upstairs and downstairs flats, but only casually – making their acquaintance in a friendly way without becoming over-involved, which might have created problems. The upstairs lot I hardly ever saw – they used the outside iron stairway, clattering noisily up or down to get in or out of their flat. But I *heard* them – at weekends when they must have been at the pub and got over jolly so that shouts and hoots of laughter usually followed them in; they also argued, loudly. The family consisted, if they were a family, of two attractive working daughters and a sweet, tiny mother. My artist friends from London, when staying with me swore, when occasionally hearing what sounded like a screams coming from upstairs – not joyful sounding screams, that the place was a centre enabling unmarried women to painfully redeem their respectability in the community; the jest was not intended as unkindly.

The retired couple downstairs could only be described as *nice people,* and they really were – saying the time of day pleasantly should I meet them in passing, but keeping to themselves otherwise. They were also tolerant, perhaps needing to be – for my flat was not always a haven of quiet, or convention. Although I suspect they quite liked having someone from the Art College upstairs – with all that that might imply in an obviously conventional neighbourhood, that is, as long as a degree of respectability remained. I imagine also, that my arrival on the scene as a strange but not unpleasant man living alone, brought a hint of excitement into their normally uneventful lives.

I became more convinced of their tolerance when, arriving back from college one late afternoon, on opening the front door to reach my flat upstairs, I found a briefly penned note on the bottom step. After only a few weeks in occupation, reading it, I was not unreasonably horrified at its implication.

That week, a friend had been up teaching for three days, occupying my spare room. Whilst staying he formed a close liaison with a young, not unrespectable but certainly easy-going young person. The opposite sex most likely found my friend attractive because he was an artist – a painter up from the big city, tall, bearded and a handsome man to boot. Bringing her back to the flat – presumably to sleep, was giving the old couple night after sleepless night – that apart from the embarrassment they like as not felt. What was happening was patently obvious when I read the note they'd placed at the bottom of my staircase. It very politely pointed out that *their* bedroom was directly under my spare room. Would your friend, it asked, kindly desist from bouncing about all night – for one thing the noise kept them awake, and for another, their bedroom light bulb – dangling only on flex from the ceiling had finally packed it in!

Life in the flat was otherwise uneventful during those first few weeks. I was beginning to enjoy waking up early morning to find the spacious room flooded with yellow summer sunlight coming through the broad expanse of brightly illuminated white-canvas curtain. I would lay still, cogitating, while blankly staring up at the white, ornamented ceiling rose from which hung a massive white-tissue Chinese lamp-shade. The ceiling rose by now had become a friend – my sleepy unfocussed gaze occasionally metamorphosed its repeated sculptured wedge-shapes into a circle of sheep's heads, as seen in plan-view – their noses pointing inwards to the centre. It was definitely a friendly circle of creatures, conversing – I was glad they were there, sharing my white, uncluttered now familiar room. Apart from teaching and creating the new, often discomforting images I was making, I was leading a less emotionally charged life – continuing more calmly the serious self-search I'd begun last Autumn.

Chapter 20

Things perceived

I was contemplating the form or appearance my next work might take, and what it would attempt to convey. I knew loosely what I wanted to say – implant as the essential root within the structure of the materials I would use to fashion the thing taking shape at the back of my mind. In a dictionary I'd read that this conceptual *thing*, might better be described under the word *phenomenon*: Phenomenon: 1. A fact or occurrence that appears or is perceived, esp. one of which the cause is in question. 2. A remarkable person or thing. 3 *Philos.* the object of a person's perception; what the senses or mind notice... (Oxford Concise 1995).

The definition also promoted a sense of mystery at the same time as applying to the slowly composing image in *a* mind – in this case my mind. Nowhere near a specific image yet, it was still consistent with something I had thought about quite often lately. It would be pretentious to imagine that I might make a gesture or an offering to the World! But if I felt strongly about something then bollocks and to hell with it – I would do whatever I could to make the point, pretentious or not!

Sitting at my kitchen table this late Friday evening, returned from a lonely pint at the pub – I had only now read the final chapter of Huxley's Brave New World. Written in 1932 it foretells of and foreshadows unpleasant *things* to come – things that were already happening to a minor degree by 1965. I imagined there would probably be even worse ones in process by the time the third millennium rolled up into place. It was a brilliantly written book of sinister, imaginative story design. The clinical descriptions of conveyor belts endlessly carrying along test-tubes and glass bottles containing artificially fertilised semi-human embryos are horrifying. The end product of these genetically manipulated creatures is a range of controlled sub-human species. Classified under the Greek letters Alpha, Beta, Gamma, Delta, etc., the letters denote higher or lower degrees of mentality. Some scientifically designed foetuses are programmed to mature as morons – bred with physical attributes suitable only for undertaking tasks requiring sheer manual labour; these creatures were registered lower down the scale in alphabetical terms.

In the era of *FORD* – the measure of Time in the Brave New World derived from Henry Ford's innovatory idea of conveyor belts for producing mass products as opposed to the one-off civilisation Aldous Huxley knew in 1932, is no more. Our present generally un-doctored psyche possesses a capacity for developing intellectual concepts; it experiences sensory feelings which give rise to chance events, individual forms of expression and emotional decision making – all of these are *OUT!*

In this Brave New World, one segregated region, the

Reservation, remains – wherein unadulterated humans of original mind and body continue to exist, living tribal and supposedly uncultured, once normal lives. Looked down upon as primitive remnants of the *old world* these real people live as outcasts. One man among them, taken out of this – his native background, is introduced as a freak among the genetically modified, counterfeit beings of the Brave New World. Known in the book as Savage – estranged in an unrecognisable world he becomes bewildered, unhappy, and immeasurably shocked at finding himself surrounded by emotionally barren, synthetic humans who lack the capacity to grasp matters outside of their own contrived world, and who cannot think and feel as us humans do – or love in the way we today do! Neither can they experience let alone understand any of the *old world* urges and insistent desires surging through poor Savage's veins. Therefore – his behaviour, natural and normal to himself is seen as abnormal, hilariously comical and violently antisocial by the mutant, ersatz inhabitants of the Brave New World into which he has been cast. The book ends tragically. Should such a civilisation overtake us I thought – what a catastrophic happening that would be. It would be the retrograde scientific creation of an uncivilised, dehumanized world totally devoid of human consciousness, empathy, compassion and love. Thank God for this world right *now* as it presently exists. It maybe becoming over populated by an ever hopeful even if a frequently downcast medley of people, but people who 99% of the time entered into it via Natural causes and natural means – conceived in passion they were born of natural childbirth.

At this time the vulnerable embryo remained beyond the tinkering of unnatural sciences and the probable genetic emasculation of humanity. Here in my world happiness and suffering live side by side; and cruel and callous as the suffering brought about by wars, famine and floods, plague and poverty seem, humans are still able to rise above these distressing facts of life, show kindness toward one another, and possess a consciousness enabling them to act freely, and above all to *Love!*

Sitting alone in the quiet of near to midnight, sipping a hot drink before going along to bed, my mind was a jumble of thoughts, less defined than I would have wished. But by this time I had come to know that for *me* thinking and feeling merged – rational lines of thought arrived only when material considerations arose. But despite inner confusion and laboured thought, the direction my work would take and its intentions were already on the way to being established – if only subtly they were steadily compounding. Somehow, if nothing stood in the way, and I was pretty determined it should not – then the images I made would mirror, somehow, the horrors of the Brave New World and reflect the spiritual nature of the human plea implicit in the poem by MacNeice; I would read it once more – tomorrow.

The ideas gelling within me concerned the sense of value placed upon each single member of the human race – from the simplest to the most knowledgeable, from the most unfortunately ignorant to the very wisest. Who at this Time on Earth knows what a child entering the world might accomplish, create – or alternatively destroy? No one, unless they or you believe in an omnipresent, omniscient God who might finally interfere. Science might today predict the physical make-up and gender of the tiny human/animal gestating in the womb – but surely it would not wish to ultimately determine the brain's precise mental formations which throughout the history of Man only loosely, not specifically, determined the pattern of a human life before it actually came to be lived. How mass suicidal for Mankind it will be to change that process of Natural evolution – it will also be destructive of whatever spiritual truth life contains. Truth is surely a reward, begot and perceived by people undergoing the largely self-determined, often excruciating enterprise called living – living out what we call Life. But most often it's a life of anxious times which, by error and misbehaviour, happiness and sadness we accumulate learning and thereby instil a small measure of hard earned wisdom within our human psyche, soul or whatever. If such extreme or even near extreme genetic modifications to the human species completely took over as predicted in Huxley's Brave New World – then 'Goodbye!' our far from perfect but remarkable civilisation. Perhaps as we know it in our present worried but *Brave old world* terms it would ultimately disappear – *forever and ever!*

The ultimate question, I imagined, was whether humans should retain the God or Nature-given right to the foetus as it comes – pure and untouched no matter how bad or good the particular life might turn out to be. A really daft question I thought – obviously the option cannot be taken before birth so who decides, the parents or the experimental scientist? The moral predicament demands god-like decisions not legalised ones – and who truly should make those but God or loving parents to be. I supposed one would have to admit to special cases of saving both parents and child from a miserable life of severe physical or/and mental suffering. But in the end, interfering without serious cause in another person's pre-life form seems to be a move against majestic Nature.

My final fazed thought after failing to achieve any rational conclusion was – that the child *begat* by an animal yet *biblical* act leading to conception and Nature's miracle enacted within the womb, *is* the only true future – which I soon realised was no progression of a conclusion at all, really...

It was late, I left off heavy thinking at that point and retired to bed, hoping I would sleep soundly. Tomorrow I was going up North to visit the children. Not having seen them since before my time in hospital I must do so. Having rung through to arrange the visit I was very much looking forward to our meeting. Any possible uneasiness about my seeing them was a fear due to the closeness of a certain house. But I would only be staying for one night with a newly made artist friend; there would be little opportunity for a momentary weakness.

*

The six hour train journey provided more time for meditative thinking. My mind turned to various subjects such as my life and the appalling mess I'd made of things not so long ago. I also thought up one or two of my better, more worthy accomplishments – if that is what they were in the light of the painful consequences brought down upon myself and others. Do good acts balance out bad ones I wondered – attempting to reassure myself? It was not altogether my fault, was it – the way things had turned out; much of it I blamed on an inherited need to *make* – to make Art, create things!

All the good that could be said about the situation when I eventually got round to thinking *why* I needed to fashion objects – make sculpture or works of art, was that it was a compulsive need to do so; I also believe it was a wish to effect, move people feelingly, emotionally in some way – like when they were impressed by a poem or made to feel good looking at a famous work of art. Apart from all that – it now provided me with a living, and in these more recent times a purposeful way of life with an ongoing desire to create something good, worthwhile, even important! So there was always something ahead to work for and to achieve if that were possible. But best of all it was teaching me to understand more about life, about myself – stirring up deep, serious thoughts to do with things I might never before have even glimpsed, dreamed of previously – never mind known. The unhappy down-side of being more of a free spirit, leading a less controlled yet creative life among other similarly less conventional, aspiring people – artists, was the relationship problems which brought hurt to others and which I could not, most times, wilfully help. I suppose I'd been thrown into the deep end – it being the characteristic Bohemian society which free thinking and imaginative humans appear to inhabit.

The other aspect of my life – that search for myself, or my more real self – well at least I'd cleared away lots false trails. Unfortunately that had often been at other people's expense and confusion. I have already implied that straight thinking was never my best attribute, and anyway – I had also realised that too much rational thinking kills the imagination, prevents it coming into free play. Perhaps it's when intuition joins up with ones imagination that more subtle, other-world insights emerge. For instance – that there just might be deeper, or higher levels of mind or forms of super-awareness which do exist – are an *actual fact*. This was something I had always seriously wondered about, considered – which was something confirmed for me in years to come.

*

Creativity, art making at its ultimate level, can really become a time consuming, isolationist, selfish activity demanding costly payment in terms of relationships – it did for me anyway! The only excuse I can invent to expiate some such wrongs is in convincing myself that the artist gives something invaluable to society – offering the public an art form which translates life at a more deeply perceived, intense level of seeing and feeling. The artist attempts to transform mundane experience into the less ordinary, into something higher, more intense – oceanic in feeling, spiritual and extraordinary, either in poetical conceptual terms or by sheer visual beauty.

Art aside, I had used people, inadvertently, naively, lacking the will not-to-do – yet not entirely unknowing of what I was doing. I was at times helping myself to what was on offer at the expense of the person's delicate feelings. Using people was getting what you wanted from them even if you were not necessarily thinking in directly grasping terms. Physical love and affection were the things I had most exacted from women; but, I wished to believe that I had never taken these without something of my own given back. And I never intentionally hurt except in anger; but regrettably, out of anger I certainly *did* give hurt.

I found myself comparing animals to us human-animals. For the lower animals as we call them finding a mate is largely a biological urge, although with some species it results in lifelong partnerships. It is not always so with us humans – often, once the sexual attraction is exhausted, has been got out of the way and the loving becomes threadbare, then more than likely furious confrontations of dissimilar personalities take place. And because we humans often talk too much – without thinking, the talking invariably leads to argument and sadly and often the argument turns into something not too far from hate. Fortunately and thankfully this did not happen to me or mine. God! What inane, even insane unpredictable systems humans are. Perhaps the way of the Brave New World is better after all?

I became bored – it was a six hour train journey. My thoughts took a softer turn, reversing time, thinking back to the women I had known in my later years. There'd been three special ones since I left the army in the late 1940s, and others who were special in their own way. Yet, aren't all people that – special! But the three I really came to know and loved, *each* played a unique and important equal-to-anything-ever part in my life. Never mind art, career, or whatever, these lovely generous women had been the desired and determining milestones on the Way. And it was ever despite all the male to female fallings-out we'd had and *because* of the magical fallings back-in again – we'd loved. The sad endings with each which I invariably and unhappily brought about were never meant to be cruel, although they must have been! I did love them all – in different ways because that's how love is, as I understand it – different people call upon different things in you, bringing out qualities of good, not so good, and sometimes exceptional things better than good; that was the way it was, the way life is, I thought. There'd been my wife, how sad I made her – happy sometimes but very sad in the end – and to say I was sorry was ineffectual, a futile gesture implying an altogether inadequate sense of sorrow.

And there was another lovely person who made life

sustainable and fun at an almost despairing time when I needed just that; I disappointed her by appearing to relinquish the great affection I felt by falling seriously in love with someone else. This someone else relationship had been the last, a near to fatal one. But no matter, I would always be grateful to those three women for the love given to me. And to those other, lesser known lovely women who had shown kindness and affection in sharing with me a little of their own invaluable lives. Had I known it, one more special person was to appear; and already had – distantly.

Weighing it all up – I thought there'd been good times, some not so good, and some times exceptionally bad, but all had been important and a part of the inestimable experience life offers to an occasionally foolhardy, yet open-to-chance person sufficiently daring to test Life out. And saying this it is not as though I'm dismissively disowning my wrong behaviour – I am merely owning up to being not entirely an uncaring person who is sometimes actually kind. Yet neither was I always or even now selfless – I am just *me*!

Getting up, I made my way along the carriages to the buffet car, swaying from side to side mumbling, 'Sorry, sorry,' to passengers I unavoidably bumped on the shoulder. Back with a cardboard cup of scalding hot tea and a boring but expensive sandwich I sat down intending to dismiss further thoughts about myself and the whys and the wherefore of us as people. I attempted instead to sip the impossibly hot tea between bites of sandwich as the countryside flashed by and the train rattled noisily on its way up to Leeds.

However, true to form my thoughts quickly introverted. This time to consider serious but more congenial subject matter – my intended work. By the end of the journey North I knew exactly the first step I would need to take before I began work on the idea taking possession of my mind. It meant obtaining knowledge of a special item which was to be the essential and significant part around which the whole concept and its structure was to be built – God knows where I would find it! Considering the purpose of the work – I knew this to be the crucial element deciding its eventual success or its turning out to be a dismal failure. That particular worry apart I was beginning to enjoy the old sense of excitement and anticipation for the formal adventure involved in making this *thing* (yet indistinct) in my mind's eye. Also, for the first time ever, I knew beforehand the real purpose of the work I planned and the intention behind its creation. Of the object, or the sculpture – what it would look like I had no specific idea; that would have to come, to be worked out bit by bit as the invention of the mechanics needed and the construction of the image progressed – this was when the work would begin to take on a formal life of its own.

I would be wilfully exploring formal ways and means – shaping materials, and demanding discriminative judgements from my now more experienced formative mind. I would be allowing myself to become obsessed to the point of brooking no interference in bringing this *phenomenon*, this thing, into being and out into the open. I would gamble with shape – hoping the emerging image and its final presence would fulfil its manifest purpose; the sculpture would need a forceful image in order to grab a spectator's attention.

If at this early stage the proposed work remains obscure I would trust my instinct to begin with – and believe in my usual sense of commitment to an ideal; trusting also in the unseen muse who continues to infiltrate my mind with exceptionally mad ideas. Apart from the quasi-moral reasons of why I wished to create this *thing*, I wished also – as artists do when plagued by an idea, to see what it looked like completed. I would begin work with those ends in mind, hoping against hope that the object finally standing there would visually *shout out* its intention.

I knew without any shadow of doubt that it would not in the slightest way reflect the accepted beauty of a conventional work of art or necessarily reflect even present Art – because the world was fast changing beyond recognition, changing right now, this very minute. But the object would definitely come to belong to the Art of the latter half of the twentieth century and be a work expressing the feelings and perceptions of an artist living at this time. It would demonstrate serious concern for the people of the Future.

When it was actually made, existed in reality – no matter how unacceptable it turned out to be visually, would not the fact of its creation and arrival in the world prove it to be the result of an artist's desire for the beautiful – for beauty existing in conceived form not the conventionally beautiful in appearance. No, this was to make the world beatifically aware of the God like form within the man made form which would be the artwork. In other words what I came up with might be unsightly rather than pretty – its intentional antipathy to the norm of aesthetic appreciation blasting out the message of its meaning forcefully, calling out a cry of warning against the possibility of a coming barren world – a fast approaching almost here and now Brave New World, The sculpture would be a cry for the safeguarding of the *Good* the *True* and the *Beautiful* within the virginal, immaculate emptiness of a newly born child's mind – a *natural* child. Indirectly, if the sculpture was successful, it would speak from the Past to point to the Present, warning against an abhorrent Future – an empty of humans future. The *thing* I would make manifest would be a very small gesture – the only gesture I as an individual might make.

*

Once up North I would enjoy being with the children and they with me; we would be sad once more when the time came for a further parting – but there would other times for us to get together. And while I was there I would meet with my wife and reaffirm an affectionate friendship – one that would last for ever.

I also looked forward to my return to College on Monday morning and getting back to work with a mind concentrated upon a special machine – yet to be devised.

Chapter 21

Bits, pieces, the machine and conclusions

We were on our way towards an annexe of the local hospital – it was the Medical School my friend from College told me. Once in the building I recognised the pungent smell of formaldehyde. It took me back to hobby days of photography when I was about fourteen – the chemical was to do with hardening photographic prints after they'd been developed and fixed. Now, walking down this narrow corridor I realised that the smell was connected with more serious things. My friend was about to introduce me to a professor of anatomy. The stench in the place was overpowering! I had come not knowing exactly what to expect. Glancing through an open doorway to my left I saw a number of white-coated people assembled halfway around a table – peering down at something. Elsewhere one or two others were bent doing things to what looked like, to me – from this distance, a long piece of brown, ribbed bacon. It took only seconds considering I knew where I was to realise with a jolt that it was obviously part of a once human body. Squeamish at the best of times, to find myself walking in what normal minded people would quite literally take to be a chamber of horrors was even more disturbing.

But there was no time to dwell on the fact, a door at the end of the corridor opened and out came the man my friend had brought me to see. After an introduction, having previously told him over the telephone my reason for coming and what it was I wanted, my friend explained once more that his colleague wished to have a look at an embryo, a foetus or whichever – if that was possible? Certainly it was possible, said the man, casually agreeing to a request which seemed to me to be as extraordinary as asking to see the man in the moon.

'Come this way,' said the professor, leading me into the room he'd just left – my friend followed.

Following him in there was a shocking, almost frightening experience – it was an encounter with the flesh and bone of the human body I would never forget. The place was a long, narrow storeroom for the remnants of bodies and things once contained within bodies – some probably taken from living ones! The sickly chemical stench, stronger than ever inside the room, combined with the earlier shock to my senses on seeing white coated medical students hovering over the brown lump on the table was difficult to stomach – a stomach which now felt indecisive as to whether it could! I had not actually seen death close up before, never having been in the vicinity of a dead body with opportunity to contemplate it – even during my army days. It was not that I felt fearful of death – it was just the idea of corpses and gruesome dismembered bodies that worried me. In one way, I reckoned it was good that the ones here – the bits and pieces of bodies had come to be of some use before fulfilling their foretold biblical fate of – from dust to dust. It would probably be more like ashes to ashes when the students had finished fiddling with the bits I thought, gloomily. Visually over sensitive, it was the dissected parts of the cadavers I felt alarmed at seeing – worrying that I might disgrace myself by passing out!

A quick glance round the narrow room had shown me two huge stainless steel tanks – wide and long enough to contain whole, or parts of whole dead bodies. The tops of both tanks were draped over with white cloths – I dreaded to think what might be floating beneath them. Shelved around the walls just above eye level were bottles and jars – glass containers of *things*. These things were various inner and external anatomical parts, pickled and floating in preservative – probably once belonging to the unseen horrors in the man-sized stainless steel tanks.

The professor interrupted my scanning by pointing up to the shelf behind me – turning, I saw a sickening yet pathetic sight which immediately smacked of the images conjured up when reading the Brave New World. The shelf was lined with glass jars inhabited by tiny, almost transparent fleshed foetus in various stages of growth. They were little dead human bodies which might have grown up, matured into living big ones once – had they been given an opportunity to do so. They would not necessarily have become happy people, but surely people! They each now, at least had a separate jar for their temporary entombment before experimentation should that take place and finally destroy them.

The professor was absent-mindedly murmuring to himself as he reached up to the shelf – his forefinger casually tapping each of the jars containing a foetus as he went along the line; he appeared to be seeking a suitable specimen.

'Yes! Here's a good one,' he said to me over his shoulder, 'This might do...' and he lifted the jar down, keeping it upright, careful to prevent the formaldehyde slopping over the open top.

Facing me the professor balanced the jar on one hand and firmly grasping the bottom rim he reached in to extract the miniature person – holding it between his fingers over the jar, letting the clear preservative drip away...

'Here!' he said brusquely, thrusting the still wet foetus at me. Astonished, I was forced to take it in my upturned cupped palm, suppressing a shudder as the cold, wet, pitiful little body came to nestle there. Watched by the professor and the friend who'd brought me I looked with something like horror at the thing resting on my hands – horror mixed with a sheer sense of wonder I suppose. Well, here it was, wasn't this what I had come for, to see! Yes, but without this totally unexpected flesh to flesh, or dead flesh contact – it was something I certainly had not dreamed could happen!

The foetus, curled up, measured less than five inches in length – resting on its side as though in sleep it did not quite reach the last joint of my middle finger. Its once pink flesh was now grey, near translucent – the body appeared to be fully and perfectly formed. Its curved foetal position obscured what sex it might be – the tiny legs, bent at the knees, complete with doll-like feet and toes were crossed over at the ankles. The hands and splayed out tiny fingers were held poised between chin and bent knees, not quite touching together; the eyes, hooded over, allowed it to appear content and peaceful in death.

I returned the foetus to the professor who replacing it carefully back in the jar handed both jar and its contents back over to me. He then walked over to a desk, obtained a brown-paper bag from somewhere and came back to slide it down over the jar – concealing the lifeless little occupant.

Protesting, 'I only wanted to look...' I said. 'So that I'd have a better idea how to make one, sorry, model one in clay,' I corrected myself. 'You're letting me borrow this...?'

'No, take it...' the professor interrupted me, 'You can have it. It's yours,' he said – grinning!

It was too much. I was not immediately sure I wished to own this absolutely real, dead thing – this foetus. I felt afraid somehow, never in my life having lived through what seemed to be such an absolutely surreal life and death event. I wondered what the hell I was going to do with it – the foetus. Having gasped out a worried, 'Thank you,' I left, holding my incredible new possession carefully upright well out in front of me.

Making my way back to College alone, my mood was sober, yet at the same time I was elated by what had just taken place. I was fully appreciative of how much this miraculous acquisition in the jar meant to me. Passing people walking the opposite way to me – *their* minds I thought were occupied with the everyday goings-on of ordinary life where astounding things rarely happened. I wondered again at the inconceivable secret thing concealed beneath the brown paper covered jar held out anxiously before me. I imagined the disbelief – the absolute horror and probable repulsion passers-by would exhibit if, *if*, I slid the bag off to disclose the foetus floating inside the glass jar; and my God, what if I accidentally dropped the thing on the pavement? Quickly arriving back in college, avoiding students and staff wherever possible, aware that those I did see eyed the brown paper covered jar with great curiosity, I sought the safety of my tiny office. After a further almost disbelieving examination of the foetus I placed it in a cupboard – reflecting on how extraordinary events turned out, and odder still that things seemed to come along to fill the slot of my demanding need exactly at the right time; perhaps my muse had something to do with it?

I would need to consider how best the foetus could be used. Which ever way or by whatever means I chose to build it into the artwork I contemplated, it was to be the hub, the metaphorical heart and soul of the work. The look of the object – the image of the proposed machine, was at last beginning to form more clearly in my mind.

That night in the flat, dawdling at my typewriter, a glass of wine at hand, I considered the day's events. It *was* a day to remember I decided – intense, gruesome in a strange sort of a way but worthwhile. I'd been more than glad to get out of there – the anatomy place. And never by any way-out stretch of the imagination had I expected to come away with the actual entity which was going to make this coming work a significant phenomenon – make it real to myself, *and*, I could only hope, very real to other people – I typed up the day's events:

Unborn!
White translucent flesh
pickled in glass -
tiny hands crossed,
as in older death.
One hundred and twenty days,
fully formed, what sex...?
Garrotted – the severed cord
torn from the belly,
who grew you...?

Placenta to the pigs,
you to the shelf
suffocated of soul.
Now I have you-away
from the sickening stench
of death and formaldehyde.
Between thumb and forefinger
the spirit drips away...
you are no bigger than my hand,
beautiful and unsuffering.

*

'Why not cast it straight in bronze?' my friend suggested. We were discussing how to solve the problem of actually presenting the foetus within the sculptural works – the mechanics of doing so and its image; I was about to begin working on the thing – it was out of the question that I could exhibit the foetus in its preservative in a sealed glass jar as the focal point of the artwork. Apart from the engineering difficulties that would entail, even the open ended art scene of the Sixties was not yet ready for such a cold-blooded image.

No, it would need to be translated into bronze. Doing so should not reduce its impact – after all, it would be an actual life-cast and closely exact to a true replica of a four months old *unborn child*. The sight of a foetus was not altogether the common sight it would be in years to come – so that for its Time the the artwork would still be stepping outside of existing boundaries and established art conventions. It would also be visually powerful – but I had no intention of worrying whether or not it turned out to be a pleasant experience for the Art viewing audience of the later 1960s.

Contrarily I wished for the opposite – for it to surprise and to shock in order that its impact and purpose might be felt.

'I think you're probably right,' I replied to the suggestion of directly casting the foetus in bronze. Elaborate mould making would be too long a process, and at that moment I did not want the whole College to know I was using a human model – even a dead one, or that I had such a thing hidden away in my office. My boss, I was told second hand, had not been altogether pleased when told about my idea and the odd thing in my possession. He wanted me to be discreet and not spread the news around. I imagine this request gives out some idea of the measure of the visual and moral constraints of the 1960s – compared to the anything-goes-attitude of almost fifty years on, and which continues into this third millennium.

'Right...!' said my sculptor friend, 'Bring it round tonight when everyone's gone and we'll put it straight into plaster – asbestos plaster,'. He then explained exactly how the foetus would be cast directly in bronze.

The mould making was a bizarre affair – and a touching one. I carried the glass jar complete with its inert little inhabitant round to the sculpture department where mixing bowls, spatulas and plaster were already organised. When everything was ready I lifted the foetus gently out of its jar and carefully placed it once more upon the upturned palm of my hand. As it lay there – a tiny dead creature-thing, unnatural and out of context in its present environment, it appeared as sad and pathetic as when I first saw and held it. I thought, this barely lived in body will soon cease to exist upon Earth – it was to be cremated.

While I held out the lifeless foetus, its upper side was invested with a thick coating of asbestos plaster – a material which hardened reasonably quickly. Lifted from my outstretched hand and turned over, its underside was given a similar coating – but this time funnel openings were left to act as inlet and outlet, or access and exit for the liquid bronze which would eventually be poured in. It now became necessary to remove the entombed foetus somehow from the hardened block of plaster – in order to leave the negative impression inside quite empty. The only way to achieve this without damaging the delicate inner moulding of the plaster was by cremation. The mould needed to be baked in a ceramic kiln until the actual plaster glowed a dull red – and remain at that same temperature for some hours. The process dried out the mould completely and at the same time it would ensure that all the ex-human substance would be consumed – burned out with fire and flame.

However, before entering the kiln the wet plaster needed a day or two to dry out – slowly. This would allow me ample opportunity to think over what I was actually about to do. During this time my overworked imagination continued to ask useless questions about the life of the unknown foetus before it was aborted. I speculated on the man/woman events leading up to its conception – how had its parents met and fallen in love, or had they not loved? Was this dead thing then – once safe and nurtured in its mother's womb, merely the result of a carnal act of passion, or more crudely – the result of a one night stand. Whatever the manner of its conception I wondered who the begetters were? All such sad questions were unanswerable riddles. Even knowing this my mind wandered uselessly on wondering what unavoidable factors brought about the decision to terminate the pregnancy? Had there been a choice – a yea or a nay vote for the life or death of the poor little bugger whoever he or she was, or would have been? My conjectures were in no way a search leading up to any form of judgement one way or the other; the questions were no more than a level of concerned curiosity tinged with compassion.

No, the present questions were to do with belated concern for the once human, once living though unborn *thing* I possessed for this short period of time – which was soon to be consumed by fire. Then it would be safe – for nothing thereafter could again harm the material body of the foetus; its phenomenal time here on Earth would be at an end – God knows where lay its soul – somewhere holy?

I debated if there was the possibility of a degree of feeling and anticipation experienced during the traumatic and unnatural process of abortion – was there pain? Who on Earth knew of this, or could say for sure that there was *not!* It seems highly likely there *must* be some measure of awareness – of intuitive *knowing* during the pre-birth period. There *were* people who claim to recall sensations of being in the womb – so I have heard! In the event of the foetus being aborted – prematurely expelled, unwanted – did these suspected traces of awareness in the womb mean that the unborn child sensed something dreadful was about to, or was happening? And did it feel pain, physical pain – ceasing only with the final rude violation and severing of the umbilical cord thus ending the symbiotic relationship of mother to child and child to mother?

God! what was the use of allowing my mind to witter on like this, what earthly good could come of it? But such thinking at the time probably helped strengthen my conviction and fixed a resolve to get on with the making of the artwork – the machine.

Two days later, moments before committing the mould

to the kiln, I self-consciously mumbled the Lord's prayer over it. Still abject at what I was about to do to the foetus embedded within the plaster block – burn it out, I found myself muttering further words of comfort for the soul of the *thing* about to be consigned to the flames. The consoling thought came to me that should there be one – a soul in subtle existence, then it might become aware that its Earth-form would live for ever in hallowed bronze. At that point – I quickly placed the mould into the already fired kiln, protecting my face from the burning, fiery heat as I did so.

*

Getting to College early the following morning I went straight to the kiln room. A time-switch, operating during the night had switched the kiln off – it was now cooling. Peering through a spy hole in the fire-brick door I saw that the dried out block of plaster looked cool enough to risk removal. Asbestos gloved – everything was still hot to the touch, I extracted the mould carefully and gently placed it on a nearby bench.

There might be ashes inside – although I would have expected that the body of the foetus, helped by the spirit it was preserved in, to have gone completely up in smoke. At the moment all that was in evidence was the block of plaster, baked chalk white, resting on the bench – its inlet and outlet openings uppermost; there was nothing to be seen by peering down either. Would there be ash inside I wondered and tipped the mould upside down over the table, shaking it as I did so – if there *was* anything left inside it should easily fall out.

Not a trace of ash fell out – the flesh *must* have vapourised! I gave it a harder shake, not quite sure whether I had actually heard an almost imperceptible sound coming from inside – as though things were loose. I desperately hoped that bits of plaster had not broken away in the casting, ruining the irreplaceable shape of the foetus. Bits of things did at last fall out of the mould, recognisable bits of things – churning up pity once more as they helter-skeltered down onto the table. They were the remains of what had once been a very small human body – miniature bones, loose ribs, pelvic halves, tiny clavicles, the almost dots of finger and toe bones and other skeletal parts. Christ, I thought, how pathetic this is, and how pathetic we as humans are...

I saved the fragments, unwilling to destroy them, and some months later after embedding the tiny remains in clear plastic – buried the resulting capsule.

The waiting mould, now ready, I passed it over to my friend, who filling it would transform the empty space within into the telling image of a very small, unlived, unfulfilled figure of human shape, resurrected in enduring bronze.

When this had been accomplished I would take it on from there, doing with it whatever my intuitive voices directed – praying that both my very ancient muse, or guardian angel would not fail me; and for the sake of that little unfulfilled life I would soon immortalise, and for all those other future lives for which I felt concern – I prayed that they would guide me well...

*

Late that night, lying in bed in darkness, I felt an unexpected element of content – it must result from having gone part of the way in accomplishing what I had set out to do. Even if, in the end the planned work was a total failure it would not be because of any lack of trying on my part.

I thought back to other nights spent like this, lying thinking, about the past generally. There had been many unhappy, lonely times, full of regrets – and a good measure of self-pity in those early days. But there'd been better nights lately, and weekends when I'd readily accepted the fact that nothing fantastic was going to happen – like a beautiful woman walking through the door, or suddenly as if by magic everything became perfect and problems like money, guilt, self-doubt, doubts about work and all the other innumerable niggling gripes that enter into a person's life would disappear, leaving behind a blissful emptiness, unimaginable peace and contentment – some hope!

What these last few months had taught me was that there are certain rewards in coming to understand *aloneness* – not loneliness, that is a different thing altogether. Aloneness does not equate with loneliness, which strikes when one cannot bear being by oneself and endlessly wish for someone, anyone, to come along and fill that gap. Loneliness I finally came to recognise is the fear of being alone with a self one does not particularly like!

I recalled that first weekend in the flat – arriving there after leaving behind busy, overpowering London. I remembered the appalling silence and my sudden startled awareness of it – how odd that the quality of silence I now know seems to have changed, stillness is no longer an empty enemy. There is an advantage I had soon come to realise in having a less agitated, demanding mind which continually wished for the presence of people and any kind of excitement. Somewhere I read that Buddhists use the phrase, 'calm abiding' – apparently it helps bring about a sense of inner peacefulness. I was beginning to realise that stopping thinking endless thoughts about nothing useful really does equate with emptier mind space – ergo, peace of mind. The writing and reading I'd done also helped persuade me to see life in a wider context – broadening my perception by more outward looking, away from the pettiness of mood I still, occasionally find rising within me. Of course these difficult times remain when depression takes over and I momentarily fall back – sunk in remorse and the guilt that crashes any new found tranquillity; but those times were becoming fewer and I felt that things were working out reasonably well.

Over-tired, I fell into deep sleep. Wherever I was taken in the half-real mystical world of dreams on this particular night – it must have been to a special place, because, for some unexplainable reason, in the still dark hours of the night I was suddenly wide awake, aware of a strange but benevolent feeling flooding both my mind and body. There was no time scale as to how long the feeling persisted or any sure measure of its depth; nor could I have explained in so many words what it felt like. If asked I might have compared what was happening inside me to a vaguely similar experience at a bus stop not long ago, when a sudden, clear insight allowed me a shattering value judgement of my own life's worth.

Now, lying here in the blackness of night, as wide awake as one could get, I experienced an overwhelming feeling of anxious concern, a *sadness* – all the sorry-for-myself pains of old were gone, dissipated, completely vanished – now, sharing the darkness with me was this great sadness or enormous *sorrow* for the innumerable peoples on Earth who suffer the inescapable growing-pains Earth-life imposes upon each person from birth to death. I was filled with profound sympathy for all those who experience loneliness and separation, self-doubt and the innumerable physical pains and mental anguish life can inflict on any individual. And all of these added together with the unhappy abandonings each person comes to know – brought about by love in its various guises, by the evil of hate and by the finality of death. There was no end to the list of tribulations humans seem suffer in order to survive their three-score years and ten.

The complexity of these common fears and the resulting human wretchedness they cause came together into my mind in one all encompassing awareness – of the destructive emotional process people must undergo between their unknowing ignorance and the tortuous way each needs to mentally travel in order to arrive at any level of understanding – and hopefully a rewarding measure of peace of mind. This *awakening,* if that is what it was and I could think of no better word to explain it, came in one lump – in the form of an intuitive charge of clearly directed emotion. It could only be called Love I thought afterwards, or perhaps the feeling was more in the nature of compassion – a great human attribute which leads to the generosity of ultimate kindness and reflects the principle of Love in its highest sense.

Anyway, when the initial awareness of what happened evened out, wore off, searching the experience less emotionally I realised it *was* similar in pattern to that time at the bus stop, and once before on a beautiful summer afternoon wandering down a grassy slope with friends – it *was* a kind of *waking up!* I went back to sleep, hoping the new feeling would not go away and that it would still be there when morning came. Whatever occurred during the night had been very special. I wished that what it had brought and shown to me would stay – remain during the rest of the long journey ahead, for I was yet only half-way there...

Epilogue

The Machine stood shoulder high – a bizarre aberration of twentieth century Art. It functioned by means of a primitive mechanism at the will of whosoever might choose to use it – knowing or unknowing of its sad yield. Wrought in iron it could have been fashioned by a medieval armourer. Crude in appearance it showed no lack of skill in design or any hesitancy of intention in standing as an object of Art. The Machine's stark image looked to be the antithesis of the True, the Good, and the Beautiful – Utopian ideals once purported to help bring about the social and political perfection of Man's world.

Utilising sham, equivalent to human and mechanical parts, the Machine became a grotesque, cynical model of a crude humanoid birth-machine, a satirical phenomenon warning of the dangers inherent in second millennium life and the Future. It was also an inverse comment on the 'High Art' of the 1960s. Its apparent discordant tones mirrored the compound anxieties and moral values confronting humans conceived either in lust, or more gently out of love – all of these born as little children upon Earth.

The ugliness of the Machine by the strength of its unsightliness attempted to convey the need for people to care seriously and compassionately for future people. At its symbolic heart lay a small monument – a recollection and reminder of natural life in the Brave Old World.

Post Script: There was little doubt that the Machine would fail to succeed in conveying its good-intentions for any considerable length of time before it became a loathed possession – a 'thing' to be consigned to a deep vault beyond commonplace sight.

L.B. Circa 2008 A.D.